MW00583509

The Road Is Good

The Road Is Good

How a Mother's Strength

Became a Daughter's Purpose

UZO ADUBA

VIKING

VIKING
An imprint of Penguin Random House LLC
penguinrandomhouse.com

Copyright © 2024 by Uzo Aduba
Penguin Random House supports copyright. Copyright fuels creativity, encourages
diverse voices, promotes free speech, and creates a vibrant culture. Thank you for buying
an authorized edition of this book and for complying with copyright laws by not reproducing,
scanning, or distributing any part of it in any form without permission. You are supporting writers
and allowing Penguin Random House to continue to publish books for every reader.

LIBRARY OF CONGRESS CATALOGING-IN-PUBLICATION DATA
Names: Aduba, Uzo, author.
Title: The road is good : how a mother's strength became a daughter's
purpose / Uzo Aduba.
Description: [New York] : Viking, [2024]
Identifiers: LCCN 2023040071 (print) | LCCN 2023040072 (ebook) |
ISBN 9780593299128 (hardcover) | ISBN 9780593299135 (ebook)
Subjects: LCSH: Aduba, Uzo. | African American actresses—Biography. |
Nigerian Americans—Biography.
Classification: LCC PN2287.A434 A3 2024 (print) | LCC PN2287.A434 (ebook) |
DDC 791.4302/8092 [B]—dc23/eng/20231204
LC record available at https://lccn.loc.gov/2023040071
LC ebook record available at https://lccn.loc.gov/2023040072

Printed in the United States of America
1st Printing

DESIGNED BY MEIGHAN CAVANAUGH

Some names and identifying characteristics have been
changed to protect the privacy of the individuals involved.

To my mother, Nonyem,

who meant absolutely everything to me

—Your Zozo

Let every sleeper wake, for the sun is in the sky.

Come rise, come rise, and hear the cuckoo cry;

Cuckoo, cuckoo, wake up, be spry.

Introduction

As I write this, my mother is dying.

For years, this is how I imagined I'd begin my book. That is how much the stories of our lives intertwine. Ours was the longest relationship of my life.

When I first received the news, there was, at the core of my being, a resistance. Up until that moment, I hadn't realized that I'd thought my mother would never die. I hadn't known that she was my belief system—that I'd thought my mother was a god, even if it was a little g.

You see, my mother could do anything, lift anything, move mountains. Only a few inches above five feet, she was tall to me; she had that much fire in her. My boldness is bolstered by her sincere belief that I can accomplish anything.

I began work on this book before my mother's cancer diagnosis and continued while my siblings and I cared for her—while I prepared to say goodbye.

When I say that my mother taught me so much, even in dying,

I don't mean what she taught me in those final days and weeks. I mean the dignity with which she sat for the 495 days after her cancer diagnosis. She was then who she'd always been: loving, faithful, funny.

How could I lose her when I still had so much to learn?

Each time I set out to write my own story, the only place I thought I could begin was the end.

MY MOTHER NEVER sat me down to tell me about her life. She told stories in the way that most Nigerians tell stories: They drift in when the time is right.

I understood her past mostly through questions.

"How'd you learn to sew, Mommy?" I asked as a kid watching her from the other side of the dining room table. She was putting the finishing stitches into two identical dresses for my sister Chi-Chi and me.

"In the war," my mother said, and that was the end.

I have always been the family historian—remembering names, connections, and even birthdays, trying to piece together the past. When I asked my mother questions that had complicated answers, she tried to answer as briefly as she could, and then she would say, "That's all I have to say about that." The next opportunity to inquire would arise years—sometimes many years—down the line.

While writing this book, I began to wonder: My children are going to know about my life the way that I tell it to them. But is that actually my life?

Of course, I will share with them all sorts of things, as my mother did with me. I'll say that, as a student, I won state championships in track and field, just as my mother had in tennis. When they see my medals, will they know only that their mother was fast? Or will they also know that this speed was my ticket out of a small town, where I never really felt that I fit?

I was the only Black girl in my suburban high school's graduating class, which had pretty much been the case all the way through. Like so many Black women in America, I came into my power in a world of white, male gatekeepers. As I grew as a woman and an artist, I sometimes held back in ways that I thought would help me get ahead.

Through both the tumult of my childhood and the valleys and peaks of my career, a deeper sense of myself grounded me.

Each time the world questioned my worth, my mother challenged it. She made it clear that there was a continent, a people, and, most essentially, a family where I absolutely belonged. No matter how many times I was tested, there remained, somewhere within me, a mustard-size grain of this idea, which kept me running, reaching.

I call this book *The Road Is Good* because that's what my name, Uzoamaka, means in Igbo, the language spoken by my parents and my people in southeastern Nigeria. It sounds like a simple statement, but to say *uzo amaka* is to say that the journey was hard—that, along the way, you went through something and you are grateful.

Let's say, for example, that you were coming to see me, but your flight was delayed because of rain, your luggage lost, the traffic into the city crazy.

"How was your journey?" I might say, as I opened the door.

"*Uzo amaka*," you'd say, stepping over the threshold. It was challenging, but it was worth it.

The significance of a name is an essential part of Igbo culture. If you are a native speaker and hear someone's Igbo name, you know that person's story without even knowing them. You have a sense of whether they are an only child, for example, or the last of many. You can determine, even, whether their conception was difficult and the circumstances around that: Were the parents elated, or was there a long delay that caused fear and concern?

Our names are our introduction to the world and, in some ways, our inheritance. Each child carries the burden and the blessing.

I continued asking my mother questions even as I knew time was running out. As we mourned her passing and celebrated her life, I brought some of my questions to family and friends. It wasn't easy to sit down and remember, but as we did, my mother's voice came alive again. News of our loss spread, and people, even some strangers, reached out to me with stories, photos, and even a book that mentioned my mother.

Each person's story comes into view in pieces; often the story changes, as you learn more about yourself too.

This is a story not about death but about life.

This is my mother's story as much as it is my own, even now that the fire inside her has been passed to her children and their children. Even as I continue to discover it.

Part I

My American Dream is for you
people to live your dream.

—*Nonyem Aduba*

Chapter 1

My mother had many sayings, which my siblings and I call Nonyemisms.

"My American Dream is for you people to be able to live your dream," she often told us, her children.

My mother was always calling us "you people."

First-gen American kids often seem to have parents pressuring them to be doctors or lawyers. While academics and career prospects were very important to my parents when I was young, they cared more that we were well-rounded. Very few of the Nigerian children I knew here in the US were playing sports or musical instruments like my siblings and I were growing up. But then, my family is very much in the business of not missing an opportunity.

The soundtrack of my early childhood included the thunk of a tennis ball against the garage or the more staccato basketball on the driveway, courtesy of my brother Rich. He also played the drums, which, to me, made him impossibly cool. Older, eight years older, Rich seemed, from my pesky-little-sister vantage, like a club I couldn't get into.

Rich has dimples and thick hair, which he wore high back in the early '90s. I tried to join him when he was on the couch with his boom box, rocking out to Run DMC or Queen Latifah. I learned every word of Public Enemy's "Fight the Power," or at least enough to nod along, mimicking the way I'd seen others move, as a way of bonding with him. Sometimes he'd humor me; mostly he'd tell me to scram. By the time I was eight, old enough to have strong memories, Rich had his driver's license and his own freedom.

My sister Onyi is two years younger than Rich, so we had more time together under our parents' roof—especially after a knee injury sidelined her soccer career. If Rich seemed, in some ways, like a big kid, then Onyi was a little adult. She was politely patient with me, pretending not to notice when, during her sleepovers, I'd shimmy up to her friends halfway through their movie. She let me loll around her room as she listened to Bon Jovi and Guns N' Roses. The eldest daughter, Onyi was what my mother called a "parentified" child: the one getting my younger sister, my brother, and me ready for school and out the door in the mornings and otherwise filling in for—or, in my parents' words, "representing"—the adults, who were busy at work. We Nigerian families *love* a representative.

This isn't to say Rich didn't do his share. Onyi dressed us, but he was in charge of making sure our teeth were brushed in the mornings. He and Onyi got special permission to leave high school in the middle of the day and walk over to the elementary school for our parent-pupil lunches. The summers when she and Rich were in charge, nap times went on into the afternoons far longer than they should have—and far longer into our childhoods, as well. Sometimes my big brother and sister needed a break.

Back then Onyi wore glasses with very thick lenses, and her long hair fell in a loose-waves perm called Hawaiian Silk. She has a bright, bright smile, with a gap between her two front teeth just like mine—though I always thought hers was beautiful. I wanted to wear every outfit she owned, especially her prized knockoff Benetton set: a narrow black knit skirt and a matching cropped sweater with a red-trimmed neckline, which read, in a white banner across the chest, "Local Hero." It was hopelessly out of style by the time she handed it down to me. I proudly wore it anyway.

Even Onyi had her limits. She absolutely would not let me have the lead on the dance numbers we all made up together in the family room. We often pretended we were New Edition, even if Rich and Onyi were the only ones who were actually approaching their teenage years. My younger sister, my brother, and I, all still in the single digits, sang backup, which was very much key to the whole scene reflected back to us in our sliding glass door. We too were five kids, just like the R&B group, with heads tipped back in song—even if our "microphones" were whisks, wooden spoons, and the remote control.

Onyi would give Rich the lead on "Cool It Now" and "Mr. Telephone Man," but there was no way I was coming forward as Ralph Tresvant or Bobby Brown, no matter how much I begged. No, Onyi said, Chi-Chi, Junior, and I were to hang back, like the members of Bell Biv DeVoe. At least Michael Bivins's rap on "Cool It Now" just sort of naturally stole the spotlight from Rich's Ralph: "Oooo . . . watch out!"

We also got a lot of play out of Billy Joel's *An Innocent Man*, with

Chi-Chi, Junior, and I forever the doo-wop backup on his song "The Longest Time." (Rich bowed out of this one.) To this day, if that song comes on, I am quietly bothered when Onyi leans into the verse.

Rich and Onyi are children of our mother's first marriage. Born in the US, they lived for a few years in Nigeria before coming back for good. Still, I have not once in my life thought of them as "half" anything. It's a distinction that simply does not exist in our minds or in the way we were raised.

I am the third born, but in some ways, I am also a kind of eldest: the ringleader among our family's close-spaced youngest three. Onyi was our boss, but I wanted to be the boss of something too.

While not the last born, Chi-Chi was tiny and very much "Baby Girl" in the eyes of our family, especially our mother. Obi, whom we called Junior, was also very little, with legs spinning under him, as if on a motor, so he could keep up.

Junior and I share a wild imagination, and I think Chi-Chi enjoyed having a front-row seat to our antics. She got knocked around sometimes, but as she grew, she learned to assert herself better than I ever could. Even more valuable, for a kid: She also learned how to make trouble without getting caught.

I was a precocious child, and rambunctious—never meaning harm but certainly causing some, with a mind full of ideas and not enough experience with consequence.

"Let's pretend we're bobsledding in the Olympics!" I announced, plastic sled in hand, one wintry afternoon when I was nine. My younger sister, my brother, and I surveyed the steep, unshoveled steps off our back porch and suited up. I went down. He went down. She went down, banging her head on the rail.

Chi-Chi cried, cried, cried—oh, how she used to cry when she was small.

Later that year, after the snow melted, we pushed our plastic, four-seater convertible up the super-steep hill in our Medfield, Massachusetts, hometown. "I'll be the driver," I told the crew.

Chi-Chi sat shotgun; Junior stood at the back. "Run-run-run-run!" I screamed at him as he pushed and jumped in. We whooshed down as I yanked the levers on the side in an attempt to steer, and then we skidded to a swervy stop, cracking up.

"OK, now Junior's the driver," I said, once we had pushed the car up the hill once again. "Chi-Chi, you're in the back."

It was her turn to push, but when she tried to jump in, she missed. She held on anyway, so we dragged her all the way down, the sides of her sneakers and her legs scraping against the asphalt. By the time we reached the bottom, she was crying.

"Why didn't you guys stop?" Chi-Chi wailed.

Junior and I stared at her before exchanging a quick look. Then, at the same time, we said, "Why didn't you *let go?*"

Our mother got home from work that evening, surveyed Chi-Chi's skinned knees, and shook her head. "That Uzo has too many ideas," she said, looking at me.

I did—both Junior and I did.

After watching the TV movie *Swiss Family Robinson*, about a shipwrecked family who constructs a giant tree house on a deserted island, we decided to build our own in the backyard. We spent entire afternoons after school climbing around the remnants of an old tree house that once stood between two of our trees—most of which had collapsed before we moved in. All that was left standing was the floor between the trees and the remainder of a rail that you could still lean on. Nailed into one trunk, practically flush with the bark, was a single ladder rung that you could use to scramble up.

Scrounging around the loose pile of wood under the trees, we found enough old planks to build an "extension." Then we hauled our father's toolbox out of the garage and hoisted it up onto the platform. Together, Chi-Chi and I carefully nailed one of the reddish planks out into the atmosphere. It held!

"Now, Chi-Chi," I said. "Go walk out there and see if it's sturdy."

"Why me?" Chi-Chi asked.

"I'm heavier," I said. "If I do it, it'll fall right away. And we've done all this hard work! If you do it, though, we can add a little weight at a time."

It made sense to me; it made sense to her too. I positioned myself on one end of the plank, and she slowly walked away from me to the other side. "It worked!" she exclaimed, slowly turning around.

"OK, now I'm going to stand up," I said, shifting forward, coming up out of my crouch and then carefully returning one foot to the board. I think I made it an entire half inch before the whole thing came ripping out. I froze as Chi-Chi grabbed the board on her side. "Don't let go! Don't let go!" I shouted.

"JUNIOR!" I don't know if she screamed or I did. "Get the ladder!"

And that little boy, legs pumping once again, grabbed it from the side of the house, ran it over, and put it under her just in time.

My mother saw children all day in her role as a social worker with the Massachusetts Department of Social Services. With me, she knew: Here is one who could go either one way or another. Depending on how much she stayed on top of me, I would either become some crazy person or run the planet.

"I will kill you before I have an insubordinate child," she told me once, as I was explaining why our neighbor Davy and I had turned the front windshield of his parents' Volvo station wagon into a waterslide. "Do you hear me?"

"We didn't mean to crack it," I said.

"Do you hear me?"

"If you kill me," I said, "you'll go to jail."

"And I will go to jail happy," my mother said.

MY IMMIGRANT PARENTS DID NOT understand the practice of moving around work commitments to accommodate a midday school occasion like a class party or a field trip. These boundaries were particularly fixed for my father, who worked as an accountant, with hours and commitments that we kids could not touch.

I begged him to come to school for lunch, but I always received the same answer. But one day when I was in the second grade, instead of seeing Onyi among the parents streaming in, I saw, toward the back of the group, my father dressed up in his old work suit. I was so shocked.

"This is my dad!" I exclaimed, introducing him to everyone I knew—adults and classmates. I couldn't believe he'd come. We sat down, and we had French bread pizza for lunch.

While he didn't stay long, and I couldn't follow him back home like the many kids with stay-at-home moms could, the gesture meant a lot to me.

My siblings and I often got dinner started before our parents came home. We'd learned to cook by fetching: running back and forth from the kitchen to the garage, then back again when reminded of another forgotten ingredient. Most of our nonperishable food was kept on shelves back there, in large, white plastic chewing gum containers that still had faint labels—Dubble Bubble or Super Bubble. Most of the tubs held rice; some had onugbu—sometimes called bitter leaf—dried and brought over from some relation's last visit to Nigeria. This my mother would crumble in her fingers as she would an autumn leaf, then soak and boil it before adding it to a soup with perfectly blended pepper.

When my mother was kept late at work, Onyi would corral us to chop onion, ginger, and peppers both sweet and hot. All cooked down with curry powder and tomatoes into a paste, the result was similar to a spaghetti sauce, but thicker and so much more satisfying. This start of red stew, a Nigerian staple—a sweet humidity coming from the stove, onto my face—was my childhood. Snow-dusted late afternoons, post-practice homework at the dining room table, the sizzle of plantains, and red stew on the stove.

These memories also have the sound of television in the background: My parents allowed thirty minutes, or maybe an hour, while we had a snack after school. These rules did not apply, however, to *The Cosby Show* and *A Different World*. For these the whole house stopped to watch, after dinner, in my parents' bedroom. My father in his recliner, my mother under the covers, and the rest of us cuddled around her or sitting with our backs to the foot of the bed. In these shows, we saw the best of us—a part of Black life in America so different from the endless drone of crime stories on the news.

On the weekends, my family watched movies and movie musicals in the living room, snuggled into the couch or sprawled out on the carpeting. *The Sound of Music* was always a ritual a few days before Christmas, as well as whatever the Disney Sunday movie was that week. Once we had a VCR, *The Sound of Music* fell into more regular rotation, along with *Oklahoma!*, *My Fair Lady*, *West Side Story*, and whatever else we could get our hands on.

My Fair Lady was far and away my favorite. I loved the fairy tale of Eliza Doolittle's story—her transformation from Cockney working-class girl to high-society lady. I loved the songs, especially "I Could Have Danced All Night," as well as the glamorous costumes, as we see Eliza off to the horse races at Royal Ascot or the embassy ball. Most of all, I loved the sentiment and the idea of the song "Wouldn't It Be Loverly," which is all about dreaming of something more—and getting it.

I could have had my own room once Rich and Onyi left for college, but I still preferred the one I shared with Chi-Chi, next door to Junior's. We three were always close, and by then, we knew it was to our benefit: We could have more privileges—like riding our bikes to the swimming pond on our own in the summers—if we promised we'd stick together.

Chi-Chi and I fought like cats in our tweens and early teens; we were, after all, just a year and a half apart. This narrow age gap ultimately made us even closer, or "practically twins," as we sometimes say. We have the same sense of humor and a similar laugh, with the same kind of cheesy wheeze at the end, like some Hanna-Barbera cartoon character.

"What's so funny?"

This is how it always started—Junior would hear us carrying on and pipe in from next door. In the doorway, we'd see his hopeful smile, pure sunshine and good. Then he'd come in, sit at the foot of one of our beds, and lay there with us, talking, until either Chi-Chi or I threw an elbow: "All right. Goodnight!"

Eventually he leveled up. He'd bring in a sleeping bag, fluffing it up in front of the nightstand in the space separating our two twin beds.

"Junior, *leave*!" we'd say, laughing. "This is our room!" More often, he would stay.

We slept like that for what seemed like forever. A little box set.

. . .

With a name like Aduba, I was accustomed to going first. In elementary school, only Dan Abramson came before me. I was also quick, which meant that on school field days, I led the pack. I handily won the girls' races and then went up against the boys in the finals.

"Girls don't beat boys!" The sound of Matt Monahan's voice and my sense of the other boys' raised eyebrows made me even more determined. To quote Yosemite Sam, in my family, "them's fightin' words." I pushed myself, passed them all, and my God, I was so proud.

Inside the classroom, I found real comfort in sidling up beside Dr. Seuss's Sam-I-Am and his fast-paced rhymes about green eggs and ham. Our school was part of the Pizza Hut Book It! Program, which incentivized students to read by offering free personal pan pizzas as a reward. While I needed no convincing to read more, the idea that I could exchange gold stars for a pizza of my choice kept me up with *Fantastic Mr. Fox* long past bedtime.

Besides reading, I loved writing—especially cursive—and talking, as much as possible. I was too chatty for most teachers. In my report cards, the consistent complaint, year after year, was "talks too much in class" or "distracts students with too much idle conversation." I was nonstop.

My friend Crowley's earliest memory of me is from the first grade. In it, I am dead asleep, head down on the desk. "Don't wake her up!" Mrs. Tascioni had insisted. She welcomed the break.

The other image that sticks with Crowley is from the day I brought in an entire family-size package of cookies for a snack—a snack I'd proudly packed myself, as I'd noticed so many of the other kids bringing in cookies. When Mrs. T noticed, she took it away.

I often went toe-to-toe with my second-grade teacher, Nancy Featherman: She scolded me for talking too much in class one day, and on the next, I spent the afternoon's writing lesson bent over my blue Grade 2 composition book, with its black binding down the spine, methodically listing every single complaint about her that I had.

My father saw the notebook a few days later, at parent-teacher conferences. He laughed, asking my teacher, "Didn't you say she could write whatever she wanted to in there?"

On another day, Ms. Featherman turned over our class to a student teacher, Miss Getchen. She returned to find the place in chaos and me sitting at her desk, with students asking me, not the student teacher, if they could use the restroom.

"I let them go," I explained to Ms. Featherman. It wasn't a complete banana republic. My classmates were reading, after all. I was in the very chair I felt I was meant to be in, down front and in charge.

Ms. Featherman assured me that I was not.

WHENEVER IT WAS TIME to sign up for extracurricular activities, our mother sat us down at the kitchen table and listed our choices. "Are you *sure*?" she asked each of us, every time, regardless of whether she knew the answer. Still, at the start of each season, my mother would ask as if each activity were a new undertaking, reminding me that practices and competitions meant no weekend birthday parties or sleeping in.

There was a discipline of completion in my house: When you said you were doing something, that was what you were doing.

Of course I would play the violin, just as Onyi had. Junior

would play saxophone, and Chi-Chi would do another season of tap dance and jazz. And of *course* I wanted to do figure skating again—that above all else.

I'd been a kindergartener when the "Learn to Skate!" flyer had fallen out of my backpack. I'm not sure what had spoken to my mother: I'd never been to an ice rink before. I'm not sure any of us had. But she'd called the number and signed me up, as well as Chi-Chi and Junior, and that was how our Saturday-morning routine began.

We pulled extra sweaters over our playclothes, which our family called "staying-home clothes," and buckled in for the ride to Natick, about fifteen minutes north of our home in Medfield. When we walked in, lugging the skates and helmets our parents had bought us, we were hit right away by an unforgettable smell: that lingering exhaust from the Zamboni and the slight whiff of sweat and undiscovered mildew, which would come to seem so familiar.

This scent, carried through the persistent moisture in the air, was also my childhood. The sounds—the teachers' metal blades, sharp enough to cut through meat, carving out the bass. The young students' new blades, shuffling across the surface, making a higher, tinny sound. The feeling of the cold, kept at bay by my winter jacket and pleather winter gloves, always a size too big.

From the minute I first stepped on the ice, I was hooked: Skating was a game of speed and precision, balance and strength. There was risk in skating and, for once, a great reward for my willingness to dare. I loved that.

Junior and I took to skating like fish to water. He moved quickly into hockey; Chi-Chi, after a few years, chose ballet instead. I continued on the figure skating path, promising my mother that I would stick with it. The ice time wasn't cheap; I knew.

By the end of elementary school, skating had become my life. I practiced before school and sometimes left school early for ice time or travel competitions.

I could find no match for the wonderful, free feeling of speed under my skates, the cold air racing past my face—what I imagined flying must feel like. I loved the precision required to create a look or execute a move; I even enjoyed the challenge of building my strength to perfect that move's full expression.

One early fundamental was the waltz jump—taking off on the outside edge of one foot for a half-rotation jump, landing on the outside edge of the other foot. Nailing it was a point of pride, but I quickly moved on to something I felt would be more impressive. I practiced taking off while skating backward until I could land a toe loop, but what I was after was the axel: the feat of a turn and a half in the air and a confident finish. Then I would know I had arrived.

From the start, my focus was on the big kids: the teenagers who seemed like professionals. I was fascinated by the command they had over their bodies—how smoothly they glided, how quickly they stopped. I wanted to be over there with them, doing exactly what they were doing, instead of where I was, with the little kids, doing the little-kid stuff. I actually believed that I could just glide up and blend in with them, just as I'd so often tried at home with Rich and Onyi. I stumbled and fell endlessly, trying to perfect my program.

WITH OUR FULL SLATE of extracurricular activities, our family did a lot of leaning on other families in our neighborhood—especially the mothers. My mother's demanding work schedule was a rarity. At the time, very few women in our town worked outside the home.

My siblings and I benefited greatly from our neighbors' generosity: Mrs. Trasher picked me up on the way to drop her daughter, Aly, at figure skating. The Browns across the street often got Junior to hockey. Luckily, Chi-Chi's ballet lessons were in Medfield, within walking distance of the school. She got there on her own and then later caught a ride home with Holly Gudaitis.

To reciprocate, my mother saved up all her vacation time for the start of each summer, when she ran an informal, two-week tennis clinic over at the high school. She had the experience to do so: When she first moved from Nigeria to the United States in the early 1970s, one of her first jobs was coaching the sport at a private school in Connecticut. She and my father were not ones to push, but I know she had hoped that one of her kids would fall desperately in love with the sport.

My mother certainly tried to kindle a passion in us. On those tennis clinic mornings, she was the one home to make us breakfast. She packed our van with lunch bags, snacks, and all of us kids and then drove around our neighborhood, stopping for Ryan and Holly and Erin and all these friends whose parents had been so wonderful to us. The van idled near the court as we kids unloaded the canvas bags stuffed with tennis balls, the ball hoppers, and the blue, plastic one-gallon Coleman water jugs. We stacked them all against the chain-link fence and then dragged them in as she parked.

We spread out on the court, and Rich guided us through our warm-up stretches. We ran sprints—"suicides," we called them—from baseline to center line and back again. We practiced our strokes and our serves until tennis balls covered the courts, and then we took the ball hoppers to scoop them all up and start again.

These weeks were my mother's way of giving back—her opportunity to take our neighbors' kids off their hands, watch them, and produce an activity for them. I think she was also repaying a debt to our family, or maybe to herself, making up for the year's inevitable missed moments in fifty weeks of full-time work.

My mother knew that in suburban America, parents expressed love by creating predictability. For us, that meant these active, sun-soaked mornings, the carpool, the feeling of the still-cool courts on my palms as I stretched. I loved seeing Mommy in her element, in the moment, doing something that we rarely saw her do, which was to relax.

My siblings and I were clear that our mother was good at tennis, but years later, we'd learn that when she was in college, she had claimed the West African Singles Tennis Championship title.

We didn't buy it at first. My mother did love a great joke, after all. Then, when she returned to Nigeria for a visit, sometime around 2002, she flew home with the trophy.

Chapter 2

Medfield was a typical New England town, by which I mean that it was small—about eight thousand people and six stoplights—and very white. In our well-to-do suburban area, the majority of our classmates' fathers were professionals—doctors, lawyers, accountants, teachers.

The kids lived by unspoken ideas about who mattered most, depending on whether you lived on Indian Hill and your dad went "into Boston" to work in one of the tall, shiny glass skyscrapers you saw when approaching the city, or you lived farther out and Dad worked in one of the brown, closer-to-the-ground corporate offices near the local mall.

Families in Medfield were made up, mostly, of two or three kids. There were a few households with four kids, but never five, as we had. I knew of exactly one family, the Oscarsons, who had more kids than we did. They had six. Watching them navigate life as a family, attending school and activities, was like watching a moon landing.

We were one of a few Black families in town, and on top of that we were Nigerian American, which in the 1980s and 1990s often felt like too much to have to explain. We were the Black family, "but not *Black* Black," as some of my classmates would say, as if the distinction were some kind of compliment for an achievement—a "By Jove, they've got it!" Pygmalion-level transformation. Neighbors and friends were surprised when my mother spoke the Queen's English; seeing her, they hadn't expected her "weird accent."

I cringed on every first day, hearing teachers, instructors, and new classmates stumble over my Nigerian name—the full version, Uzoamaka, or even the short form, Uzo. "Call me Zoe," I begged my mother, reasoning that it was so close to her nickname of Zozo.

"If they can learn to say Tchaikovsky and Michelangelo and Dostoyevsky, then they can learn to say Uzoamaka," she told me. We never discussed it again.

I had plenty of friends growing up, but with some of their families, I felt a subtle uneasiness. It wasn't so much the kids as the parents who didn't want to play with me. I sensed their caution and uncertainty from the slightly irregular questions they asked in response to our invitations.

"Will you be having anything spicy?" one of my classmate's mothers asked my own.

Some of my closest pals on the playground had homes that seemed off-limits, except for their birthday parties. There, even though we were all in T-shirts and shorts, I sat with my spine extra straight, as if I were wearing white gloves and my Sunday best. As if I might look down and discover mud all over my feet.

Erin Stanley, with her blond bobbed hair, big blue plastic glasses, and welcoming spirit, was the exception. I hung out at her house without reservation and invited her to mine, or to join my family on trips to the mall or the movies. Around her, I felt safe.

The Stanleys had moved to Medfield from Newton, a more diverse suburb closer to Boston, where my family had once lived too. Mrs. Stanley was a teacher at Newton North High School, home of the kids from New Edition. I couldn't get over the fact that she had taught Ronnie.

Unlike many in our small town, the Stanleys didn't seem to be caught up with a lot of the status concerns at play. They weren't jockeying for friendships with the "right" people, which isn't to say they didn't have those friendships. Erin's bond with many of those Indian Hill girls lasted through high school.

Lovely Mr. Stanley, who had come from a simple background, always knew how to make me feel welcome. I didn't have to edit myself with their family. If—or when—I was loud, I knew I wouldn't be viewed as anything other than a kid being loud.

Erin and I mixed into each other's family seamlessly. She was there for our movie marathons, lying on the floor with the rest of my siblings as we watched musicals, which the Stanleys loved as much as the Adubas. *The 10th Anniversary Dream Cast in Concert* recording of *Les Misérables* is still my favorite; it's the one Erin's mom and her Aunt Janet loved best.

The Stanleys also introduced me to the Beatles—records that my parents recognized but did not play in our home. I can still see Mrs. Stanley with her pixie cut standing alongside Aunt Janet, shaking their heads like Paul and John as we listened to "I Want to Hold Your Hand."

On the countless sleepovers at Erin's house, we'd finish our pizza dinner with Mr. and Mrs. Stanley and head down to the basement, arms full of soda and snacks and the video cassette of some '80s teen flick. That's what I think of, when I think of Erin Stanley: Sunkist and Chips Ahoy! cookies and *Sixteen Candles*.

I'd seen parts of that John Hughes film, and several others, as a much younger kid, while sneaking into Onyi's sleepovers. I'd crouched on the floor, in the small corner of the hallway where I could still see the TV, to watch Molly Ringwald's character, Sam, gazing at her crush, Jake Ryan. It wasn't until Erin and I were each tucked in our own sleeping bags, watching the two actors lean in for a kiss over a birthday cake to the tune of the Thompson Twins "If You Were Here" that I understood why the movie was all the rage. Erin loved *Sixteen Candles* and John Hughes films, and now, so did I.

At one of Erin's relatives' Christmas parties, I learned about the intrigue of Secret Santa gift-giving, and Aunt Janet showed me an exotic recipe that blew my mind: white bread, crusts cut off, wrapped around a cream cheese filling and an asparagus spear, toasted.

I came home begging my mother to pick up the ingredients. She was resistant, seeing little room for an additional task in our already overstuffed holiday routine. The spread she'd planned for our party worked for everyone else. Why wasn't it enough for her Zozo?

WITH ITS MIX OF TASTES and cultures, I sometimes describe my childhood as "Igbo Interrupted." While we were very much American kids, Igbo language was the default in our home, but English gained ground each year we were in school. Oh, *this* is how it's done, my siblings and I realized, as we spoke with our friends. That's the control way. *We* are saying the variant.

Because of Nigeria's colonial history, the English on which we were raised was the British version—calling the trunk of the car the "boot," and so on. I was surprised, in the school cafeteria, to hear my classmates ask for "veg-ta-bles," as I was so used to hearing that extra *e*: "veg-e-tah-ble." I was even more shocked to see my uncle Bertie's name in writing, having only heard it as "Battee." Saying "burr" at the top, as my friends would, seemed just as foreign as calling him by his given name, Uncle Ogugua.

All five of us were constantly code-switching, whether we were on the school playground in our jeans and Nikes or headed into the city on the weekend for a meet-up with other Igbo families at the Museum of Fine Arts, Boston. Code-switching was—and still is—the daily armor we put on to face the world. It's saying "yes" and not "yasss," or "how are you?" and not "*kedu?*" We adapted to be heard—so our thoughts and ideas carried the same weight as everyone else's.

My parents played by these rules too: They had their traditional clothes—their "trad," as we called them—and they also wore Western clothes, just as they had when they were young. Back home in Nigeria, however, those Western trends *and* their nation's attire were seen as equally valuable and chic. In America, only Western clothes relayed your most sophisticated, professional, elegant self.

Knowing this, my siblings and I insisted, sometimes harshly, that our parents lay off the trad around Medfield. I didn't think much about their feelings on the matter; far more important was the fear of extra attention from our school friends, many of whom saw the clothes as a kind of funny costume. Our parents didn't want to cause us hardship, so the *aso-oke*, *ankara*, and lace fabrics stayed in their drawers. They tucked away their *ichafus*, hung up their *agbadas*, and went to our ballet recitals, sports banquets, and concerts in the expected suits and shift dresses.

As super aware of our onliness as we all were, there is no question that Rich suffered the most. He was eight years old when my family moved to Medfield from Newton; when he started school, he was called all sorts of horrible names, like Monkey or African Booty Scratcher—that was a big one, back in the day—and much, much worse. As he waited for the bus, kids stole his lunch and then insulted him on the drive, telling him to go back to Africa. With few friends at school, he was constantly picked on and provoked.

One of Rich's chief tormentors lived in a red house just around the corner. Years later, his mother would wave at me as I was out riding my bike. I wouldn't wave back, instead glaring as I rode by. Those are bad people, I thought.

When Rich was twelve, he came home from school one day fresh from another beating. "You keep telling me I can't fight back," he cried to my mother, "and they keep fighting me and taking my stuff! It's not fair!"

"Ricky," my mother said, "if these kids come at you and start hitting you, I want you to just . . . so . . ." She'd had enough. "Just knock one of them," she told him. "I'll deal with it."

As God would have it, the next time those boys came for Rich was on a weekend. Rich was playing with his soccer ball, and my mother was at the kitchen sink, washing dishes, and so watched through the window as the neighborhood kids walked into our backyard. They kicked the ball around together for a bit, back and forth. Then Rich passed the ball to one kid, who punted it over the fence and the rarely used railroad tracks beyond so that it landed in the woods.

When that same boy next lunged toward Rich, my brother took our mother's advice. He threw his fists back at him, ultimately blackening the kid's eye.

The group quickly dispersed, and my mother came out.

"It's OK," she said to Rich. "I saw the whole thing." She ran for my father. That afternoon, the three of them walked around to each of the bullies' houses, beginning with the boy with the black eye.

"Do you know that my son comes home every day, telling me that *your* son said—" My mother rattled off the insults, this this, that that, and then listened in silence as the parents expressed their disbelief.

"Your child is never to bother my son again," my mother said, "or we are going to involve the police."

A black eye doesn't go away immediately. In a sixth-grade class-room, it's definitely something that gets noticed.

"What happened?" asked the teacher that Monday.

"Ricky hit me," said the kid who started the fight with my brother.

"Get up," the teacher said to Rich. "You're going down to the office now." The principal suspended him on the spot and then called my mother at work.

An hour later, my mother and my father sat together in the principal's office with Rich's teacher.

"So you suspended my son for blackening this boy's eye," my mother said to the principal. "Did you ask my son how it came to be that he hit that boy?"

The principal shook his head.

"Mm-*hmm*," she said with satisfaction. My mother had this way of interrogating people: Even when she already knew the answer, she still needed to be sure about the level of stupidity she was deal-ing with.

She turned to the teacher. "Did you ask that child what it was that caused my son to hit him?"

"No," the teacher replied.

"Did you know this child actually hit my son, and my son hit him back because he was defending himself?" asked my mother, adding that she and my father had already been around to talk with the other parents. "Go ahead and see that what I'm saying has actually occurred."

The teacher apologized. "I didn't know—"

"You didn't know because you didn't ask and because you didn't care," my mother said. "You assume my son has done something that he did not do, not even imagining—could never imagine—that these racist children have been harassing my son at his bus stop, at your school. My son has not said anything to you, but he has been telling me all this."

She straightened herself. "Now let me tell you something right now." (Now let me tell *you* something: When my mother said this to me, it was about to go down unlike any other way. This woman was getting ready to knock me out.)

"Let me tell you something," she repeated. "If ever I have to leave work to come to this school again for something like this, I will sue you. I will sue this teacher. I will sue this school. I will sue this town. This school will go from the Thomas Blake School to the Nonyem Aduba School. Do you understand what I'm saying?"

That question ended the suspension conversation. Rich, the principal said, was free to go back to class.

As hard as it was for us to be different, I have never in my life wished to be white. Good hair, according to eight-year-old Uzo, was *The Cosby Show*'s Rudy Huxtable. I didn't yearn for the long blond hair my friends coveted. I didn't want what they had; I wanted more of *me*.

At school I stood out, but not in any way that was considered valuable. I was visibly invisible. So I loved seeing my Blackness, in its perfect natural state, promenaded positively on television. *The Cosby Show* and *A Different World* reminded me that the parts of me so often overlooked had worth. Inside, I was confident they did; I wanted everybody else to see and appreciate their value too.

I could talk with my friends forever about fan mail to early-1990s heartthrobs like Jonathan Taylor Thomas and Prince William, who are both white, but my first TV crush was Brandon Adams. I first saw him in a 1989 all-Black Disney TV remake of *Pollyanna*, called *Polly*, playing orphan boy Jimmy Bean. The morning after the movie aired, I went to school ready for a deep-dive lunchtime discussion about Jimmy Bean's curly brown hair. I launched right in and was met with blank stares across the table. "What's a Polly?" asked one of the girls.

Not one of them had seen the movie or even heard of it. I was confused, given that we had watched and gabbed about all the other TV movies premiering on the Wonderful World of Disney. Why had they all skipped it? Had Taryn, the one biracial girl in our school, seen it, and had she seen what I had? While I didn't have the language to understand my difference, I knew instinctively that I should keep my Jimmy Bean crush to myself.

For this reason, when Talitha—another Brown girl—moved in, I automatically had a partner in crime. She knew everything I knew: She wasn't going to ask to touch my hair or why there were beads in it, why it was "so greasy," or why I always braided it "like that."

I assumed that we would be friends, and we were. Her family had a beautiful home, and I spent a good deal of time there. We didn't do anything remarkable together, but it was remarkable how well we *fit*.

With Erin, I didn't have to be extra polite: I could be myself, and I was understood and accepted as such. With Talitha, I didn't even have to worry or wonder if some weird joke was going to be made. *Did you spend too much time tanning?* Still, what I wanted most of all, at school, was to find community in being Nigerian, just like the community enjoyed by the majority of my Irish American–leaning classmates.

I did have this experience at Igbo meet-ups on the weekends. Saturdays meant driving into the city, no matter what, to where the characterless museum classrooms of the Museum of Fine Arts, Boston transformed into a kind of social club. These were get-togethers that were typically standing room only, featuring a rotating cast of characters—often thirty to forty people—from greater Boston's growing Igbo community. There, among their peers, my parents' week of hard work seemed to melt away. They pulled out their trad and seemed lighter somehow.

It didn't matter if they were tired from the week, or even if, because of conflicting commitments, we'd arrived super late. (We were often late, I'll add. On the spectrum of early, prompt, "CP Time" (or "Colored People Time"), and then "African Time," which is a whole time zone unto itself, my parents were somewhere in the middle.) We'd sail into the room filled with aunties, uncles, and students, all chatting over the music. There was dancing, heated debates, and even arguments. Often we young kids were tossed into another room, where the main instruction was "Don't knock anything over."

The adults sometimes brought the two rooms together for an educational interlude. They taught us the Nigerian national anthem, which we all committed to memory—still a source of great pride for the elders. There was a cooking class, a dance troupe. All reminders of our roots, our history, our culture.

When my parents first arrived in the US, most of the Nigerian families that came through the Boston area lived in the city, among other Black people, in neighborhoods like Dorchester or Mattapan or Jamaica Plain. If they were able, those families sent their kids to private schools, where they—as we—were "only ones." As family lines became more established in the US, more and more of our Nigerian community moved out to the suburbs. A very close family friend of ours, for example, lived two towns over in a well-to-do place called Westwood, comparable to Medfield in size and demographics.

My parents, among the group's original founders, were waypavers—the first of each of their extended families to settle in the United States. Their younger relatives and friends could immigrate with the faith that they would never be alone. We often hosted them upon arrival; long after they settled, we remained a kind of home base.

We were a particular haven for the college students—my father's brother, my Uncle David, as well as our cousins Ike and Chudi, the eldest son of my mother's sister Adora, all spent time under our roof. Born and raised in Nigeria, all three earned scholarships to Framingham State University, about fifteen miles north of us.

At six feet, six inches, Chudi was a towering figure, with legs like a giant. When I was three, he'd hoist me up to eye level and ask, "What's the air like up there?" Sometimes I'd balance on the tops of his feet, giggling, as he walked around.

There were no formalities between us; Chudi's grades and other important documents were sent to our family's mailing address. He knew that he could walk in the door at any hour and find in the refrigerator home-cooked Nigerian food he could heat in minutes. If he needed to chat with his aunty, it wasn't anything restrained over tea; my mother took him into her bedroom and closed the door, as she would with any of her children.

One of Chudi's most vivid memories of my mother is of a phone call and a request that he come out to the street to meet her. "Aunty Nonyem insisted she would not meet me in the building," he told me many years later.

Framingham State had sent his first-semester grades; my mother held them in her hand. "She gave me the letter, and I opened it up to see," Chudi said. "When I saw it, she told me, 'You know, this is very disappointing.'"

"Yes, Aunty, I'm going to try," Chudi had told my mother.

"You kidding?" my mother had told Chudi. "Trying is not the word. You will make it. Not just try. You will do it. You didn't come here to fail."

My parents took a similar approach with my Uncle David, who, ten years my father's junior, was treated more as a son than a brother. When he was first at Framingham State, my father picked him up on the weekends and drove him around town to ask for job applications. Later I'd watch out the window for Uncle David's yellow Oldsmobile Omega, bought for just $300, to turn the corner onto our street.

To my siblings and me, Uncle David was a cross between uncle and parent, keeping an eye on us after school and joining the cheering sections for skating competitions and basketball and softball games. He came along on our family outings to a local state park close to his campus and followed our car all the way down to Washington, DC, for vacation. At our family parties, Uncle David was often pitching in as much—or likely more—than we kids did.

Family and close friends always offered to help, or to bring something to our house, on birthdays or Christmas or the Fourth of July, but my mother's response, always, was that "we have everything." It truly felt like we did, on those days, out in the backyard, with the rich scent of jollof rice floating through the open windows and Fela Kuti's horns on the stereo. There was plenty to eat and drink—soups, stews, snacks, and pilafs, enough so that guests who chose to linger on into the following meal could make another plate before saying goodbye.

Several times a year, our guests' cars lined up on both sides of our quiet block, parking all the way from one end of our street to the other. For the biggest events, weddings and graduations, the street transformed into a kind of catwalk: the perfect setup for all these women and men peacocking in their fine-fines.

Now, you will never see a group of people more swagged out, well-tailored, regal with a pop, elegant, or floating in all their glory than Nigerian people in traditional dress. We love to dress, and we know how, choosing fabric, craft, and design the likes of which have never been seen . . . or, if it *has* been done, then clearly it has never been done so well.

Our driveway was on a steep decline, so we kids were responsible for helping our aunties negotiate their heels on the way down. "Give me your hand, *Uzoamaka*, help me," they'd say, still parading, trying to keep their cool as they landed in the grass, perhaps even timing their steps to Chief Stephen Osadebe's "Nwanem Ebezina" trumpeting through the speakers.

Last to arrive, always, was my Aunty Oby, who was for many years my mother's youngest sister (until my Aunty Uju came along), and was the queen supreme when it came to style. On every occasion she and my Uncle Uche came in their matching trad, the height of fashion for married couples. Tall and curvy, Aunty Oby always arrived blinged out, her beautiful hair poured into a matching *ichafu* and a full face of perfectly applied makeup. Her full name, Obiageli, is typical of a youngest child and perfect for her: "one who has come during a time of plenty."

Every wedding is a major occasion, but Uncle David's took the cake. The music was bumping, as my parents had set up one of those big box speakers—the kind with a tripod stand—on the porch and another on the grass in the backyard. That is another thing about Nigerians: We don't think the party is going until the speakers have that too-loud, radiating hiss. No matter the occasion, it was the old Naija music, the high-life music, playing. Fela playing, or Prince Nico Mbarga's "Sweet Mother," cranked up way too loud.

This was the soundtrack, the flavor, the feel: the late-afternoon sunshine, the men playing draughts. The women in all their hues and bright patterns, preening and gossiping.

Oh, she came with her big gold chains. She didn't see my bracelet, though.

Did you see what my doctor son has brought me?

The new car? BMW.

At some point my father's cousin, my Uncle Rufus, and his wife, my Aunty Grace, would slip away, change into the most old-school trad, and return ready to perform. Uncle Rufus played the African pipe, and Aunty Grace was a dancer; they enjoyed a kind of fame for it. Whenever anyone was having a party, the question always was, *Can Aunty Grace and Uncle Rufus come?*

For Uncle David's wedding, someone brought in a drum, which they started beating over the music on the stereo. On this cue my aunty and uncle began, building on the rhythm, with my father egging them on.

My father's signature move was to pick his leg up, turn it out at the hip really big, and then slam it down on the ground. He did this again and again, up-boom, up-boom, faster and faster, dancing closer, until people were really charged up. More and more guests began to dance, and really dance—the men with puffed chests, as if they were warriors, dancing together. The women, with Grace holding court, almost like chickens, bok-boking around.

My father leaned in with his cash, spraying the money in Grace's direction while she continued dancing, jokingly encouraging him. Then he started up again with the one leg, exaggerating, playfully indicating, *Grace, don't make me do it*, a kind of comedic threat, until both legs were going and the rest of us had crowded in.

This was how my father worked a room—first being serious, then turning on his megawatt smile, as if to say, *OK, you've got me*, and then becoming more and more gregarious, laying back in the groove until it was time to pull away. Then he'd joke and play again. This was my father: charismatic, wickedly charming, moving in different circles, always reaching for more.

The party went on late into the evening. As my parents and siblings walked back up the driveway to say our last goodbyes, we were surprised by how many of our neighbors we saw. One couple was sitting out on their front steps. Others had pulled out lawn chairs. Still others were out taking a walk on the nice evening, lingering near, trying to catch a glimpse.

Chapter 3

I have always kept a journal. This I owe to my mother, who bought me my first small diary when I was nine. It had a tiny padlock and was covered in soft-textured blue-green fabric, with little pink-budded vines running up and down in parallel lines. I treasured it, as I'd grown up watching her lying in bed, filling up her own books.

My mother often wrote in lined notebooks, occasionally stacking two handwritten lines on every narrow rule. Sometimes her "journal" was just a scrap of paper where she could scribble some account of what was happening in her life.

Watching her keep to this routine, with great peace, is what made me want to do it too. Keeping a journal was a very adult thing to do, in my mind, even if my mother's practice began when she was a small girl.

My mother told me that when she was a child, she had a dream about a relation's passing and wrote it down in her journal. She told her mother about it too. A week later, that person passed away.

Then, a little later on, she had a similar dream about someone else and did the same thing. About a week later, that person passed, and my grandmother took that journal away. For how long, I don't know.

My mother could *see*. I don't know if you believe in any of that. But I do.

While my parents are not from the same town in Nigeria, or even the same state, they are both Igbo—from the same region and people. This is important to note, as Nigerians are not all one tribe or culture. Before British colonialists drew a map over the land, Nigeria was actually three separate nations, named for the major tribes: Igboland in the southeast, Yorubaland in the west, and Hausaland in the north.

My father's family is from a small rural village inside the town of Achi, in Enugu State, an area of Igboland that was once a coal mining stronghold. Obosi, my mother's hometown, lies about fifty miles west of Achi. It's close to Onitsha, a big port city on the Niger River.

In all my time hearing stories from the elders, I have never once heard anything ill said of Obosi. The same may be true of Achi, I suppose, but during my parents' day, Obosi was a hot spot. Home to a huge market, it has great historical significance, as it was once the capital of Igboland; it's also one of a few areas still governed by a traditional kingship.

Although densely populated and well developed by many African definitions, the Nigeria my parents knew as children in the 1950s and 1960s was very different from the Nigeria of today. It was still quite rural. In many ways, life there was as it had always been: The toys my mother and her sisters played with were baby dolls made of crossed sticks, which they lay in beds of piled sand.

To hear it from my mother's generation, life back then was better. There weren't concerns about banditry and kidnapping, my Aunty Ifeyinwa told me. "There was nothing like this hatred, religious bigotry. There was one Nigeria, and everyone was just happy to get together."

My uncles described it to me in this way: You could put a letter in a mailbox, and it would reach its destination. Food was widely available, the markets bountiful, and, thanks to the railway system constructed by the British, the job opportunities in other cities were plentiful. You could take a train to school, even; if it were a longer ride, you could rest in a sleeper car. The system created more connections—and brought in more commerce—within the country and beyond. It carried my mother's family out of poverty too. After my grandfather finished his education at a school run by the Government Department of Railway, he worked his way up to become a railway manager and conductor.

Raised with Igbo traditions, my parents were both Anglican, educated in the Christian missionary–run schools known to be the best. *Their* parents' and grandparents' generations were the ones who first began practicing the Christianity that European missionaries brought a century earlier. My father's family especially worked hard to share our faith, hand in hand with Western education.

My mother's father, Egwuenu, was known for his progressive beliefs. The Igbo translation of his last name, *Anyaoku*—so my mother's family name—is "Eye of Fire." And Anyaoku means two things in our culture: great drive—great push, more literally—and sharp tongue. A dominant gene, as you can see.

Having lost both of their parents very young, my grandfather and his two siblings made a pact: When the time came, they would raise their children together. This is what my family has come to know as the Anyaoku way—the philosophy that family is king and that there is strength in numbers. Both Egwuenu and my grandmother Alice Nwakaego shared all they had with the extended family. By pooling their money, they believed, they could *all* get to a better place.

My list of uncles and aunties seemed limitless sometimes: My mother is one of ten, biologically. We also count the cousins she called brother and sister, so we really say that she's one of fifteen. When she and the young ones were all home together in Obosi, on holidays, she was the mediator—settling quarrels among the four, five, or six playing together.

They were all one, eating from the same pot, with no distinction of "my mother's side" or "my uncle's child." No half brothers or step anything, as is now the case for Rich and Onyi, born of a different father, and Chi-Chi, Junior, and me.

This was the way, in Nigeria: The family compound included multiple homes and room for more. Plenty of extra space in anticipation of a bright future.

My mother's parents traveled often, sometimes living far away from Obosi—a practice that was rare in those days. This gave them a broader view of the world than they would have had otherwise, in a place with few highways or buses or cars to traverse it.

My grandfather Egwuenu was stationed for a time in Zaria, an ancient city in northern Nigeria that was once the capital of the Hausa kingdom. As there were no railway quarters, the family lived in town, where they were in the distinct minority—both as Igbo people and as Christians. (The Hausa people are predominantly

Muslim.) They tried to fit in, attending the local schools and gaining, through practice, an understanding of the cultural norms. My mother's youngest siblings spoke fluent Hausa before they spoke Igbo.

Back home in Obosi, my grandfather was known for his belief in education. That meant his daughters didn't stay home, as was common for the time and place, while the sons pursued dreams of working in government, law, or medicine. (Think American society is patriarchal? Multiply that by one hundred, and you're in Nigeria.)

Their village is said to be one of the first in the Igbo community to give girls equal access to Western education, and my family went far above that. "Whosoever has the intelligence and wants to go to school, I will be sure to assist them in going," said my grandfather, according to my mother, who quoted him so often I can almost picture him saying this to me. Of the family's children, eight were girls; each one of them went to college, and many went on to pursue advanced degrees.

Creating these opportunities for so many children came with a high cost. While most of the men of his stature owned an imported car—a Volvo, Volkswagen, or the like—my grandfather made do with a bicycle, riding it to the station or to the market, where my grandmother traded fabrics. "Where is your car?" his friends teased, knowing full well that tuition fees were his priority.

Nwakaego, my grandmother, also understood the power of education. A secondary school graduate, she was studying at a local women's college when she met my grandfather. I've been told many times that she was a brilliant cook—and that she did not suffer fools. A "tough lady." This was the party line.

A progressive marriage like my grandparents' was rare. As the story goes, my grandfather's first response to a suggestion was often, "I have to discuss it with my wife."

"A firebrand, like your mother," my Aunty Ifey told me. Tough or not, let's just say the women in my family know what they like.

My grandmother loved fashion—her dresses, her jewelry. She lived to shop too, even as my grandfather tucked away every penny, wearing the same railway uniform, khaki on khaki, each day of the week. Ignoring the wishes of her husband, as the story goes, Nwakaego pierced her girls' ears. For days my mother and her sisters tucked their newly bejeweled lobes under headscarves, fearful of being found out.

Still, with so many mouths to feed, my grandmother, like my grandfather, was industrious. Her style sensibility was put to good use at the local market, where she traded fabrics. My uncles and aunties helped her take the bolts of cloth down in the mornings and then returned, after school, to help bring it all back home.

In one of the few childhood photos of my mother that I've seen, she is standing, eyes shining, head shaven, barely smiling, among five of her siblings. She's the only one in the photo touching anyone else. Her arm is slung over her little brother, my Uncle Ifeanyi—a baby with no shoes, who somehow still looks strong. On the other side of Ifeanyi is my mother's older sister, Ifeoma, her very best friend, so quiet and shy that my mom often served as her protector. Behind Ifeoma is Emeka, the eldest of the fifteen, whom we would later address as Adazie, reflecting his chieftaincy title.

On the opposite side of Uncle Adazie stands my Uncle Bertie, though the bright, buoyant smile that defined him is nowhere to be found. I'd later learn that this was the first time he'd had his portrait taken. Still, even stony-faced, his spirit seems to leap out of the photo.

My mother's affection came from a childhood knowing affection. Her best friend, Ani, from boarding school, envied the way my grandfather engaged all his daughters—loving, supporting, listening to, and believing in them. Father and growing girls laughing together, hugging, just wasn't done.

He believed that they were just as capable as his sons to find their own way. While culture's tradition dictates that the father of a bride receives a payment when his daughter marries, my grandfather told each of his girls' fiancés' families to "give me one British pound, for culture's sake." That way, if there were ever a problem, there could be a simple, ceremonial return, and she'd be out of there.

I can imagine Egwuenu and his daughter Nonyem together in Obosi, both young and vital. I can see him fanning the flame of her curiosity so that it persisted in her spirit and in her mind. My grandfather was deeply inquisitive, according to my mother; surely her love of reading was born from his questions. She received and passed along the same message to us: If you want to know more, you shouldn't be afraid to find out.

My mother and her siblings graduated, succeeded, and scattered. While this was typical of Igbo people, their generation had access to an entirely new sense of possibility. Nigerian oil was first discovered in 1956 in Oloibiri, in the delta south of Obosi; as production ramped up and pipelines were built, the economy boomed.

My mother found a job as a teacher; her siblings and peers worked across the country as engineers, technicians, merchants, and government ministers. They lived elsewhere, returning mostly on holidays to Obosi, where they were greeted as members of the elite. I can imagine my mother, looking as she did in her college portrait, heading home for Christmas on my grandfather's train. She steadies herself in her seat, notebook balanced on her lap or a small suitcase, writing about her hopes for her students and how her semester has gone.

During one of these holidays, my uncle's car sat in the driveway of my grandparents' compound; inside sat his driver, waiting for him. Two aunties' cars were there as well. One had driven in separately from her husband, who'd followed in their truck, carrying a few large items down from their home in Hausaland.

My grandfather was standing outside when an old friend walked by. Gesturing to the five cars in the compound, the friend said, "What are you doing with all of these?"

"Remember when you used to tease me about my bicycle?" said my grandfather with a smile. "*These* are the cars I was buying."

EDUCATION WAS A LIFELINE for my father, who lost his parents and three older siblings when he was very young. The generous aunties and uncles of the Umuigwe clan fostered my father and his orphaned siblings. Achi, their hometown, had a vibrant sense of community, with traditional ways of maintaining order and a loving culture centered around the wisdom of the elders.

Much smaller and more rural than Obosi, Achi had neighborhoods with dirt roads and buildings topped by roofs made from tightly woven native grasses. Many homes, including my father's, began as one room with a dirt floor. On market days, young children took brooms to the streets to sweep in front of their family compounds.

On this side, my family can trace our beginnings far, far back, all the way to Igwe, the region's traditional ruler. *Umuigwe,* the name of my father's line, means "descended from the king," and according to my father, who once wrote down the lineage for me, this is how his family unfolded: "Descended from Joseph Uzodinma Aduba, who descended from Adubaokpasuo, who descended from Okoroafor, who descended from Okorohugwo, who descended from Igwe, who descended from Aham."

My father's father and grandfather were "great athletes and warriors," in the words of my father: "Uzodinma died unbeaten in his choice of athletics, wrestling." They were also men of faith. The founder of a church in Achi, my grandfather was one of the first teachers to come out of that church's school. Like my father and his siblings, our earlier ancestors were familiar with the toll of war. My great-great-grandfather died "with a bullet lodged in his chest from a war against a neighboring village in Enugwu Agu."

After his parents' death, my father, the eldest, went to work to support his three younger siblings as soon as he could. He followed his late father's example and, after primary school, enrolled directly into a teacher's training college in Lagos. When he moved for a job, he often took along with him my Uncle David. "I was like the Visa," Uncle David once joked. "Don't leave home without it."

The teaching work was steady for my father, and when the younger ones returned home from school, they handled the household—cooking, sweeping, and handwashing the clothes. With their participation, Achi's church and school grew; so did our family's sense of possibility.

When I was a child, this was all I knew of my father's past. A few stories floated in during family visits, but he was not at all forthcoming. There also were not as many family visits. Unlike my mother's family, who traveled and lived in all corners of the world, all of my father's family, save my Uncle David, still lived in or near Achi.

"You know," my father sometimes said, when we were young, "your mom—she grew up with a lot." My mother would protest, but there is truth in that. Having and not having looked different then, in Nigeria, than it does now, in America. My father did not speak of his parents, but when you lose your parents at age twelve, is there anything to tell?

My mother had access to education and relative privilege, and her greatest wealth was the support of a closely knit extended family. My father was the beginning of the line for his family. The top. There was no one above him.

Chapter 4

W hen I was in third grade, I noticed piles of furniture collecting mysteriously in one corner of our garage. Sears delivered our new couch one Saturday afternoon, and our old three-seater went back there too.

"Why is all this stuff just sitting there?" I asked my father.

"Oh, it's for when we move back to Nigeria," he said.

Nigeria? My mind leapt to the often-echoed parental threat: *Look at you, being so rambunctious. If you continue with this, I will send you to Nigeria.* My siblings and I had been raised on the classic immigrant hardship stories: In Africa, electricity comes and goes, we'd been told. The children have to fetch water for the family, to drink and to bathe.

That would be my life too? Surely the slaps on the wrist or bottom that I'd gotten at home would not match what was possible in a place where *teachers* could hit you.

No way, I'd think, feeling as if I'd just been scolded. I'll straighten up and fly right.

As time passed, though, I got used to this idea of going "home"—even excited about it. I felt a pull to this place I'd never seen that came alive through my relatives' stories. While we now knew a significant number of Nigerians living in the US and abroad, the wealth of our lineage, on both sides, remained in Nigeria, and my parents were each incredibly close with their families. There was something delicious about knowing that, over there, I had cousins who were exactly my age. (The ones we saw at Igbo meetings in Boston were typically Onyi's age or older, or Junior's age and younger.)

We knew many in our circles—including the family of my Aunty Rachel, my father's cousin—who had gone back. From that conversation with my father forward, when I gazed at the stack of housewares, I saw this life that my parents had built in a different way. I felt as American as any of my classmates, but for my Nigerian parents and their peers, the idea never was to stay.

Many of them left Nigeria in the 1970s, fleeing a country torn apart by civil war. Some came as refugees, some, like my father, on scholarships. Whether they settled in the US, the UK, Canada, Australia, or elsewhere, they sought the opportunities and skills needed to rebuild their country. The relative prosperity they worked so hard to create was a means to this end—a return.

I imagine that when my mother's younger sister, my Aunty Oby, came to America several years after my parents, she and her peers had a softer landing, with family and community established and thriving in the US. They wanted to stay, even as parts of the economy began to improve back home and a true transition to democratic rule seemed likely.

Then, just as plans for our return were coming together, the political winds shifted once again. The optimistic phone calls and plans were replaced by news of an annulled presidential election; the ascent of yet another military dictator, General Sani Abacha; and brutal attacks on the press and pro-democracy activists. Concerned that life could revert back to the Nigeria they'd fled, my parents shifted their time line from stacking housewares in the garage to "Well, let's wait and see." Then the conversation stopped altogether.

As a child, I thought I understood what a huge exchange it would be, moving to Nigeria: We'd trade certain creature comforts for close family. But I didn't know the half of it.

In the US, there's an honor system: Electricity is provided based not just on how much you have paid but on the shared understanding that you will pay. A hard day's work does, in fact, equal a hard day's wage. It had never occurred to any of us, growing up in Medfield, that because of a military coup, the banks could close, leaving us with no money and therefore no food. My parents remembered this life in Nigeria all too well.

It became clear that the "nice American life" that my parents worked so hard to establish—especially "nice," considering their own Nigerian childhoods—did not guarantee us a "nice Nigerian life" in this uncertain future. The promise they were building in our minds and in our garage gathered dust, then collapsed.

In the end, my father simply was not willing to roll the dice. As is true for so many immigrants who arrive at a place with the hope of returning home, when it came time to do the deed, we didn't.

OUR CONVERSATION DOWNSHIFTED to what some might see as a simpler dream—a family trip to Nigeria. My parents began to save, but still, with seven plane tickets required and limited time off from work and school, the idea seemed almost as distant and ambitious as our moving there.

Then, one day, my grandmother Nwakaego called, asking to see all of her grandchildren as soon as possible. The weight of that request, plus the happy news that in the summer Uncle David would marry in Achi, our family's village, sped up the clock. We couldn't save and wait to do what we wanted; we had to do what we could.

My mother had been back to Nigeria most recently, taking along Junior when he was just a baby. Rich and Onyi had lived there, as children, and had their own memories and feelings about going back. And so my parents decided that Chi-Chi and I—the only ones of our five who had never been—would travel over with our father once school let out.

We flew Pan Am—a double-decker plane with an upstairs that we weren't allowed to go to. When we finally disembarked, it was into a blazing heat, like the rush of an oven, turning foreheads, palms, and suitcase handles sticky with sweat.

We walked out of the airport gate and into the crowd, and I could feel my father's demeanor change into something I'd never seen in America. His eyes darted, as if something could very quickly transpire. I didn't know the reason for his concern, but I knew that for us, the look on his face meant we shouldn't wander off. As we passed armed men with semiautomatic machine guns, I understood that Chi-Chi and I had to stay close—and for real. This wasn't like the Natick mall, where we were warned to stick together, even if the food court beckoned us. At Lagos's Murtala Muhammed International Airport, it seemed that a similar distraction could create heavy consequences.

My father, sister, and I stood near the airport curb with our suitcases, searching for the metallic blue Volvo belonging to my

Uncle Ifeanyi, my mother's brother. It was late afternoon; the slanting hot sun beamed into car grilles and fenders. I looked around, realizing that I had never seen so many Black people in my life: Black people out in a world absent of white people, a sight I had witnessed only at family weddings and other Nigerian events. When I say Black, I mean Black like me: chocolate, sun-kissed— everyone I saw had that kind of sheen about them—and steeped in their Africanness. Here I was in a place where I could see myself, my family, at every turn.

Uncle Ifeanyi finally arrived. As we hurtled down the road, with Chi-Chi and me in the back seat, I stared out the window. The dirt was red in Nigeria—as if we were on Mars. I gripped the thick pleather of the back seat as we raced the setting sun, and I remembered that here, armed robbers—area boys, as they're called— were said to come out after dark.

We drove through downtown Lagos, through crowds and car horns blasting, and arrived at my uncle's garden apartment. The first things I noticed were the grate on the front door, the padlock, and the size of the deadbolt. Though I knew we'd be safe inside, I had a strong sense of threats outside, real or imagined.

We adjusted to the time change and got to know our many doting aunties and uncles, and I began to relax. Chi-Chi and I now understood: These weren't costumes that our parents were wearing; these weren't special occasion foods. *All* the men here wore trousers and short-sleeved button-downs and slippers in the house, not just my father. This was where all of me was from.

There is a word in the Igbo language, *ikune*, that speaks to the welcome you feel in your mother's home place. It means "the authority you are given." In every home we visited, Chi-Chi and I were honored guests, encouraged to take freely. The treatment made us feel both fragile and coddled—like "eggs," as Uncle Ifeanyi joked. If there were a big tree on the side of the house, its first fruits would go to me before even the children who lived there. If I felt like watching something on TV, the other kids had to change the channel—something that would never fly with my siblings back home. When we stayed with my Uncle Bertie, my mother's brother, my aunt served us anything we wanted to eat, even if she had to make it. The fabric she had in the house was meant to become clothes for my sister and me.

After a few days we went on to Achi, my father's village, which was about nine hours east. Traditionally, this was our home: In Nigeria, the children of a family belong to the father.

Unlike my mother, whose family traveled often, my father was the first of his family to leave Achi. Now he was a successful accountant bringing home his American children and his brother, Uncle David. The family would not only celebrate the return of two sons; there would be a wedding besides.

While there were dirt roads across Nigeria, the drive to Achi was through the bush. We pulled up at a modest house built back into a palm grove, a fire for cooking out front. Nearby was a giant mound of dirt marking a spot that our father said would be our family's home one day. For now, it was just an idea—a barren hill with a metal stake driven through on one side.

Chi-Chi and I were excited for a wedding, but even more so to meet young cousins—peers who not only looked like us but *felt* like us. Together we all slept on the floor, head to toe.

These cousins, especially Chidimma and Uche, the daughters of my Aunty Mercy, made us feel not only welcome but famous, almost. They had an outsize love for America, all the way down to the peanut butter and jelly and tuna fish that we privileged

American kids brought in our suitcases. Later, they boasted to their friends about having tried animal crackers—the humblebrag of humblebrags. We taught them our hand games and shared our books on tape—*Goldilocks and the Three Bears* and *The Ugly Duckling*—which chimed when it was time to turn the book's page. A jackpot for any child in those days, and especially a Nigerian child, who couldn't find such a toy in any market. My cousins loved them so much that my father, feigning begging, guilted us into leaving the tapes behind.

A few days into our stay, a brown goat appeared. It was medium-size, tied to the stake atop that mound representing our family's future home. The next morning, a group of women poured into the compound before dawn; the scent of spices from their large cooking pots filled the air by first light. Chi-Chi and I joined the other girls and women out back by the fire, cutting vegetables and rolling and cutting dough for chin-chin, which the aunties would fry up in pans of hot oil while the kids ran around outside.

The afternoon grew late, and I heard the sounds of drums in the distance, a kind of fife poking through. As the music advanced, the older kids nudged the rest of us back into the house. "You have to come now," said one when I resisted.

From the size of our crowd and the feeling of anticipation, I wondered if the wedding was about to begin. The music grew louder, and finally I relented, finding Chi-Chi and following the wave of kids back toward the house. The aunties were waiting for us, standing along the path and in the doorways. "Inside now," they commanded.

We complied, but Chi-Chi and I lingered near the doorway, taking turns peeking out, trying to catch a glimpse of the action. The men in our family greeted this parade of men, and together they all encircled a masked man wearing a kind of shaggy, blackish-brown costume. It was an ancestor—a masquerade, they called him—coming back to them to bless the marriage.

This masquerade had a wide mouth in a kind of turned-up smile, the likes of which I'd seen only on dragon costumes for Chinese New Year. He seemed like a giant, towering on stilts above the other men. With large gestures, he danced to the drumbeat, waving and pointing a finger at man after boy after man after boy, as if he knew something—almost as if he were admonishing them. His other hand held the tail of some kind of animal, maybe a horse or a cow, which he used as a fan and fly swatter.

As the music and the dance continued, some of the men began waving machetes in time to the rhythm, as if they were trying to tame this ancestor. Others, including my father and my uncles David and Augustin, sprayed money at him. Through the cracks I watched as they danced, joyful and joyous: A wedding was coming, and now this masquerade—a lifeline, carrying spirits of the dead—had arrived.

I leaned my left shoulder a little farther against the door and felt a tug on the back of my dress. "They will beat you, badly, if you go," Chidimma whispered in my ear. Only men could speak with the ancestors, she explained.

Then the door slammed shut. The shutters too. As the house had no electricity, Chi-Chi and I found ourselves cross-legged on the cold concrete floor in total darkness. We could hear the women going out the back door to continue cooking. Only my Aunty Vickie, my father's sister, stayed behind, urging us cousins to keep still.

The other children didn't seem frightened, but I was. To me, the darkness felt ominous, but more than that, it felt lonely—as if everyone else were aware of something we didn't understand.

Through my nervous breathing and the squirming around me, I could hear the music growing still louder. Faster. Then, atop that swirl of sound came an equally frantic bleating—a noise I'd never heard before.

I didn't know what was happening, and I don't speak goat, but somewhere, in my spirit, maybe I had a sense. That noise sounded like panic: very loud, very loud, and then silence. No sound at all.

The door opened again a few minutes later, this time wide enough for us to push out into the yard. Chi-Chi and I trailed behind the crowd of cousins walking toward the place where the aunties were standing over their large cauldrons. Once again we picked up our games, this time by firelight. In the midst of all the activity, I saw the goat inside one of the hot cauldrons. Its head hung lifeless on the pot's edge, facing the night sky. Its tongue was sticking out.

"They killed that goat," I said to myself, each word standing up on its own, straight and scared and plain. I'd never seen a dead thing before. My imagination took off as I wondered how life could lose its light so fast.

"It's dead, they killed it, and we're going to eat it," I told Chi-Chi. This felt both matter-of-fact to me and completely impossible.

Animal sacrifices—a sign of abundance, of thanksgiving, in our culture—are a part of life in Nigeria. If we hadn't been there, I doubt the other children would have been shut away. They were likely told: *Those kids, those Americans, don't kill goats on a hill; they put them in a farm machine somewhere, and the meat returns in a package.*

I felt a shadow over the rest of the evening. Chi-Chi and I didn't know what everyone else knew.

The ritual, which would become more familiar to me during later trips, would never feel easy. I would stand in the same spot many years later, to witness my Uncle Augustin's lastborn son, a child then just eleven or twelve, holding the head of another goat for a similar purpose. Still I shuddered; still I was the American kid who wasn't used to such things.

In this rite of passage was a huge responsibility: For there to be life, you have to take life. You may not want this to be the case; you have no choice but to join the club.

I thought to myself: How very young boys are, in our culture, when they're expected to become men.

WITH JUST TWO DAYS left in our family's trip, we prepared to leave Achi and take what was known as the Old Road to Obosi, my mother's place. We set off late in the day, and we arrived at the compound in almost total darkness. By then Chi-Chi and I had grown used to nights with little light—so different from our home in Medfield, with a thousand hums and glows.

My Aunty Ifey, whom we knew well from the US, was now caring for my grandmother at her home. She'd waited for us, opening the front door carrying a small lantern. She led us straight into a bedroom, where a tiny figure was propped up, wearing a headscarf and cardigan.

I approached the bed frightened. Realizing that Chi-Chi was hanging back, I stepped forward, taking one of my grandmother's hands. I was mystified by how worn and leathered it was. Rough and yet strangely soft. Her fingers felt heavy as I held them. Substantial, even in their obvious weakness.

"How's Mommy?" This voice of my grandmother was as distant as the light. The other adults in the room were silent, motionless.

"How are you?" my grandmother asked us in Igbo. "Are you being good for Mommy? How's school? Keep working hard in school, please . . ." And over again, "*I nụgo?*" "Do you hear me, do you understand?"

Chi-Chi and I nodded, listening, as we stood together at the side of her low bed. I felt awed—and a little proud. Everyone I knew had a grandma, and now, finally, I had one too.

My mom, I said to myself, has a mom. It was a strangely new idea. As hard as it is for any child to imagine their parents as children, it's all the more true when you've never seen any evidence of their acting in a childlike way. I'd never heard her say "Mama" on our end of an expensive phone call, kept as brief as possible. The surprising fact that she didn't come into the world grown and whole—that she had to learn to become a mother and a wife— meant that one day, I too could fill those roles.

My mom had not always been the mother I knew. She was once a baby this woman lying here had carried. I wondered, for the first time, whether my mother missed her mother. Then the pride faded as I realized that my grandmother was also the oldest-looking person I'd ever seen. I sensed the fragility of her life just as I had when I'd held my infant cousins or my friends' tiny baby sisters and brothers.

We could not stay long. We had to return to Lagos to prepare for our flight home. On the drive back, I recalled a few early memories of my grandmother, from when I must have been about three years old. They were more like half memories: dreamlike and hazy.

In one, she is at home with us. She's leaning over the tub in our bathroom, bathing weeks-old Chi-Chi, having come to the US for the first time for the Igbo tradition of *omugwo*.

When a woman becomes a mother, it's believed to be her own mother's responsibility to ease her into the new role. The mother stays with her daughter during this period of *omugwo*, taking the child during the day, handling the cooking and cleaning, so the new mother can get some rest and relief. Meanwhile, the new father sends money and food back to his father-in-law, who is now without his wife, so he can hire someone to help with his home.

Like *The Lion King*'s Rafiki holding up his baby Simba, it's supposed to go 'round and 'round, this circle. In our culture, as well as many others, it's understood that caring for your children, and your parents, is not only your responsibility; it's the highest currency.

There is a lesson to be learned here, America.

The way my mother described *omugwo* was like water, quenching a thirst she didn't even know she had. When you leave a country as she did, you do so with no assumption about when you'll see any of its people again. I can only imagine how much work was involved, arranging for my grandmother to come over. Still, the way my mother recounted this rite of passage was as joy—pure joy.

In another memory, my grandmother is sitting near the entryway of our kitchen, in the seat where my mom would normally sit to watch the TV on the counter. She has the chair pulled out, so I can't squeeze by.

There is no sound accompanying either memory. But even if her voice wasn't there, her presence was.

My father, Chi-Chi, and I arrived back in Lagos at the home of my Uncle Ifeanyi. As we got out of the car, we saw his eldest son, my cousin Chubi, outside waiting for us.

"Grandma died," Chubi said through the iron gate.

But we had seen her just hours earlier. How could someone who was very much alive, who I had just met, in the space of a minute—seconds, even—be gone? Death felt nearer to me then. Life had been taken, was often taken, even as I had been unaware.

We sat with our cousins while our father picked up the phone to call our mother; several minutes later, Chi-Chi and I crowded around the phone to hear her voice.

"How are you? Are you OK?" my mother asked, before we could speak. "It's good that you saw her. I am glad you got to see her."

From the other side of the world, I sensed a shift. Chi-Chi too. We were only children then, but we knew. On that call, we were all children.

On the flight home I leaned over the tray table, scribbling in my journal, trying to capture each person, each drive, and every detail of the landscape: the grace of the giant palm leaves in Achi, the layout of the Anyaoku family compound, the view from the street as well as the inside. I wanted to get down in words the taste and texture of the food, the rules of each new game I'd learned.

"Dear Diary," I began, thinking of my mother's beautiful handwriting and feeling myself drift away. Over the years, as I'd fill in book after book, I came to see my journals as a space to put feelings I didn't know I could say out loud.

The journal I kept for our trip to Nigeria had a stiff, kelly green cover. Three gold, round-headed prongs held in the lined paper my mother had bound inside. It was fitting that it seemed more like a report cover, as this was the first time that accounting for my story felt critical. The details mattered. I wanted to remember all the sights and sounds.

I felt a clearer sense that it was possible to forget, or, in the case of my grandmother, to be forgotten. I didn't want to forget her any more than I already had; there was so little of her already. I didn't want any more of her story—my story—to be erased.

I began that journal in a way that felt formal. From the time we embarked, my goal was to provide my mother with a firsthand account of our experiences in her homeland—our homeland. I knew that she wanted to be squarely seated among us, and to breathe in our time as her own. I worked to keep names sorted and relationships clear to the best that my elementary school education could afford. Just the facts, ma'am: dates, locations, times.

After meeting my grandmother, my "Grandma," I realized that all she was—all my mom was—was so much bigger than my quick surface description. I needed to help fill the passage of time between them, bringing back home my answers to Grandma's questions, as well as my observations. I wondered: Did my grandmother have a smell, and, if so, what was it? I wish I had thought to take that in. I know transporting that detail would have meant so much to my mom.

As I continued to record our time together, I found that the pages had expanded past a book report, the "required reading," and writing had become a pleasure for me. I wanted to have my own piece of my grandma, my own memories.

As we crossed the Atlantic, I added every single detail I could remember of our interaction with my grandmother. Every question, every move.

I would never see Grandma again. I had hardly seen her before, so what, for me, had died? The chance to have a grandma—to use that word with loving frequency, as I'd heard my friends use it. The chance to be a grandchild.

We returned to Medfield, to a home filled with visitors and food. For once, someone else was hosting. But my mother was still presiding over the conversation, which, for the first few days, centered around funeral preparations: who was going there, who was coming back.

We already knew that there was no money for another plane

ticket, but that did not make the situation any less devastating for my mother. While she was not technically her mother's eldest daughter, her elder sister, Ifeoma, had died of cancer young—at age forty-four. For this reason, my mother was a kind of acting eldest, a role known in our culture as the *ada*.

There are no nursing homes in Nigeria; caring for one's parents when they grow old is the charge of the *ada*. In this way, in those years of transition, the *ada* becomes a sort of mother to the family. The role of the eldest son, known as the *diokpa*, is to manage the wealth and property he is to inherit. He does the organizing, the fundraising, and the handling of funeral costs; she handles the preparations. She is the one who chooses the clothing and casket, and she washes and dresses the parent for burial—a final act of human loving-kindness.

I had been crushed that my mother couldn't come with us to Nigeria, and I now felt doubly helpless. I couldn't bring back my grandmother; I couldn't even help my mother feel better.

"Yep, that's OK," chirped Chi-Chi when she learned upon our return that her seventh birthday party, a huge topic of discussion on our trip, would be canceled.

"Mommy's very sad," said my mother, patting her hand.

When I told my mother about my journal, I could see her pride. I readily produced the book; I didn't mind even when she asked to keep it. It was, by some measures, the last living account of her mother.

Chapter 5

Sunday mornings were sacred in our home, not to be touched by friends or sports or activities. A blessing before a meal was a daily practice. I saw church as an hour of space for us to express gratitude and remember that God loves all of us.

Though the community at Medfield's Church of the Advent was made up of our town's very traditionalist, quiet, conservative folks, the environment inside the church's walls felt very open-minded, welcoming, and spiritually liberal. The focus was love above all things—all we need and all we need to do.

The message coming from the pulpit was to be good, treat people well, and, most of all, give thanks. Just as strongly present among the liturgies and the Bible readings was song: I grew up steeped in choral music, as, for our congregation, faith and music were so deeply entwined.

I didn't know much about sin and absolution until I was in college and first sat in Boston's Trinity Church, next to my friend

Jessica, and heard only fear from the pulpit. I felt shocked, my eyes sliding across the iconography inside the glowing stained glass, thinking, Where is that written? I'm not sure that I even knew, until then, about Leviticus—the implications underscoring the "thou shalts," the fire and brimstone, judgment and condemnation.

Christianity came to Nigeria in the sixteenth century, when the first missionaries navigated down the Niger River. Under British colonial rule, it truly took hold. The Book of Common Prayer, which my family uses, is a fixture of the Church of England. It guided the primary and secondary curricula when my parents were young.

My father's father helped to establish the Anglican congregation in their hometown. Many of my relatives' most joyful memories, on each side, surround the church. When each of my parents came to the US, they sought out the Episcopalian church, the Anglican Church's American offshoot.

My parents taught us that gratitude is our deepest connection with God. My mother believed you could lean on God for positivity, protective covering, or just to get through. If you did, as she did, then you had to appreciate everything He sent in your direction.

Faith can be tough for a young person. Though I grew up knowing God was real, I also came to understand that life could be hard. I often wondered why God wasn't helping me in the ways I was asking.

He will, my mother insisted. She had seen it happen in her own life.

When my mother was five, out at the market with my grandmother, she suddenly realized that she couldn't move. Sitting on a large rock, she'd heard her mother ask her to fetch something. She'd attempted to move her legs to stand up but felt—and, equally horrifying, she saw—nothing happen.

By this time, in 1946, polio was very much a concern in Western countries such as the US and Sweden; a vaccine was already under development. The threat of this contagious and often debilitating virus was not as well-known in Nigeria. Still, my grandmother, by the grace of God and the work of the March of Dimes missionaries, immediately recognized the symptoms. She threw my mother over her shoulder and ran to the hospital.

There, the local doctors told my grandparents that my mother would never walk again—a prognosis that the family refused to accept. They believed that there was something guiding my mother. The meaning of her full name, Chukwunonyelum, is "God abides with me." I've heard it said that it is a name given for the loss of a child, though my mother knew of no such happening for her parents. Still, I like the idea of her name holding a force—God's or otherwise.

Their abiding faith did not mean, however, that their daughter could just sit in the house and expect to recover. As the book of James says, she had to pray for healing and also work for it.

Certain that, with God's help, their daughter could overcome her illness, my grandparents decided that they would take her by train to Port Harcourt, a city a few hours south of where they lived. My grandfather's sister Afulenu was a nurse at a teaching hospital close by, which had good treatment options and good physical therapy.

"All I remember of this time is the pushing on my leg, pushing on my leg," my mother told me when I was in high school. "I'd be trying so hard. I'd want to pull it back, and they'd say, 'Nno, keep exercising until it's straight.'"

Ifeoma, two years my mother's senior, moved down to Port Harcourt to keep her sister company—and to help. The nurses handed her a little switch and told her to watch my mother on the way to school: "Force her to put her foot down," they said. "If she doesn't, you have to be whipping her, making sure it stays on the floor."

Such harsh treatment seemed impossible to Ify; the two girls were best friends. "I don't want to hit you with this thing," she would tell my mother tearfully. "But they say I have to."

"But I cannot put my foot down! It hurts!" my mother would say in reply.

Then they would both sit down, together, to cry. "We would get up, and I'd start walking the right way, until I went back to walking the way I was used to," my mother told me. "And then we would cry again."

This was how my mother taught herself to walk once more, and to do so without so much as a limp. Only if you trailed behind her, looking very closely, could you see that the heel of her left foot never really touched the ground.

My mother returned to school when she was steady enough, and she learned to play netball, a game similar to basketball. Soon she joined the school's team. Concerned, the administrators at St. Michael's Cathedral Anglican Church called my grandparents, reminding them that their daughter was "a cripple."

"Tell her that she has to sit out," they said.

"So you say that my daughter is 'a cripple,'" said my grandmother. "Did my daughter complain of any problems?" When she heard no, my grandmother countered: "Well, then I think she is not a cripple. She should play like the others."

After netball, she picked up tennis, growing into a phenomenal athlete. My uncles and aunties admired her inner fight. "Oh, your mother was in all the sports, and you know she had polio," they'd tell me—a little tip of the hat. "And still, even, to be so strong . . ."

What polio took from my mother, and what she had to restore, made her ever so much more aware of her body and, I think, even more grateful for what it could accomplish. She instilled in her children a willingness to dare and try—to explore our full selves without fear of condemnation, or fear of whatever else people fear their parents will do when they take a risk.

My siblings and I sometimes wondered what might have been, if any of us had pursued tennis. Junior once asked my mother why she hadn't insisted we try, but she was never like that—a "stage mommy." She cheered us on, always, but there was never an agenda. No cursing, sideline coaching, or any of that.

She was less invested in our winning and more in how we prepared: "How hard did you work?" she'd ask. "Do you think you really put in the work?" My father, on the other hand, loved the victory. He too was a great athlete: I had seen pictures of him in his tracksuit, jumping over hurdles. We understood that he was very, very quick, as was my Aunty Mercy. As am I.

My father loved seeing his children celebrated. Quietly humble on the outside, he would drive as far as needed, and to as many stores as necessary, if he knew that one of our names was in the newspaper. He loved all of us, but he was especially captivated by Junior, his last born. His son. He made his best efforts to be part of all phases of his growth: practices, games, friendships, relationships. He was a true believer in everything Junior thought possible for himself—and, as my mother was for me, a true champion for the things Junior could not yet see as possible.

IF, IN OUR HOUSE, sports were the main course—and they were—then they came with a heaping side of the arts. The flute and violin, drama club and knitting—they all spoke to my parents, who didn't come from a place that had such options. They enrolled us in as many activities as possible, pushing us academically, physically, and creatively.

My mother told us that if she had been fortunate enough to grow up in the United States, she would have been an artist. And now that I'm an adult, I can admit that she was single-handedly responsible for the artwork for every school project I did.

Any time my siblings and I were able to choose our focus for a school project—a book report, say, or a story about a "Hero of Mine"—my mother insisted that our subject had to be somebody Black. I don't remember wanting to write about Amelia Earhart, but even if I had, she wouldn't have been an option.

"You get enough of that," she said. "You don't know anything about your own people."

My mother could not believe the erasure of Black people in our world history lessons; her shock over our absence was nothing compared to her surprise by how few Black people figured into our *American* history books.

"I know more about your people than you know about your people—than white people write about your own people," she once told us.

She took every opportunity to tell us: "If I went to your American school, if I walked away with the education you received, I would think the only Black people in the world who ever did anything were Martin Luther King Jr. and Harriet Tubman.

"Tell me again, how is it that you have never heard of Sojourner Truth? Marcus Garvey? Shirley Chisholm? *They* are your American heroes." What about world history, or African history? she wondered. "Nelson Mandela? Nnamdi Azikiwe? Kwame Nkrumah? Chinua Achebe?!"

My mother had come to this land of so-called opportunity feeling like she had won the lottery. She hadn't considered the implications of life as a Black woman in America as she was hopping and skipping to that plane.

Both she and my father had been aware of the civil rights movement. *They* knew who Martin Luther King Jr. was, they knew who Malcolm X was, and they knew that things had been bad. Still, the Civil Rights Act of 1968 had passed; they thought things were getting better. Now, having discovered that she'd landed in a country that actively worked to make Black people feel like they were nothing, she was determined to reverse engineer her own children's experience.

My siblings and I also grew up in the '90s, steeped in the Pan-African movement—aware of people, including our own friends and relatives, going to Nigeria or Ghana to learn more about themselves. We were painfully aware of the apartheid in South Africa, and we knew all too well too the ways more subtle racism played out right at home.

Both of my parents impressed on all of us this idea: You come from somewhere with a history and a culture, which means that you have worth. That's true for your family, Nigerian people, and *all* Black people, even those whose histories have been abducted. Even your awareness of that unspeakable tragedy should not eclipse the root knowledge that we all began on the mighty African continent. Your life is not disposable—whether that means your academic life, how you use your life, or how people treat you in this life.

The psychological grip enslavement has over some of our people persists now, even though the physical bonds were broken. We still have room to claim our legacy as descendants of survivors. Bondage, Jim Crow policies, systemic racism still prevalent today—this all might feel like hard history to hold. But don't be fooled into believing that our history is anything other than invaluable.

"I never knew there was anything wrong with being Black until I moved to America," my mother said.

WHEN MY MOTHER arrived in the US, she lived with her first husband—Rich and Onyi's biological father—in Connecticut's Litchfield County, which was then 99 percent white. As the couple were settling in, a few of their new neighbors invited them to a party. There, as introductions were made, a well-appointed white party guest nodded approvingly at my mother's new dress. "How did you learn to wear these clothes?" asked the woman, shaking her head in amazement.

Having sewed the dress herself, my mother launched into an earnest explanation of the pattern type, the fabric choices. Neither the subtext of the woman's response nor the other new neighbors' surprise at her facility with English registered to her. Only later, when she was applying for a teaching position at one of the local schools, did the implications become clear.

My mother arrived for the interview, and a secretary at the school's office greeted her and pointed her down the hall. Taking her seat among a few others, my mother waited. She looked around at people wearing jeans and T-shirts, fearing she was overdressed. She watched as others were called in, her time slot coming and going.

Finally, she caught the eye of one of the school officials. Upon hearing that she was there for the teaching position, he raised his eyebrows. "Come with me," he said.

Not even a minute into her interview, which began hastily soon after, my mother was aghast. What would have made them think that she was there for a custodial position? This she couldn't help wondering, while endeavoring to politely correct them.

The answer to this question is what she would, years later, come to understand as racism. She'd been dressed to interview for a teaching position, but all the school secretary had seen was a Black face, like many of the custodial candidates. This ridiculous thought—that, because of her skin color, she would not be able to teach, to speak the language, to dress herself appropriately—would dog my mother no matter how she tried to fit in. She would grow exhausted working to prove her right to belong.

Sometimes, when we were growing up, my mother's mind drifted back to that party in Connecticut, her neighbor's comment on her dress, and the later, harsh revelation of its context.

"I was so mad," she said.

There's a subtle distinction between "mad" and "angry," and I learned about it from my mother. She was known to throw a slipper in angry frustration if we weren't cleaning up, or to shout when one of us didn't listen or do what she'd asked. This anger was like an unexpected tornado, showing up quickly and likely to upset anything in its path. When she was mad, it was like watching clouds gather into a hurricane out at sea. A focused power, intentional in its direction, whose force is unimaginable until observed on land.

This is how my mother addressed the high insult of racist behavior. She clenched her fists in frustration, as if the offending person were right in front of her. Her reaction wasn't always loud, but we could sense there was a roar caught in her, like a lion, and the pressure and presence made you sit up a little bit straighter with the realization that someone had done something . . . bad.

To see her mad was to know that, without ever having experienced anything close to her story, something like this could also happen to me.

Chapter 6

By middle school, I was starting to have more crushes on boys and wanting them to like me back, while also understanding that their definition of beauty was blond hair and blue eyes. I, then, believed that I was not beautiful. How could I be? There is no clearer binary than one from a culture rooted in colonialism, which defines skin tone as either "white" or "black." If blond was beautiful, then I was the antithesis. It felt like very simple math to me.

But I could see the beauty in my own family, and especially in my sisters. Onyi, whom I idolized, had the most gorgeous hair I'd ever seen. Chi-Chi had always been thought of as cute; she was tiny—toothpick skinny—with wide-set almond-shaped eyes and perfect, equally tiny teeth, like a row of Chiclets.

I was not alone in seeing them as extraordinary. At Nigerian functions, greeting aunties we hadn't seen in so long, my siblings and I would line up, trying to smile, as my mother reintroduced us.

Oh! Is this really Onyi? So smart, so pretty.

That's Chi-Chi! So slim! they'd exclaim, reaching out, cupping her chin, really taking her in. Grasping her hands, stretching each arm out to the side.

And ah! This Uzo, with her figure skating. So talented.

Wasn't it supposed to be pretty *and* talented?

I spent a lot of time in those days looking in the mirror at my own eyes, my own smile, sadly wondering how they measured up.

I didn't care, as a teenager, that the space between my two front teeth—the Anyaoku gap, as my family called it—was a sign of beauty and wisdom in Africa. All my friends had braces, and they'd come off revealing straight, "perfect" teeth. My mother ignored all my pleas for the orthodontist, so I stopped smiling in public and especially in photos. I practiced speaking with my mouth mostly closed too.

If she saw me posing with a group, my mother would make a "smile" gesture, fingers framing her mouth's turned-up corners, cheeks high in the air—even if she wasn't personally taking the picture. That was the only thing in the world that could make me smile less.

I'd loved dressing up since Chi-Chi and I wore our matching, homemade flower girl dresses to Uncle David's wedding. I began to linger in our parents' bathroom, staring at the shelving over the toilet that was packed with tubes, canisters, and bottles. I grew curious about the significant time and energy that my mother and the other women in my life put into their own looks.

My mother's biggest piece of beauty advice was: Not too much. She loved red lipstick, but it was a muted red. She wore a little bit of powder but always let her face come through. Perfume, just a dab—but always, always perfume before leaving the house: Elizabeth Arden Blue Grass.

Her one essential practice was washing her face every night. Even when exhausted, with ninety thousand things to do, she carried this ritual like a badge of honor: "I don't care how tired I am." She really got into it, setting up the bathroom as if indulging in a spa treatment. From the kitchen came a plastic basin filled with piping-hot water alongside a really cold washcloth. Then she got underway, moaning with pleasure as she washed away her makeup and her day. I never heard my parents make love; thanks to this nightly routine, I'm pretty sure I know what it would've sounded like.

She carried herself well, and yet I often thought that she wasn't as vain as she *could* be, at least compared to some of our other family friends and relations, whom I'd never seen not fully dressed, without jewelry and makeup. Even on her most terrible days, my Aunty Oby still had an eyebrow. She still had a little something going on.

"She was the most beautiful one . . ." my mother sometimes would say about Aunty Oby or about Aunty Ngozi, her younger sisters. "I wasn't that beautiful."

"Mom, don't say that!" It really, truly hurt my heart so much to hear those words. "No, Mom, you *are* so beautiful." I reminded her of her college portrait—her full lips set; her dark, almond-shaped eyes fixed, brows lifted; her quick wit shining through. I couldn't imagine her living under the weight of thoughts like mine. But maybe all women did.

My mother tried to be gracious, to clarify: "I'm just saying, there weren't rounds and rounds [of suitors] coming to, you know . . ." Then she'd wave it off. My mother knew that she was funny, that she was fearless, and that she had a personality people liked. Even if she, like I, had some insecurities, she knew her strengths, and her confidence shone through.

Plus, my mother, like all her sisters, had inherited a great fashion sense from her mother, my grandmother Nwakaego.

"Was she vain?" I once asked, when I'd overheard her say as much to my Aunty Oby. In what felt like no time, my memories of my grandmother's last days were crowded out by these old family stories and treasured black-and-white photos from long-ago family parties.

Picking up one of the pictures, I surveyed my grandmother's dark lashes, off-the-shoulder neckline, and white beaded necklace. Gorgeous.

"Very vain," my mother said with a laugh, peering down from behind me. "But we all loved her for it."

I WORE MY HAIR naturally as a kid, relying on my mother for the conditioning, cutting, and braiding. In the 1980s, my mother had a Jheri curl, which was tightly coiled, well-shaped, and worn high. Onyi too used chemical relaxants sometimes; her beautiful long hair held looser curls, which came through a separate treatment. She had gorgeous hair with great movement, and I wanted the same: Hawaiian Silk. Finally, one spring weekend when I was in the sixth grade, I was allowed to go to the salon to get it.

I assumed the salon would be like the one I'd walked past a number of times in Medfield, with clean, new white floors, big front windows, and lightbulb-framed "Hollywood" mirrors. Women walked out of there looking like movie stars. I imagined myself doing the same, hair cascading down my back like Rudy Huxtable's, but even more curly.

There was no place near Medfield that specialized in Black hair, however. My mother drove Onyi and me toward Boston to Roxbury, a neighborhood where people looked like us. She dropped us off at a salon on her way to some errand or appointment.

It was a far more humble establishment than any I'd seen in our surrounding towns—smaller and seemingly short of staff and hands to clean. I didn't know if this was as nice as a salon for Brown girls could be at that time, or if it was simply the best my parents could afford.

Regardless, I was excited—excited to be made beautiful.

In the chair, feeling as grown-up as anyone else there, I tried to ignore the pungent smell and my tingling scalp as I waited—and waited—for the relaxer to take effect. Finally, I followed the stylist over to the sink, helping her arrange my neck and shoulders over the dark porcelain. I felt some tugging as she washed; then I felt some more tugging. After what sounded like a soft gasp, I felt more vigorous scrubbing and much less tugging. I sat up for a minute and looked back at clumps of my hair in the sink. "Almost done," sang the stylist, guiding my face back around and my head down, racing to wash out the rest.

She settled me under the dryer and disappeared, leaving me with no idea of what to think. My searching hands reached beneath the hood of the dryer and detected sections of my hair missing, but I couldn't get a sense of the damage or how it would affect this wavy style that I had dreamed of for so long.

A new stylist walked over to greet me, holding a pair of scissors. "Just have to even it out," she said cheerfully.

Directing me into a chair spun away from the mirror, the new stylist began cutting, cutting, cutting. Onyi stood watching nearby, nodding slightly, despite my growing concern.

The new stylist turned me around to reveal my little Michael Jackson Afro.

Tears came immediately, and they didn't stop as Onyi and I sat together in the waiting area, searching out the window for our family's Dodge Grand Caravan. Now, is there anything wrong with an Afro? Absolutely not. My mother had a similar style in a portrait I loved, but that was from 1984. In Medfield in 1992, in sixth grade, this was definitely not the look.

"I'm going to fix it," Onyi said, over and over again, as I stared at my faint reflection. "I'm going to fix it. As soon as we get home, I'm going to fix it."

"How?" I cried.

". . . Hoops?"

My eyes narrowed. Onyi can fix anything, but I was skeptical.

"What happened?" was the first thing out of my mother's mouth as the van door rolled open, confirming my worst suspicions.

As soon as we got home, Onyi ran to her room, where she manufactured a long, thin, peaches-and-cream-colored scarf, narrowed at the end, very Stevie Nicks. She sat me on the bathroom counter, facing her; she picked and picked at my little puff, folding the bandana, tying it along the side and putting a large gold hoop earring through each of my pierced ears.

She lifted me down and spun me around to face the mirror.

"No," I said.

"You don't like it?"

"I look like a pirate," I said, shooing away Chi-Chi, who was trying to catch a glimpse.

I felt a kind of sadness—one that wouldn't even bring tears. The times I'd explained Black hair were innumerable. The questions began as far back as I can remember, and they continue: *Is that all your hair?* It was especially frustrating, given how little effort I'd put into it.

What would my friends say now? Or worse, what *wouldn't* they say? What would be behind that saccharine *Oh, you cut your hair!*

And most importantly, what would Kevin Roof say?

In the end, the silver lining of the whole disaster was that Kevin Roof, the boy I'd had a crush on forever, walked by me in the hall and tossed a compliment my way: "Uzo, I like your hair." I'm close to saying that it made my whole year. A year of multiple head-bands, I might add, a rotation that grew on me over time.

Kevin Roof, who would go on to be voted "Best Looking" of our senior class, was everybody's delight. Still, I'd argue that there were no Kevin Roof crushes like mine, which went on, uninter-rupted, from the day he moved to town in third grade through high school. There wasn't a love story, dream, fantasy, you name it, that did not feature Kevin Roof, even if I couldn't imagine him even considering me. His take cast some significant sunshine on the ex-perience.

Eventually my hair grew in, and Chi-Chi and I got braids, which we rocked from middle school into high school. Braids were easy and effortlessly cool, particularly when worn by Lisa Bonet's char-acter, Denise Huxtable, in *The Cosby Show* spin-off *A Different World*. I wanted that hair, those clothes, that life.

During our spring breaks, Chi-Chi, Junior, and I stayed with Onyi at Cornell University, in Ujamaa, the Black student dorm on campus. The scene felt like *A Different World*'s fictional Hillman College, and it *was* different for Onyi: Her boyfriend and her best friends were all from the Bronx.

We suburban kids taught them how to Rollerblade; they bor-rowed our skates, puffing their open winter coats behind them like capes on the way down the hill. It was the least we could do—

they'd saved up their cafeteria guest meals all semester so we could have breakfast together.

Onyi spent money that she didn't have taking us to the arcade and the bowling alley; when she was in class, we hung around the dorm with her friends. There was something else, somewhere else, other than Medfield, I learned, and it was great being somewhere else.

At home, I still sat at the same lunch table, with the same girls, but I was losing patience with the petty dramas that had begun to creep up all around me. Someone decides, for no reason, that she doesn't like another one of the girls seated there but won't say so—to her face, anyway. Instead, the whole group begins eyeing the new outcast, hinting at horrible things whenever they are in earshot of the popular boys one table over.

I tried to expand my circle, and the rhythm of bell changes and hallway chatter seemed like a good opportunity. For a while between classes, I joked around with two older boys: this guy Trevor and another kid, Luke, whose sister was in Chi-Chi's class. We weren't friends, but they had some classes in our hallway; for a while, we went back and forth with friendly teasing. Sticks and stones—some banter and color to anticipate in the middle of the day. I didn't have many guy friends at that point, so I welcomed the attention.

Seeing them around the corner one day, I made some typical if snarky comment. This time, instead of their usual spit-back, Luke said, "Oh yeah? N———"

Like a fucking bullet hit me. He and Trevor laughed at my frozen expression.

People say that word has no power. It *has* power. There was nothing I could say back to match what was said to me. "Cracker," "white boy," anything like that would be but a gnat to them. So easily brushed off.

There was certainly no one in whom I was going to confide about this—no teacher, no friend. So I walked to the bathroom and hid in a stall, quietly crying, scared and really, really lonely. Where had they learned that, I wondered, in a place with no Black people? I remembered when I'd learned it, in the third grade, watching an episode of a Friday-night sitcom. I remembered too what my mother had said: "If ever anyone would call you that, you come to me—tell me."

"What are you going to do?" I'd asked her.

"I'll fix it," my mother had said.

Now, staring at the bathroom stall door, I knew there'd be no telling my mother. I knew how much headache and hardship this very sentiment had caused her over the years. I didn't want her to have one more thing to fight.

That's the power of racism: Eventually, it will shut you up.

With that word, the marble that had been rolling around in my brain dropped into its ultimate landing place. I had not been shot, but with a single word spoken, I could feel the hit.

To me, that word meant: *I see you—I've seen you—and you are not like us. When I want to, I can dismantle whatever equality between us you think exists.*

ON MY FIRST DAY of eighth grade, Chi-Chi ran up to my locker on a bell change. "Uzo," she said breathlessly. "There's a new Black girl at school."

"WHAT?" I was so excited. Oh, thank you, God.

"She's in your grade, I think."

"What? Oh my gosh!" I rushed into the auditorium for our class assembly, scanning, scanning, scanning, until I saw her, sitting there in the front row, in a bright yellow dress. On both sides of her were empty seats; I walked up and took one.

"Hi, my name's Uzo," I said. "What's yours?"

"Simi," she said.

When I asked where she was from, she told me Wayland, a town about a half hour north. We sat together in silence for a few moments as I tried to place her. She was definitely not white, but she seemed . . . fair, to me. Could Chi-Chi have gotten it wrong? Was she mixed race?

"So, are you Black?" I said.

"No," she said.

"Are you sure?"

"I'm Indian," she said.

"Good enough," I said. We are going to have an outside experience together, I thought. And we did. Even better, we were both first-gen, forced to field the same questions, as was Karen Leong, whose parents were from China. *Why does your house smell like that? Why do your parents dress like that? Sound like that? What is that accent?* Our parents saw one another at sporting events or in the grocery store, and even though they were from completely different cultures, they connected.

Simi was funny and didn't know it, which is, to me, the most hilarious type of humor—an effortless, toss-out-the-jokes kind of way. She'd say that she was the big nerd and I was the popular one, but I don't know about that. I just know that I made much more of an effort to please, a skill that, to her, came naturally.

That first morning, I invited Simi to join my table at lunch.

But after spending one lunch period there, Simi chose to sit with another group of girls. I didn't blame her; the back-and-forth happening at my table was exhausting.

"Why are you picking on her?" I asked a tablemate one day. This particular girl had been the subject of whispers herself, and now she was giving the same treatment to someone else. "They were giving *you* shit however many days ago? Are you doing this so they'll forget about it?"

That day, the girl zipped her mouth. I think she wanted to disappear, knowing that she hadn't quite outrun her own bullying. The table was quiet as the group half remembered the past few days and their most recent enemy.

As the school year progressed, I continued to look around the table, thinking more and more of how little I had in common with these girls. By the time my birthday rolled around in February, not one of them had made my party's guest list.

Of course, they found out anyway. "Uzo, are you having a birthday party?" one asked during lunch.

"Yes," I said, taking my place on the bench, not wanting to seem intimidated.

"Who's going?" she continued. I began listing the names, and when I stopped, she asked, "That's it?"

"Yeah," I said.

"You're not inviting anyone here."

"No," I said.

"If those are your friends you're inviting, then why do you sit with us?"

"I've been sitting here since sixth grade," I said.

"But if we're not your friends, you shouldn't sit with us."

"I can sit wherever I want," I told her.

The next day, all the girls at my now-former table posted up at an empty table nearby, sending me a clear signal. I took my typical seat at our original table, my stomach on fire, my eyes hot with tears. If I were white, there'd have been no question: I would have been red.

"Why don't you come sit with us?" I heard a voice behind me and turned to see Kristin, a friend since the first grade. She held her lunch tray, sensing the breakdown in social order.

"No thanks," I said through closed teeth. And for the rest of the week, God bless her, Kristin brought her lunch over and sat with me.

I saw her walking into lunch that Friday and insisted she go back to her regular spot. "I don't want *you* to catch fire," I told her. She agreed.

Eating lunch by myself wasn't so bad, I told myself, as weeks and then months passed. It was a great time to read or write in my journal. At first, books were a useful prop and distraction. I could keep my head in my notebook, starting whatever run-on sentence might carry me to the lunch bell. Soon, journaling became a comfort—a place to firm up my conviction and release the pain of my isolation. If my eyes caught someone else's, it could very easily turn into a "Burn Book" full of insults, like the one Regina George created in *Mean Girls*.

The truth is that I felt exposed and embarrassed. I often came home crying at the end of the day and trying to hide it.

"Zozo, *o gini?*" My mother's voice was warm and soft as she asked me what was wrong. Standing in the bedroom doorway, watching me pull my covers over my head, she suggested that perhaps I'd been hasty, ignoring Kristin's invitation. She sat on the side of the bed and listened.

"They were being *mean* to this other girl, and they were mean to me," I said. I wouldn't let these girls get away with bullying me; I was not wrong. I had spoken out, and I wasn't going to change my position.

I sat alone until late spring, when, with about a month left to go in the school year, I started sitting with another crew—the "outsiders," with the flannels and Converse One Stars and a vaguely skateboarder vibe.

By then, I sensed that anyone I cared about had moved on. I'd moved on too.

I'd been nervous, at first, going it alone. I felt hurt, but I was never scared. Not only was I OK leaving that crowd behind, I was in a better place. I was stronger than I'd thought. Not a follower but a leader—even if it was an army of one.

I IMAGINE THAT for every girl who skates, there is a moment when she begins to watch the sport differently—when her focus widens beyond strength and skill and sharpens around artistry and grace. Suddenly, success is not only about landing the jump but also about its lines and execution—its *look*.

For me, it was around the same time that I began lingering in front of the bathroom mirror. I had become one of those older girls gliding across the ice—the ones I admired when I was still learning the basics. Now my peers and I stood on the precipice of *Are we doing this for play or for real?*

I'd wanted it for real from the beginning. Since I'd first watched Debi Thomas in the 1986 Olympics, and later Jill Trenary, I'd wanted to mimic their elegant posture and modern dance–like floating, pouring such style into one explosive jump after another.

I wanted to *be* Surya Bonaly, muscular with dark chocolate skin, unapologetically skating bare-legged as she landed her backflips. Back then, there were no skating tights to match our skin tone.

By the beginning of high school, I was landing triple jumps and entertaining even bigger dreams of what I might be able to achieve. I began working with coaches out of the New England Sports Center in Marlborough, about an hour north of Medfield, and practicing at the Skating Club of Boston. My coaches guided me along the Ice Skating Institute's testing path, which presented a series of skills to master and perform in front of judges. They also prepared me for competitions, which became a huge part of my life.

I often set my alarm early to make ice time by 6:00 a.m.; at the sound of the final bell, I ran straight out of school into my mother's van. I worked through as much of my written homework as I could on the drive, knowing I'd complete the rest in the stands.

If I didn't have a coaching session, I'd use the time to break down my sequences into single moves and combinations, lingering on the parts that needed refinement. Some days were easier than others: My loop needed work; while I did the triple lutz's three rotations in the air, the blade of my skate hit just a few degrees short of 360. Still, I was close, and the only thing higher than that complicated lutz was the triple axel—something that only two women in the world had executed in competition.

I knew that I was good. My ribbons and medals accumulated, joining my siblings' in our living room cabinet, along with our trophies. So I next set my sights on the US Figure Skating Association—a gateway to the Olympics. When I qualified, I immediately looked ahead to the senior test requirements, as only skaters of that level were allowed to join Team USA. That is what I wanted: that level of respect.

These competitions were even farther away, down to Martha's Vineyard or up to Lake Placid, New York. The travel was exhilarating; by the time I took the ice, I was already on an adventure. The experience of competing was equal parts thrilling and humbling.

In the middle of one competition, I finished my performance and searched for my mother in the stands. I found her in her usual place, underneath the heater. She couldn't stand the cold. We sat in the bleachers for a while, watching the others, and then she said, "This is going to be your last one, Uzo."

"Yeah, right," I said.

"No, you are going to have to stop," she said. Her voice held a new kind of finality. My mother had hinted at this before, but I hadn't wanted to listen.

It had just become so expensive, she explained. To get to the next place, to invest even more, was simply not possible.

I knew that skating was stretching my family. Beyond the ice time and the gear and the membership fees, there was the gas, the lodging, and all the meals besides. For this road trip, just like the others, my mother had planned out the food we would need and loaded up coolers and thermoses. We took the bus; sometimes we shared hotel rooms with friends. I knew that even with all those adjustments, our efforts still weren't enough.

The sport cost a college tuition, my mother reminded me, as I stared at the stands across the arena. My parents already had two children in college, and three others were heading there. I knew all this, of course, but I hadn't had a single clue that this conversation was coming.

I don't remember how I delivered this news to my coaches or how my ice time wound down. It seemed to happen that quickly, and I was that devastated. I'd worked for what had felt like my whole life, following the constantly moving goal of figure skating excellence. If not for that, then what?

I mourned the loss of this one special thing that I didn't have to share with my siblings. This opportunity for concentrated, one-on-one time with my mother, who, I knew, would go back to spending her afternoons at work. Still, my disappointment was deeper than those personal losses.

I knew that others valued my skill in this unique sport, with its art and athleticism. I valued it too. My mother had placed her value on her intelligence, quick wit, and confidence. My beautiful sisters had their brilliance and ease. I had my talent. It was who I was—what I had to trade on the playground.

As winter's coldest weather dug in, I bummed around the house doing nothing or, when I was really ambitious, watching TV. My mother offered to drive me to Natick's open skate on the weekends, but after such a rigorous schedule and strict regimen, the loops around and hot chocolate after were not satisfying.

After a while, my mother decided I'd wallowed for too long. She walked into the living room one day and stood over the couch, looking down at me. "You need to go and find something to do," she said. "How about a spring sport?"

I stared up at her, laying my paperback across my chest. "There's nothing I want to do," I said, and I meant it. I hadn't played soccer as a kid; by then it was too late to start. I had exactly zero interest in doing anything that might compare me to Golden Child Onyi, the star of the softball team in her day. To anything my mother suggested, I said no, no, no—even though I knew we weren't having an argument so much as she had issued an order.

A few weeks later, I was standing at my locker and spotted my old elementary school gym teacher hanging flyers nearby. I walked over to one, remembering that he was also the high school track coach.

He waved in recognition. "Come to our preseason meeting," he said.

I knew that I was quick; he did too. I agreed to go to the meet-and-greet, and to my mother's delight, I was on board by the end.

The after-school practices got underway, and I was drawn in by the sport's simplicity: Start, run, finish. While skating had a certain degree of subjectivity, here the outcomes were always clear.

I could satisfy the craving for competition I had discovered. I improved when I pushed myself, and I pushed—knowing that when it was time to race, I would feel and see the faster time. I knew what happened when I didn't train: I'd scramble, trying to figure out how to win and inevitably falling short. I didn't take kindly to defeat.

During my freshman year I qualified for spots at invitational meets, where schools from across the state came together. There, for the first time, I was surrounded not only by girls who were interested in what I was interested in, but girls who looked like me. Brown girls from different schools—some who really seemed to be having a great time chatting it up.

By the Falmouth Invitational semifinals, I recognized a few of the girls at the starting lines. I decided to step out of my teenage comfort zone and do the unheard of—try to make new friends.

The races began, and I began eyeing a group of Black girls sitting together, cheering on one another. They were all sprinters; most were from the top track schools in the state. I loved how bad-ass they were, creating with every step in their respective races a wider, more insurmountable gap, leaving the next girl in the dust.

There was a swagger to that—one they carried as they walked off knowing they'd won. Then the game face would fall away. They seemed happy to hang out with girls on other teams—even their competitors. I figured this worked in my favor.

Now, I understood by that time that many social circles require a kind of "card" as admission. Ask any high school student: If you want to rule the drama club, your audition for *Les Mis* better be next level. If you want to sit with the fastest girls on the track, you have to show up with a race time they'll respect.

At the risk of how this sounds, I knew I could deliver—even as a freshman. I was young, but I was fast; I was already receiving attention from college coaches. I belonged there, I thought. I had my card—the talent—to sit down.

These were girls who might want to know that Jimmy Bean was still hot: I'd seen Brandon Adams guest-star on an episode of *Roc*, the all-Black Fox sitcom. (Actually, that episode was super sad, I'd tell my new friends, because it was about gang violence and Brandon's character gets shot at the end.) But then, had they seen Brandon in that episode of *Fresh Prince of Bel-Air*, playing Ashley's boyfriend, when they went on a mini-golf date with Will, who was being crazy overprotective the whole time? He was suuuuuuuuuper hot there too.

I walked by their group slowly enough to hear their conversation about favorite teachers. "Oh!" I chirped, sitting down on the grass, nonchalant as could be. "That reminds me of my teacher Miss Fratollilo! She was the one who introduced me to Shakespeare through *Romeo and Juliet*. Like, I don't even know what it is about the writing. I was totally hooked after that."

The silence that followed felt as if a record had scratched and stopped.

Uh-oh.

All five girls looked at me, first stunned, then with wide-eyed bemusement.

"*Whyyoutalklikethat?!*" one girl finally asked.

I couldn't think of what to say.

She tried again. "*Youthinkyouawhitegirl?!*"

All I could muster in reply was, "What did you say?"

"I *said*: Why. You. Talk like that," she said, slowly enunciating each word. "You think you a white girl?"

Then she bent down to tie her racing spikes, chuckling as she shook her head, having revealed me as a wannabe and a fraud, and therefore deeming me unworthy of further interrogation.

By then, the other girls were all too happy to fill the silence.

"She says 'like'!" squealed one, pointing at me.

"Girl, I ain't never heard no Black girl sound so *white*!" said another.

"Don't you know you *Black*?!" a third chimed in.

Then the nail that closed my coffin: "She think she somebody."

Their laughter filled the air, smashing my heart to pieces, as they stood up to find another place to sit, far away from me.

I felt two things as they walked away. First, I felt confused. *Of course I know I'm Black*, I wanted to say. *I'm Nigerian, for fuck's sake, my name is Uzoamaka. My entire face screams West African. How could I not know that I'm Black?*

I also felt devastated, knowing they were talking not about my skin but my community. I was frustrated with my parents for putting me in this position. Opening my mouth, I'd revealed that I didn't have the only thing that mattered to this social club: my African American Express.

Although I was Black, I was not a part of Black American culture in the way these girls were. For that reason, it didn't even matter how fast I was. All that mattered was that I didn't have their same swag or their shared vocab. They would still say that I couldn't come in.

"Zozo?" asked my mother, who'd walked over, eyebrows raised, to the grassy area where I was sitting.

"Nothing," I told her, suddenly busy stretching. I balanced on one foot, holding my other ankle in my hand. Stretching out my quad, I stared intently at the track, trying to think of anything else. A fancy track, polyurethane, with just the right amount of give—a deep maroon color, with bright yellow lines separating the lanes. A chain-link fence beyond, and green, green grass. I remembered the long drive here and that we were almost to Cape Cod. Then I tried my best to snap back into focus.

I won my semifinal easily; a few in that group of girls cleaned up in their respective races too. By the time the call came for the one-hundred-meter finals, I'd formulated a new approach to win them over. Winning them over was what I so desperately wanted, even if I'd no longer play such games at school. The stakes were higher: I was living in a desert, and I was thirsty.

I walked up to the area near the starting line, where the girls were all standing in a circle, talking. "Guuuuurrrrrlll," I said to one, "let me tell y'all how, like . . . Let me tell y'all what I been tripping on."

The girl's raised eyebrows told me what I already knew: The words rang false.

She rolled her eyes and turned back to her friends, who also ignored me. I was left with no other choice but to walk away, and so I did, eyes fixed on the straightaway.

This was my worst fear confirmed: Because of the way I spoke, the school I went to, the town I grew up in, I would never have a circle of great Black girlfriends. No matter where I was, I would always be exhausting myself, proving to someone, somewhere, that I was like them. No, *I know exactly what you're talking about, and I love that too. I've been there too. I am so at ease, and you are too.*

A voice interrupted my despairing thoughts: "Is it cool if I sit here?"

I looked up to see a Brown girl, my age, with a warm, bright smile; wide-set eyes; and the purple-and-white uniform of Boston Latin, a no-joke magnet school in the heart of the city, one of the top, with one of the deepest benches of talented athletes in the state. I was impressed.

She introduced herself as Monique Tubbs and explained that she was also in the finals. I briefly introduced myself, and then, for a moment, we sat together quietly. Monique seemed more soft-spoken than the other girls; for once the nonstop talker in me was working double-time to not utter an extra word.

There was no way I was sabotaging this.

My plan worked for a while, actually, until Monique asked, "What's the matter? Don't you talk?"

"Depends on who you ask," I said. My spine tensed for the onslaught.

Instead, I heard a laugh.

We came from two different corners of the world, Monique and I—two different "Blackgrounds." I grew up in the mostly white suburbs and got a ride to school down the block; she was bussed to Boston Latin from Roxbury, a neighborhood just south of the city known to be a center of Black culture. Still, we were both freshmen. I discovered, right away, that she had the most joyful laugh.

She didn't decide, before knowing me, who I was, what I was about, or whether I was cool enough, dope, down, whatever. She got to know me first, and she saw me—not someone else's idea of who I should be.

We chatted until the race officials called us onto the track. Walking over to the starting line, I passed some of the girls who'd laughed at me, but I didn't even look their way. All I thought was that for the first time, there might be a friend to congratulate at the finish line.

"Runners, take your mark," the line official said, signaling.

We seated our feet in the starting blocks.

"Set." With the final cue before the gun, we all sprang up to the ready position, our senses heightened.

Now, the thing about the one-hundred-meter dash is that just as you're about to introduce any new thought outside of *run*, the whole thing is over. All you can do in the short time you're given to race is hope that everything you've worked on at practice will apply in this moment, when you're most tested.

The crack of the gun behind me, I didn't see a soul ahead the entire way. In my final few steps, I sensed someone right on my shoulder. Had Monique clipped me there, at the end? I couldn't tell. I almost didn't care.

The race was done, and we were doubled over, gasping for air with our hands on our knees. When we stood up, we high-fived each other, still catching our breath as we waited for the results: first place me, second place Monique.

Monique and I would see more and more of each other over the years; we competed against each other often. It would soon become clear that inside Monique's demure personality was a sharp focus.

She was competitive in the best, healthiest way. Our friendship grew stronger with each invitational, and as the years went by—and especially during our senior year—I loved watching her grow into a truly exceptional athlete.

Eventually, those other girls came around to get to know me as well, with only a few keeping their distance. But by then, I couldn't be bothered. I'd rather go it alone than exchange who I am for someone's—anyone's—idea of what I should be. I was more than enough, my own experience equally valid.

Chapter 7

Of all my mother's many sayings, this one may have been her favorite: "I've never heard of nothing coming from hard work." I don't know that we ever saw her do anything else. This was especially true when times were tight—and times were often tight, with five busy kids and a huge cast of aunties, uncles, and cousins still touching down in the US. When we were most stretched, my mother took on second jobs and other side hustles.

We barely noticed how much she juggled when we were little. All that had registered was: When Mom works at McDonald's, we can get a Happy Meal whenever we want! We loved loading into our father's car in the evenings, rolling up to the drive-through, and clamoring to the windows to see Mommy in her uniform. McDonald's, after all, was where young kids of the 1980s went for the best possible birthday parties, with paper crowns and freely flowing "orange drink." We got the food we loved, and bragging rights to boot.

My first job—all my siblings' first jobs—was a paper route. Upon learning that *The Boston Globe* offered $5,000 academic scholarships to any student who kept up a paper route for four years, my mother signed up each one of us as soon as we were eligible.

When my mother later heard that kids also received a paycheck for their work in addition to the scholarship, she took on more routes for us. And when she learned you could earn even more by picking up the stack of papers directly from the newspaper's plant and distributing them to the paperboys and -girls in the neighborhood, she began setting her alarm an hour earlier and doing that too.

Rich completed his route in the traditional paperboy way, on a bike, setting off at 6:00 a.m. with a sack of papers slung over his shoulder. Somehow Onyi got out of her route and Rich was delegated to do it. By the time I turned twelve, and with Chi-Chi and Junior right behind, our mother had maximized every efficiency of the paper route delivery system.

She'd learned that we didn't have to forfeit Rich's and Onyi's routes once they went to college, so she kept them, and added a few others in between. I'd assumed my route also would be completed by bike, as Rich's had been, but in order to serve all our customers, my mother chauffeured us across Medfield's neighborhoods in our family's van, the empty bench in the back stacked high with newsprint.

We had a system: Each child did two days a week before school, and then, on Sundays, we'd all get up early and put the big paper together. First came the Living Arts and Metro sections on Saturday; two kids would stack that up. In the middle of the night, or in the early morning, the rest of the paper would come. By 5:30 a.m., we were marrying the pieces together. One of us would work with our mother to stuff the interior sections of the paper inside the front page, then place them inside their individual plastic bags. The other two loaded the papers into the car.

We took off as the sun was still rising, my mother behind the wheel and one of us riding shotgun: window rolled down and hand on the door handle, ready to shove each *Globe* into a mailbox or toss it onto a driveway. Some of our customers had annoying requests, wanting their paper wedged in a screen door or underneath a specific rock; one of the back-seat kids would fulfill those wishes. The remaining kid hunched over in the back seat, still stuffing the last of the papers.

My mother did all this before she went to work; on the weekends, she came home in time to dress for her fourth job as a retailer at Sears. Beloved by her coworkers in the lingerie department, she was even more of a hit with the customers. Her social work background helped her counsel women through their purchases with a light touch, treating their search for the right bra as the personal crisis it so often is. I know she also welcomed the time to discuss the next trends and to window-shop in the mall on her lunch break—an actual break.

By then we were years past the gleeful drive-through visits to McDonald's, and our delight over our mother's second shifts had diminished. The discount we could get on a Sears prom dress couldn't make up for the worry I felt about my friends bumping into my mother at the mall. No longer was I bragging, "You guys, we got McDonald's apple pie—our mom is the coolest!"

I could almost hear my friends' voices in my head: *But your mom is super smart!* and *Doesn't she have a job in the city?*

I knew that my parents were not the first in Medfield to sweat trying to make their kids' dreams come true. Surely there were other families in our well-to-do town finding creative ways to make ends meet. Still, without anyone in the community having articulated this to me, I believed that our family would not be looked at with the same consideration, empathy, and understanding as a white family in the same situation. I knew, even then, that we are not all equally vulnerable.

The Adubas already stood out in Medfield, and the facts of our Blackness and our excellence existed as a kind of unspoken exchange. While we didn't have the biggest house in town, it was clear that we had worked, through our talents and merits, to build an exceptional life—a wall of protection from the insults that Chudi, Uncle David, and even Rich had to confront in earlier days. I feared that even a whiff of financial strain, an experience so common but nonetheless stereotyped as inherently Black, could put all that at risk.

I couldn't articulate this as a teenager, and my siblings and I certainly didn't discuss our family's financial situation in this way—or at all, really. As we weren't privy to our family budget, we assumed that some of this scrappiness was simply our mother being our mother.

We heard her litany: "Your school fees, your ballet, Junior's hockey, our mortgage . . ." Still, we thought she was overreacting when she refused to order soda at the Friendly's restaurant in Medfield. "We're not in Nigeria anymore, Mom," we'd say. "The extra dollar isn't going to make a difference to the mortgage."

In this vein, Chi-Chi and I tried to convince her to quit her job at Sears.

She did not care.

One Saturday afternoon, my sister and I went to the mall, stopping by Sears first to drop off something for our mother. We scaled the moving escalator as fast as we could; once we'd completed our errand, we planned to leave just as quickly. We didn't want to be seen with her.

When we saw the stack of clothes our mother had set aside for us to try on, we began to bicker, our teenage stress levels rising until all three of us were snapping at one another.

"Why are you even working here?" Chi-Chi asked.

"Chi-Chi," my mother said, "if you don't want to try this on—"

"This is ridiculous, Mom," I interrupted. "You have a master's degree. This is such a waste of time."

We continued on this shameful track, insisting that she didn't need the job—pretending or maybe even believing that she was there for the escape, the discount. The idea that the extra paycheck was not necessary was much easier to believe than the truth, which was that the extra income *was* necessary, every newspaper and bra, every candy bar sold and can returned.

My siblings and I all kept up our paper routes, though by high school, I was making more money working three days a week waiting tables at Friendly's, as had Rich before me. My schedule was a lot to manage, going from work to school to practice to work and then back home for homework, rinse and repeat. I wasn't as savvy as my siblings, who put aside some of the cash they earned before handing over the rest to our mother; I typically kept only a dollar.

I didn't think to pocket more; I was too afraid of getting in trouble. Now I see that Chi-Chi was the wiser one, tucking a little extra in her sock drawer, paying herself first. While she didn't spend it all, she had options. It turns out that when it came to Royal Pizza and the movies and hanging out downtown, that extra dollar did matter.

WHILE TRACK PLAYED a central role in my high school life, its place on my priority list became second to the arts—particularly music. This shift happened in the fifth grade, when the part of me that had always been a big talker became a full-fledged performer.

That year my parents had signed me up to take two sciences. While reading my form, scrutinizing the chosen schedule and my grades, my fifth-grade teacher, Mrs. Bruno, turned her plump, Mrs. Claus–like face toward me: "Why?"

"Because they want me . . . because I can?" I said.

"Don't you want to do something fun during the day?" she asked. When she saw my smile of assent, she scratched out that second science and scribbled me into concert choir class instead. I didn't say anything at home, feeling safe in the fact that the whole thing was Mrs. Bruno's idea.

My choir teacher, Mr. Hersee, was a white-haired man who seemed, to me, a kind of full-grown elf. He loved music and loved kids; he even stood up when he played his upright piano, so he could see us better.

I'd never sung outside of church, but I loved standing in the large group, flipping sheet music and preparing for the big performance. I shied away from the solos, assuming that the kids who did community theater would be picked.

"I noticed you walked right past the sign-up sheet for year-end concert auditions," Mr. Hersee said to me one day after class. "Why is that?"

"I don't know any songs," I said.

"You don't know *any* songs? Sing me something," he said. "What do you like to sing?"

"Songs on the radio, I guess," I said, shrugging, as that didn't seem to be what he was talking about. Those weren't "official" songs.

"What song do you like on the radio right now?"

"Whitney Houston's 'I Will Always Love You'?" Embarrassed, I stared at the far corner of the ceiling as I responded.

"OK," he said, "let's sing a little bit of that." He rolled out a D major chord and looked at me.

I nodded, beginning softly with the song's first tentative "I-i-if I . . ." until I was singing, and singing. The initial cringing I'd felt in the sides of my neck and my shoulders fell away as a warmth spread across my chest. I was free, almost invisible, but in the best way, disappearing into Dolly Parton's lyrics and connecting with the described heartbreak.

All of a sudden, Mr. Hersee stopped playing and looked at me.

"You're going to go home," he said. "You're going to tell your mom she needs to go over to the Music Nook in Milford and buy the sheet music for 'I Will Always Love You,' and that's what you're going to sing in the concert."

"OK," I said. That would mean two performances—a Tuesday evening, for all the parents and families, followed by a Wednesday afternoon with the whole school.

I followed his directions, enlisting my mother, who was thrilled. When she'd signed me up for church choir, I'd bristled, as it had meant I had to wake up even earlier on Sundays. That reaction had disappointed her, but now, I'd landed on a kind of singing that we both found exciting. Immediately I began rehearsing at school, but also in the shower, in my room, down the hallway, and—

"UZO! SHUT UP!" screamed Junior. "Go downstairs!"

I didn't care. I had to practice, had to keep vocalizing, breathing, hitting my notes, stretching my range—

"MOM!" Junior again. "Can you tell Uzo to stop singing? I'm trying to do my homework!"

"Uzo," my mother said quietly. "You need to give them one hour."

"But—"

"I know," she whispered, "but maybe later, when he goes to hockey."

. . .

SITTING, SWEATING, in the van's back seat on the way to the first performance, I stared into my lap at Whitney's piercing brown eyes underneath those loose curls. At the top of the sheet music, a light blue W and H stood at attention, keeping watch over the rest of her name. This is going to be a disaster, I thought; my dread only grew as I took the stage and the concert began.

I questioned whether I had a right to a solo. I saw myself forgetting all the words, down to the title, and making an absolute fool of myself, which I imagined could result in spontaneous combustion. I was afraid of being seen by the school and, worst of all, seen as someone so arrogant as to think she could sing anything in the world of "The Voice," Whitney Houston. I heard the words of my high school track rivals echoing in my head: *She think she somebody.*

I walked up to the microphone, and I felt my heart catch when I saw my whole family in the audience. Then the piano cue came in, I began to sing, and I lost sight of them. No longer did I feel the eyes of an entire choir on my back. There was only Mr. Hersee's piano and my own voice, just as it had been in rehearsal.

With the last notes still hanging in the air, I heard what sounded like applause. First a few, then many people in the audience stood, and I began to laugh, not because it was funny but because I was surprised and uncomfortable with the attention. I received a similar response the next afternoon and was even more taken aback. I'd assumed my classmates would make fun of me— or even boo me off the stage—for thinking that *I* sounded like Whitney. I handed back the mic and raced back to my position on the risers, thinking, I can sing. Not only do I like it; I'm good at it.

The next year, in seventh grade, Mr. Hersee found me a solo from the Broadway musical *The Phantom of the Opera* that didn't just work for my voice but that *fit* my voice—as if my soul were speaking.

Later that year, our class took the bus from Medfield to New York City to see *Les Misérables* on Broadway. I'd been curious about Broadway since I'd first seen billboards advertising *The Phantom of the Opera* on our drive into Boston to see relatives. The dazzling reality of *Les Mis* exceeded my imagination before we even walked into the theater.

I felt so connected to the show, thanks to the repeated soundtrack listening sessions at Erin Stanley's. She and I had listened to—no, studied—the CD recording of the PBS special *The Dream Cast in Concert*, but the performance had been just that: a concert. No scenes flowing into one another, no acting, no conflict or resolution.

As I sat high up in the balcony, watching the actor playing Éponine sing, "You will keep me safe, and you will keep me close," tears filled my eyes. I hadn't realized that the character *died*. Seeing her there, in the flesh, in Marius's arms, I was gutted. There was so much more to the story—indeed, to the entire experience—than I'd ever realized.

Feeling a rush of pathos and awe, I floated out of the theater completely unaware of Times Square's chaos around me. Seeing the show, experiencing the world of creativity and escape it seemed to provide for both the audience and the cast, was the nudge that set off my gleeful slide into the world of the "theater geeks."

I loved performing, and I lived for it—landing spots in the high school audition choirs and participating in choir festivals at the local and state levels. I signed up for the drama festivals as well, preparing monologues for judges to scrutinize and grade. Still, there was no greater high than the high school musical.

I loved the after-school rehearsals, finding my castmates in quiet hallway spaces talking about *The Catcher in the Rye*'s Holden Caulfield, independent "art house" films I knew nothing about, and every other "I'm so intellectual" conversation in between.

I admired the fearlessness and individuality they projected, with little care for how close they were to the margins of our high school's hierarchies. I even began wearing black turtlenecks to school, as they did, understanding that it was chicer and cooler, a standard style for people in NYC. Always the initials, in those years. Never "New York City."

My new theater friends understood the genius of the witches' prophecy in Shakespeare's *Macbeth*, which we read in English class during my sophomore year. We sat in the hallway one day discussing its brilliance: How indeed could it be that Birnam Wood could come to Dunsinane?

The study of *Macbeth* was a huge event in our home, as my mother had once played the title role. A Canadian teacher had brought the play to her all-girls high school in the 1950s. It was such a big deal, she told me; she'd worked and worked to memorize all the lines, which she still remembered, word for word.

I couldn't believe it: I opened the slim paperback to any scene, and she could recite it from memory. I tried to stump her again and again, marveling at her facility and the way she moved her head and her hands in expression. It was almost as if we had traded places, and she was the high school kid rehearsing. As she spoke, her passion for the arts came alive; I recognized it as my own.

"Is this a dagger which I see before me?" My mother's narrowed eyes held my gaze as she recited this monologue without effort. I saw the back of her spine straighten a bit as she filled out this huge, badass monster of a role she'd gotten to play.

. . .

ONE SUMMER, as Onyi was preparing to return to Cornell, Chi-Chi and I skipped school one day to see a movie with her in Framingham. On the way back, we stopped at an electronics store to browse through their music section: Montell Jordan, Boyz II Men, Coolio. Was I in the singles section, looking for Ini Kamoze's "Here Comes the Hotstepper"? Maybe.

There among the rows of CDs, on an A-frame, was an ad for the soundtrack to the Broadway musical *Rent*. I studied the woman's face on the poster, realizing that she had also been on the cover of my mother's *Newsweek* magazine: Daphne Rubin-Vega, who played Mimi, next to Adam Pascal, who played Roger. Something about the poster caught my eye, and when I saw the soundtrack had just been released, I decided to buy it.

On the drive home, we slid the CD into Onyi's car stereo. I flipped through the liner notes as I listened to the start: the tuning of a guitar.

"December 24, nine p.m. Eastern Standard Time."

This plucking was very strong in my ear; it felt urgent, and close, and I immediately thought it was cool. A series of answering machine messages followed, and then a very heavy rock groove. I was intrigued but not necessarily captivated until the fourth track hit, "One Song Glory." That song got me hot—the slow buildup, the heroic melody, and the lyrics as I read through them, again and again. "Again," I told Onyi, when it finished. I don't think I've ever stopped playing it.

Rent on repeat, repeat, repeat. Chi-Chi and I lay on the family room carpet studying the liner notes, even though we already knew all the words. We bought tickets to see the first national tour when it came to Boston. Unlike my experience with *Les Mis*, I had a true idea of the story and *Rent* still blew my mind. I sang along, wishing that I was able to *do* all the things I was seeing.

I was more than happy to squeeze in a play rehearsal before track practice, or the other way around. It was a lot to juggle, especially atop the homework and other activities I'd chosen, but I was used to this kind of schedule.

To be honest, I also wasn't interested in much more time to just "hang out" in those days. The girls who for years had been sneaking sips of alcohol at sleepovers were showing up drunk to other people's parties and even school events. The spiked sodas and hidden beers just didn't hold any appeal. What can I say? D.A.R.E., that 1990s health class cornerstone, really worked on me. The message of Just Say No truly resounded.

"This is bad, guys," I told my friends, the first time I found myself at a party, surrounded by booze. "This is illegal," I told them. "And also? My parents will kill me . . ."

I was thinking of the inquiries I'd received from college coaches and the possibility of that golden ticket: a scholarship. Those bottles and plastic cups were one thing that could instantly knock me out, and, as my parents had explained, there would be nothing they could do to protect me.

In our house, the heaviest parental talks about risk were typically reserved for Rich and Junior. These conversations touched on drugs but were mostly about sex—the subtext being the dangers of getting a white woman pregnant. The not-so-subtle message there: "This will end your life." My sisters and I didn't get it in quite the same way (our pregnancy talk was framed more as "This is the way America will look at you"). But the stakes of any misstep were equally clear.

Drinking itself could be dangerous. Even more so was getting caught.

One night, I'd happily offered to drive a group of friends to a dance. As the last few jostled in, I squeezed the steering wheel as I realized that I was the only sober one. *Something could happen*, I thought, over and over again in the driver's seat of our Dodge Mark III conversion van. I didn't want to be a part of this so-called fun; I also didn't want anyone to make a bad choice and drive home with somebody else. So I drove.

Something could happen. The night could take a bad turn, I knew, with one of the few Black girls in town at the wheel.

After that night, I spent more time with Simi, who was also on the student council, as was Crowley and a girl named Jean, whom we called T-Bone. We four would go see movies or drive to Dunkin' Donuts for frozen ice coffees. Sometimes we studied together.

I had more in common with them, both in terms of focus and personality. In short, they were super driven, hardworking, and nerdy as all get out. Just like me.

AFTER A SERIES OF CHORUS and bit parts, I landed my first significant role in our high school production of *Playing for Time*, an Arthur Miller play set during World War II. The story centers around a group of professional musicians, all Jewish women, who were forced to perform for the Nazis in order to survive. I paged through the script quickly until I reached the part where my character, a singer named Marianne, trades sex for food. I continued reading, my stomach sinking, my mind thinking only: My parents are going to be pissed.

Onyi had been a theater kid too, though mostly on the crew side, as a stage manager. Her one and only acting experience was in a play called *Night of January 16th*, written by Ayn Rand. The play is a murder trial, and it takes place in a courtroom. Our whole family had gone to see it together, proudly holding our programs as Onyi emerged onstage. Her character took the stand and then, suddenly, she was stricken blind because she was a prostitute.

The scene had continued, but I had been stuck. Seeing Onyi in that role had felt wrong, even from my limited, ten-year-old vantage. Before the curtain even fell, I could feel my parents' fury. There they were, showing us Black excellence: Denzel Washington's Stephen Biko in *Cry Freedom* and Diana Ross in the Billie Holiday biopic *Lady Sings the Blues*. Then comes some high school drama department, handing down to their daughter a character whom you'd expect to find on the six-o'clock news.

"The one time you put a Black person on the stage," my father had said, on the drive home. "You finally cast a Black girl, and this is what you do?"

I'd expected a similar response when I told my mother about *Playing for Time*, but instead I was met with a kind of shrugging. "Whatever you think is best," my mother said.

This woman had no problem telling me no. With the decision in my hands, I felt the slight tipping of a scale—and a lot of pressure.

What did I think was best? Any possible opportunity to get back on that stage. Still, there was no question how much the role fell into the heap of stereotypes my parents worked so hard to sidestep.

I gave it some thought and realized that I shared their feelings. To be honest, I was a little surprised that I did.

I asked the director about a different part; when I learned that wasn't an option, I dropped out. I went to see the production a few months later, and I wasn't sorry.

The following year, my junior year, I landed a leading role in our high school's production of the musical *Pippin*. By then, I knew many of the upperclassmen who had played major parts in *The Secret Garden* and *Guys and Dolls*, and I expected that the biggest parts would go to them. So I gasped when I scanned the list and saw that the role of the Leading Player had gone not to a senior but to me.

The Leading Player in *Pippin* is a kind of storyteller role; it was made famous on Broadway by Ben Vereen, who won a Tony Award for his performance. The character guides the story as well as its main character, Pippin, who is on a journey of discovery. He keeps the audience in the loop too, with monologues and solo numbers filled with charisma and soul.

I say "he," as the role was written for a man.

I put so much of my *stuff* into that Leading Player role, doing everything I loved: singing, acting, and making bold choices like leaping off the stage and into the audience. For the first time, I could feel all my eccentricities coming together and being celebrated. With the encouragement of Regina O'Connor, our director, and Mary Ann Hatem, our choreographer, my ideas were entertained and lived out loud, leaned into versus chilled out.

As the demands of our rehearsal schedule increased, so too did the requirements of the spring track season. Knowing that I needed to change into my running clothes and stretch, I'd continue the conversation about the scene anyway. "I have time," I'd say. "Let's run it again."

I did it for Regina, who had built the show for us and who took us seriously, nurturing our talent and providing a springboard. I wanted the production to succeed so badly that I'd stay as long as it took, sometimes showing up for just the last thirty minutes of track practice or staying after hours to work out with the coach.

I still loved the sport—the meets especially. I still craved the bite of competition, the fight of it, even when, early in the season,

I was really only trying to beat myself. In the later meets, the invitationals and local and state competitions, I was still chasing that glorious finality of finally clipping a rival at the tape.

But love wasn't enough. One day, during an indoor track practice, the coach came up beside me and took a knee. "This can't go on," he said, studying me.

I knew he was talking about my absences at practice, but I didn't care. *Pippin* was just more important to me, I told him.

I had already tried to quit track once: A year earlier, I'd stormed off the field after a disagreement with a coach. Chi-Chi, who was then a freshman on the team, had quit on the spot too, running after me without even knowing what had happened.

When I'd come home with the news, my parents had told me that I couldn't quit. I couldn't put that potential college scholarship in jeopardy. Still fired up and filled with indignation, I pleaded my case, but, eventually, I acquiesced. I knew they were right.

Now there I was again, ready to quit, but with more information. My experience onstage had changed my relationship with my sport and, along with it, my understanding of who I was—and wanted to be. I dug in: Until closing night, I told him, I wouldn't sacrifice another single moment of rehearsal.

Hearing the resolve in my voice, the coach tried a different tactic: He reminded me that my absences weren't fair to the other girls on the team. "You're right," I told him, sensing an opening. "I really should give up my spot."

Now he knew I wasn't being flippant.

"Wait a minute, wait a minute," he said. "We've got to figure something out."

At this point in the season, the Medfield track team needed me just as much as I needed them—or possibly even more. While I was still a child in many ways, my competitive sport put me at the center of some truly adult negotiations.

"Maybe we can figure out a structure to the schedule," he offered as a starting point.

Some adults have a funny way of flexing their power. For years, I tried to find my best diplomatic self to navigate these conversations. While I was typically the furthest thing from a pushover, when I saw coaches put their career aspirations on the table, I often felt tentative, humble, and young.

But now that I had something to protect, I challenged and pushed back—even if it was with a shaky voice.

My creative writing teacher, who was also my drama teacher, pulled me aside one day after class. "I'd like to speak with you," said Ms. Mehleis quietly.

When she closed the door behind the last student, I wondered if I was in trouble. She turned around to face me and then tilted her head, as if she were hoping to confirm something. "Have you given any thought to your plans for college?" she asked.

I was such a talkative kid that the family joke, always, was that Uzo would make a good lawyer. As the idea of college came into focus, I assumed I would major in international relations or political science, go on to law school, and then move to Washington, DC, and be a lobbyist or work on policy.

Ms. Mehleis seemed surprised by this map of the future. "Really?" she asked. "Have you given any thought about going into the arts?"

The arts. I looked at her with a kind of blankness. I really, truly had no idea what she was talking about.

"You know, you seem to have a real passion for it. A real talent," she said. "I think you can make a go at something like this." When I didn't respond, she took a breath. "You know you can go to school for this, right?"

I supposed I did, but still I could not imagine it. I loved theater, of course. I also knew movies and loved movies. One of my drama club friends, Mike Short, was an aspiring filmmaker. Sometimes we took the T together to an art house theater in Brookline, where I'd seen and fallen in love with Darren Aronofsky's *Pi*.

Earlier that year my parents had signed me up for voice lessons. My teacher was Cheryl Weiss, a former classical singer who had studied vocal performance at Boston University's College of Fine Arts. On Cheryl's suggestion, they'd taken me to Symphony Hall to see the iconic Leontyne Price, the first Black female principal at the Met, where we all felt the joy of her glorious voice wash over us.

Ms. Mary Violet Leontyne Price: Neither my parents nor I had known such a person existed, and she was magnificent, in a seafoam green–colored dress, singing gospel and spirituals and arias—songs we knew and songs we didn't know. Beneath her people jumped to their feet with applause. Can you imagine? In Boston, of all places? A woman who looked like me, with a similar vocal range.

By the end of my conversation with Ms. Mehleis, I'd felt a lightbulb switch on in my head: This is what I'm supposed to do.

I began looking into universities with performing arts programs, thinking first about a career as a film director. As I studied my options more closely, concerns about cost and distance ruled out my California dreams. Cheryl suggested I'd do well pursuing the same path that she did, at Boston University's College of Fine Arts.

My mother tried to dissuade me from this path. As much as she nurtured my love of the arts, her children were supposed to grow up and sit behind a desk, or in a lab or a courtroom, doing something easily identifiable as professional and successful. Sure, she wanted us to live our dreams, but she also understood the difference between a dream and reality.

"Did you know that BU also has an Opera Institute?" I'd say. If she didn't flatly ignore me, she'd say, "Uzo," in that singsongy way, dragging out the "o" in my name before a staccato "no" and a firm "no" to follow.

Neither of us wavered in our position. Still, as I prepared my audition material, my performance evolved and my confidence grew. So did my insistence. I think that by seeing this determination, my mother began to understand that I was not making a snap decision—and that the decision had already been made. I'd first approached my mother needing her consent; in the end, I was looking for her support.

I've heard of a tradition that a person who wants to convert to Judaism must first ask a rabbi for permission to study; the rabbi is supposed to deny their request three times, as a test of sincerity, and then come around.

"OK," my mother said to me one day, her face smooth in agreement, as if she'd never had any other idea.

"What changed?" I asked, feeling my heart lift.

"I wanted to make sure you're serious," my mother said.

THE NEW ENGLAND Conservatory Youth Chorale, my audition choir, planned a trip to Paris and London over our schools' midwinter breaks. It was a kind of dream journey, which included a performance at Notre-Dame Cathedral and another for the Archbishop of Canterbury, the head of the Anglican Church, at Canterbury Cathedral. My mother signed up to be a chaperone, and we planned to stay on after the group flew home, so we could visit with her brother and other family who lived there.

At the time, my mother's eldest brother, my Uncle Adazie Emeka Anyaoku, was at the height of his long career in diplomacy. As the third secretary-general of the Commonwealth of Nations—the association of states and republics once linked to the British Empire—he had met the Queen of England and enjoyed a friendship with Nelson Mandela. I had always looked up to him as well as my Aunty Ugoma Bunmi, a spirited woman with a sense of fearlessness and a delicious wit.

I'd recently seen them; they'd flown to Boston for the day while they were in New York for a meeting. That had been a casual, personal visit. Now here we were at Canterbury Cathedral, dressed for the occasion, walking below vaulted ceilings holding centuries of hosannas to meet outside the twelfth-century quire.

"Your mother gave me the tape of Handel's *Messiah*," Uncle Adazie told me after we exchanged greetings. "She *is* right—you do sound just like my sister." His youngest son, Emenike, had spent the summer with my family in Boston, and my mother had recorded him accompanying me on keyboard as I sang "I Know My Redeemer Liveth," from the oratorio. Aunty Bunmi raised her eyebrows and nodded in agreement.

He was talking about my late Aunty Ifeoma, my mother's protector and friend. I thanked him, looking over to see my cousin Ike standing there—Aunty Ife's second son—who had come to the performance along with his wife, Katherine.

I still light up at the memory of their proud smiles in the audience—a warm familiarity among so much British formality. "My niece," I heard my Aunty Bunmi say to an acquaintance in the crowd after, as I was making my way toward them. "Yes, that's her, yes—she sounds incredible."

Before we left London, my Uncle Adazie invited us to join him for dinner. My mother and I pulled away from the group and took a taxi to the official residence of the secretary-general, in Mayfair. The Edwardian mansion was huge, full of the glossiest wood paneling I'd ever seen. The way the house staff received us confirmed my sense that Adazie was a king.

Ike and Katherine joined us for dinner as well, and we all had time to really catch up. Ike told us about his career in finance and the brownstone they'd bought in West London, where they were raising their four-year-old daughter, Lola. "Notting Hill," proclaimed my mother, brimming with pride at another posh address.

"Aunty Nonyem, how old was I when I first came to visit you?" Ike asked. "Twenty-three?"

That trip to Boston had been his first-ever to the U.S, he told me, as he and my mother joked and reminisced. He would be happy to return the favor, he said. "Uzo, come back for a summer."

Can you imagine?

"You can go," my mother said.

"Really?" I said. Not *we'll see*? Was she just being polite?

I waited until we were on the flight home to ask if she'd meant what she said.

"If you can save up half the cost of the flight, I'll give you the other half," my mother said. I knew she'd keep her promise, somehow.

Thrilled by the idea of living with Ike and Katherine—daring risk-takers, with big dreams they weren't afraid to pursue—I worked like a dog that spring and into that summer. I took as many babysitting jobs and shifts at Friendly's as were on offer, and my mother's word was gold.

I'd never known, before my summer in London, that you could live in a *house* in the city—that such a thing was possible for regular people, and not just for dignitaries like my uncle. My chic older cousins showed me a different world. Knowing my love of music, they bought tickets for the Proms, an annual classical music festival at Royal Albert Hall. I joined them with awe, soaking in one of the city's most gorgeous concert halls.

On weekend mornings, I sat with Katherine in their kitchen, surrounded by her huge collection of teakettles, gazing out the window to a beautiful garden in the back. When I grow up, I thought, I'm going to have a life like this, surrounded by people who love art— who are boisterous and gregarious, interested and interesting.

That, I thought, was making it.

WHEN I RETURNED from my summer in London, I began wearing tank tops in public—something I'd stopped doing back in middle school, when I was teased about the dark bumps and scarring on my underarms. (I hadn't known then that the five-blade Gillette razors all my friends used weren't good for Black skin.)

While living in Notting Hill, I'd walked for weeks with the sun on my bare shoulders. I'd worn what I liked there, among the students in uni and young professionals, knowing that I was free from any idea that my family or community held. I'd returned feeling more settled in my body and my sense of style.

For the first day of my senior year, I chose a blue tank top with thin, gray straps and matching gray piping across the chest. As I looked in the mirror, situating the navy blue headband in my shoulder-length box braids, I felt that I looked exactly as I wanted to look. I felt beautiful.

For my senior class photos, I chose a few different outfits, and I borrowed a pair of my mother's earrings. I got on well with the photographer—a nice guy who put me at ease during the session, even cracking a few jokes along the way. Then, at one point, he lowered his camera.

"Why do you keep making that face in pictures?" he asked. He lifted the corners of his mouth in an imitation, as if something sour were under my tongue.

"I don't know," I said.

"Really, why?" asked the photographer. "Why aren't you smiling?"

He kept pressing until I had no choice: "I don't like my gap," I muttered.

He studied me for a moment and then said, "I think you have a beautiful smile."

While I can't say exactly what changed in me, I was born that day. I didn't give up a single flash of teeth for the photos, but I still walked away believing it, for the first time: I have a beautiful smile.

My mother hated it when I told this story. "Your entire life," I can hear her say. "I told you your entire life."

Sorry: For whatever reason, this guy said it, and I was proud.

BY THE TIME HIGH SCHOOL graduation rolled around, I was ready. Rea-dy—to get out of my house, out of high school, and out of Medfield. As I was the senior class president, I was invited to speak at our graduation ceremony. This thrilled my parents, who invited all our relations and family friends to the school and back to our house afterward.

"What do you think the dress is for this?" my mother asked a few weeks beforehand.

I was quiet for a moment. I stared at a blank spot on my bedroom wall and then closed my eyes to picture my classmates: a sea of white caps and gowns for girls, blue caps and gowns for boys. In the audience, our loved ones—another sea of white faces like the ones onstage, with a few faces of color peppered in, from Simi's and Karen's families, as well as my own.

There would be no sign of ourselves anywhere, no view of our families' histories and contributions. As we'd requested, my parents had tucked away their *ichafus*, hung up their *agbadas*, and gone to our ballet recitals, sports banquets, and concerts in the expected suits and shift dresses.

We didn't have big compounds here, as we had in Nigeria, but our community was still the backbone of my family body. There was no question that my parents' elaborate graduation party plans would include Uncle David, Aunty Oby, and so many others from our Igbo meetings and backyard celebrations. I thought about the colorful way they expressed themselves then, and I hated to think that they would restrain themselves for my benefit.

My siblings and I, we were America—as every bit a part of this country as any one of those Mollys or Matts or Scotts. Why were we trying so hard to blend in?

"I want you to tell everyone who comes that they should come in traditional clothes," I said proudly.

My mother's eyes flashed wide. "Really?" I knew that she'd already assumed otherwise; we'd all worn Western clothes to Rich's and Onyi's graduations. I imagine she asked the question to determine the level of formality I wanted beyond jeans and T-shirts and sundresses, but I was ready to give a different kind of answer.

"I want everyone there to know where we come from," I told my mother with a decisive nod. I knew that my family would be pleased, but I made the choice because of my own pride.

So much of what would be celebrated onstage at graduation—grades, activities, performance—was connected to my family's discipline and culture. I knew that, along the way, I'd softened parts of this identity, and I was no longer comfortable with that.

"OK," my mother said—at a loss for words, which she never was. That was, until she walked out the door and, like all Nigerian mothers, jumped on the phone to hen to her girlfriends about her wonderful daughter.

When the day finally came, I sat on the stage, watching as my crazy, loud, late, vibrant, and oh-so-spectacular extended family made their way down the aisles into the seats my parents had saved. It was as if their gorgeous greens, yellows, golds, blues—you name it—somehow represented the sacrifices, the journey, the heartaches, even our ancestors themselves. They walked into a space that was not their own, but the celebration was theirs.

And mine: By inviting them to be themselves, I was so much more.

My graduation party was just as crowded and just as lively as my Uncle David's wedding, and it went *late*. Many of the neighbors came by—some, I think, simply because they'd been curious for so long about what went on in our backyard. I buzzed excitedly about my plans. Though my family knew that I was going to Boston University on a track scholarship, few knew that it was to the College of Fine Arts.

"Singing," I told one of my uncles after the ceremony, when he asked what I was going to study.

"Singing? Just ordinary singing?" he asked, perplexed. "What does that mean?"

"So what is it . . . after that?" another uncle chimed in.

"Uncle," I said to him, "after that, maybe I will go and sing somewhere."

With raised eyebrows, that uncle turned to my mother and, in Igbo, said, "Did you hear what she said?"

"Yes, I know," my mother said.

"Why don't you go to school for law," suggested the first uncle, "and if you decide not to pursue it, then you can do that thing?"

"*Or*," I said, pausing as I looked at each of my elders, smiling slyly, inviting them to consider another way. "Why don't I go and try 'this thing' first? If I don't like it, *then* I can go to law school and become a lawyer."

"Ah?" they both said, eyebrows raised in a half question—one that another aunty would later echo when she asked me directly: "So we moved to America so you could be poor?"

Their generation had done something bold and daring yet risky too, with no guarantee on the other side of it. I wasn't getting ready to cross the Atlantic Ocean, as they had, but their example had prepared me in some way. I knew I could make it.

I will admit that as steady a front as I presented to my uncles in the moment, I can still remember their shared look. That concerned way of saying, with their eyes, *We've lost this one.*

Part II

I've never heard of nothing
coming from hard work.

—*Nonyem Aduba*

Chapter 8

Boston University was just twenty miles away from home, but I believed college truly could be a different world, as the television show title had promised. As much as I missed my family, I loved living on my own and building new routines. I was also pleased to find that all my time was my time: no more paper routes, ice-cream scooping, or babysitting for the good of the household.

The College of Fine Arts was full of people who, like me, *wanted* to stay late in theater rehearsal—to run it one more time. They wanted to talk about art and creation, music and dancing, film and theater and painting, and I wanted in on all of it. In both the School of Music and the adjacent Schools of Theatre and Visual Arts, I was surrounded by truly free spirits. Some were bookish, but even more had intelligence of a different sort, expressing themselves in ways I could have never considered.

In those days I saw "the arts" as a broad, almost limitless single category, as had my favorite Medfield teachers. I hadn't realized, going into this next phase of my education, that there were so many academic distinctions between theater and music majors. Forced to choose a path during the college application process, I went with what seemed clear: People liked me for singing, whether in the choir at my school or my church or during a solo for some other kind of crowd.

Three days into my first semester, though, I called my mother and told her I'd made the wrong choice. My mornings were great— I had movement classes with the theater majors followed by music theory and Shakespeare. My afternoons, however, were much more technical and dry: history, diction, pedagogy, piano. I loved singing, but it turned out that I much preferred the rolling-on-the-floor part of my day to what felt like rote work of melody, harmony, rhythm, and composition.

I told my mother that I'd already asked about switching to the School of Theatre. I would have to audition again; if I was accepted, I could start again with the new cohort the next fall. "It's worth it," I said. "That's what I want to do."

"You have to give the music a chance," countered my mother. I could hear the implication in her voice, in the unsaid. *Why, Uzo, must you always do the most, most, most?*

I relented, continuing along the path I'd begun; the farther I traveled, the more convinced I was that I'd made the wrong decision—and the harder I tried to find a way to make it work.

If my coursework felt dull at times, then life inside the big container that was art school never did. There we lived all the highs and lows of producing art, even if most people colliding with one another, students and teachers alike, were not always trained to manage all those feelings. Atop all this drama was a lot of competition, with only so many roles and solos to scrap over—and a lot of ego besides.

I was surprised to learn that there were just a handful of Black students in BU's College of Fine Arts—about as many as in Medfield High School. In our entire freshman class, I was the sole Black woman with a music focus. My vision of the college experience was informed by television and my time with Onyi at Cornell. While I didn't expect an all-Black experience, I certainly imagined that my life at BU would include more diversity than I'd found in my small, suburban enclave of Medfield.

Most of the Black students I knew—including Baron, a new friend and neighbor from my dorm—were in the theater department. Nevertheless, we created community among ourselves, no matter what our medium, and made a concerted effort to seek out one another.

I saw a completely different experience in the world of college athletics, which had a huge body of Black and Brown people—the football team and both men's and women's basketball teams, and a good portion of my own track and field team as well.

Many of my closest friends were my track teammates or other athletes, though I didn't try to assimilate or shape-shift, as I had in high school. I came into practice and social situations as myself, and I was fine with whoever gravitated in my direction. That's how I met Mary Ellen, a triple-jumper from Boston Latin, who grew up in West Roxbury and knew Monique. Pam, whom I met a year later, was first-generation like me; we talked often about pressures and parental expectations. To this day both are confidantes; we three are safe landing places for one another.

Through them and others in their orbit, I encountered men— West Indian and African men—who wanted to date me.

Me? I thought reflexively. I'm not just pretty because *I* say so? No, mine was a beauty they recognized.

This appreciation doesn't take away from the fact that plenty of them were also jokesters. I was often naive, interpreting any sort of kindness as love, in part because I was raised to believe that I was supposed to be looking for the real thing. But dating, I learned, was dating: Just because these men saw me, wanted me, didn't mean that they would hold my interest, or I theirs. Still, for the first time in my social life, I felt valued and validated, appreciated and seen.

By my sophomore year in college, I could feel my facility with Igbo language slipping. What began as Igbo Interrupted became a gradual slide that continued for years. At this point, even my parents' Igbo language had a lot of English mixed in—an almost unconscious blend. Unless my mother wanted to share something with me that she did not want overheard, we spoke in English.

I saw my family often, as they made a point of attending my choir concerts and recitals. I certainly wasn't shy about visiting home to do laundry, have my mother braid my hair, or load up on Nigerian food. Still, when we were together, I found myself reaching for words in Igbo that should've been second nature to me. A kind of sloppiness was now apparent during visits with relatives, as I had to stop to think about words and phrases. My awkward flip between English and Igbo smoothed out only if I stayed home long enough.

I hadn't realized how much just being in our home kept me connected to our culture. How swiftly that culture could be lost, if I didn't reach back for it.

This is how my daily conversations with my mother began.

While we'd always spoken regularly, I was now much more deliberate about when: every day, for just fifteen or even five minutes. "Of course," she said in her lilting way, when I first told her that my aim was to practice. "That will be fine."

The months passed, and the teacher inside my mother came alive. As we practiced, the territory of our conversations expanded, and something in our relationship began to shift. I wouldn't call ours a friendship exactly, but we were much more open with each other. A kinship.

It was a time of transition for my mother, who was now close to being an empty nester. Chi-Chi was in her first year at Penn State, and while Junior was still living at home, he was often busy, either on the road for hockey, at practice, or otherwise preparing for college in the fall.

She had grown so accustomed to a life that revolved around her children; it was hard to imagine that her hands-on mothering days were almost behind her. I know she worked so hard to provide the best for my siblings and me; we were becoming self-sufficient in that way as well, with great scholarships and good job prospects.

My mother loved to talk even more than I did, and she loved to listen. "The Vault," she called herself, meaning that when you told her something, it was as if it never happened. She made her living listening to other people, and I think she now welcomed the time to vent—and to reminisce. I tried to give her the space to do that without interruption.

It was a new dynamic, for both of us. I'd always come to her with my problems, but I appreciated that she wanted to share some of her own with me and that she trusted I could take in what she had to say. We spoke at length about my childhood, and our conversation broadened to hold more of my questions. There were more stories about her own beginnings too, as well as updates on what was happening around the house and in the community.

Sometimes we spoke about my father and the long-growing distance between my parents. Coming to America had been hard for both of them, but they'd handled it so differently. He had made some decisions that I—and I knew my mother—didn't agree with. When our talk lingered for too long in that direction, though, she'd guide it back to my studies or the plans for my next visit home.

In those days, my brothers, sisters, and I all came home for holidays—especially for Thanksgiving and Christmas. As the season neared, my mother and I discussed on our calls who would bring what, marveling at how our celebrations were created from this great mixture of different cultures. We made turkey, always, because that was what you were supposed to have, as well as lasagna next to some egusi and jollof rice. Red stew and jibo and onugbu soup and cranberry sauce and stuffing too.

All the idyllic memories of my siblings that became top of mind while we were apart were dashed the moment we were all back under the same roof. We may have grown in different ways, but the rules of old roles still applied.

Yet there was also the upside: We could still go into my parents' room and find my mother sitting up in bed, a long pillow placed on her lap, cutting coupons out of a stack of newspapers. (She was forever cutting coupons, sorting them, fitting paper clips around them.) We could shift around the books, magazines, and journals she had lying there and clear a little space for ourselves on the left side of the bed. We could help her cut coupons or just lie around and talk with her. Or not talk and just feel the comfort of being close as we lay there on that left side, facing the television, our head on a pillow fluffed up high so we could see.

IN COLLEGE I gained a far deeper understanding of myself as an artist, but two of my biggest influences were not musicians or even educators. Bruce and Lesley Lehane were a calm presence inside track and field's urgent demands. Working with them, I learned that I had a choice about where I placed my energy and focus— and that, in training, any attention directed to any other person, whether teammate, opponent, or otherwise, was a total waste.

"Just focus on *your* race," Bruce told me when I let myself get down about my performance. "Do you know how much time it takes to look left or right or behind you during a race?

"One-tenth of a second," he continued, answering his own question. "Forget about first and second place; that's the difference between winning and losing—between first and last place."

Bruce and Lesley were both tall and lanky, their heritage very much from where the Anglos met the Saxons. Bruce looked like Ichabod Crane in a red baseball hat, his long, straw-like gray hair peeking out the bottom. When he spoke with you, he never took his eyes off the track. He looked out at the long-distance runners, watching everyone's form, checking his watch before saying something deeply philosophical.

In the 1980s, Lesley had been one of the nation's best in cross-country, having won multiple NCAA titles. When we were together, however, there was no talk of past glories or medals. She was proud, but in a way that didn't shout about her accomplishments.

She still had the eye of the tiger in her. "Let's work hahd," she'd say in her hoarse whisper and thick Boston accent. She pushed me on our long-distance runs, keeping pace and then some, although she was likely twice our age. "Let's get fit."

Knowing that Lesley had once delivered on everything she was asking of me helped me run faster and push harder. It was a valuable leadership lesson: I now know that I should not expect anything from someone else that I cannot do myself.

Their focus, especially Bruce's, was beyond the sport. It wasn't about winning, or even about speed. He didn't want back that fraction of a second it took me to look over my left shoulder; he wanted me to examine what even made me want to do so.

It wasn't about what I was willing to do to win, but about what I was willing to do with my *life*.

I'd long known that I responded to a push and even a scream; I learned, through the Lehanes, that I actually respond best to a steady hand. Rather than thinking about the whole track, or the whole training program on the calendar, I focused on taking a bite out of each step. Considering a sprint or a relay this way, one piece at a time, helped me keep from falling into overwhelm, both on the track and in other areas of my life.

JIM SPRUILL WAS THE KING of cool. The full package, from the sunglasses that he never took off to the gray beard to the freedom fighter vibe; all he was missing was the beret. Everybody loved him: the Black kids, or at least the few who existed in the College of Fine Arts, and the white kids as well.

Jim was the first Black professor I ever had.

Never in my education had I experienced a Black-focused perspective or a theater environment where a Black voice was centered, beyond, maybe, "Here's this one August Wilson play." In his acting class, Jim did not adjust himself; he did not make himself more palatable or comfortable for the class's white student majority. In our studies, Suzan-Lori Parks's *Topdog/Underdog* was given just as much weight as Tennessee Williams's *Cat on a Hot Tin Roof.*

Working through scenes with Jim, I discovered monologues and long twists to stories as or even more powerful than anything I'd read. I learned that the possibilities that I believed existed for me were far narrower than the opportunity really there for the taking. With such authority, he helped me understand that I was enough—that my Blackness warranted no explanation.

I know James Baldwin's *The Amen Corner* because of Jim Spruill. I know James Baldwin, for never in my twenty years before Jim had I even heard his name. I know Charles Gordone's *No Place to Be Somebody*—especially Gabe Gabriel's "There's more to being black than meets the eye."

Jim Spruill taught me how to act, and the way he did that was by teaching me how to listen. Through him, this ideal I had about myself crystallized: I loved singing, but what I loved most about it was the real-time storytelling through a performance.

Walking up to the ivy-covered College of Fine Arts one day, I saw Jim sitting on the bench outside, having a smoke break. Returning my wave, he motioned for me to come closer: "We're doing a new show this spring—*Translations of Xhosa.*"

Written by a BU senior, Kira Lallas, it was a two-hander, he said. A play with two main characters. "We're not supposed to be working with kids who aren't acting majors, but I think you can do it," he said. "And I think it would be good if you did."

My eyes widened.

"If you were up for it, it would be in addition to all your other work. But I think you could do it," he repeated.

This opportunity changed the course of my life.

Xhosa is about a young, white American woman who spends a semester abroad in South Africa, meeting people and learning about herself and her own place in the world. I played all the South African men and women, as well as children and the elderly, while Kira played herself and all the white Afrikaner characters.

The play had a fair amount of singing, but the real focus, for me, was the character building. I had to do a lot of legwork—research and invention—in order to make each character distinctive from the last, both physically and vocally.

I stayed up late into the evenings, pouring over the script in bed, surrounded by papers, old photographs, my journal, and the script, highlighter in hand. I began listening to more South African music, especially Miriam Makeba, to study and practice the pronunciation and the different clicks.

One night I'd been working like this for hours, scribbling notes, thoughts, and questions in the margins, when I stopped with a realization. I felt . . . alive. How long had it been since I'd put this much effort into my actual schoolwork? I tried my best in rehearsal, but there was no passion. Some pieces I wouldn't even practice; I was just not interested.

This sparking of inspiration—this drive, this search for more information—was what I'd imagined the college experience would be.

This is what I had to do, I knew. I was drunk off the feeling.

I WASN'T ABLE to work during BU's school year because of the terms of my track scholarship; the summers were different. I spent the first two living at home, waitressing at Friendly's. As that third summer approached, I landed a much better job at a restaurant near campus that served alcohol, guaranteeing much more in take-home tips. If I stayed in Boston for the summer, I could bump up my shifts to full-time work and still have time to train on the college track as the summer wound down.

I planned to sublet a room from a friend, but her lease didn't start until a month after finals. The summer dorms were full, so I tried commuting back and forth from Medfield. Each day I'd take the commuter rail into the city; after helping to clean and lock up the restaurant, I'd head back out, often waiting up to an hour for the right connecting train. I'd arrive at Newton's Woodland Station, about twenty-five minutes from home, to find my mother's car in the parking lot. If I missed my connection, I'd call home to let her know; she'd drive out to the closest T stop I could find, typically all the way to Boston.

We kept up this routine until one night, as I opened the van door on yet another late Newton pickup, my mother said, "I can't do this." I stepped up into the van as she shifted back into drive. "I still have to get up early and go to work tomorrow," she said.

I sat for a while, watching her as she drove. I knew she was managing a lot. "Well, will you let me take the car?" I asked.

She said nothing, and I played out the scenario briefly; it soon became clear that the money I'd spend on gas and parking would eat far—too far—into my take-home pay.

"You'll have to figure it out," my mother told me, and then she left me to do so.

I felt frustrated. Abandoned. I knew my first-gen problems did not register with my mother, who that summer was already juggling work with hosting three of her younger siblings. In some ways, maybe, I was behaving like a spoiled child, but I felt trapped—and resentful. Only some of my friends even had to spend their summers working. Those who did had the luxury of knowing they could work a part-time job and all the money needed to keep the machine of their life going in the meantime would somehow sort itself out.

BU's women's track locker room wasn't huge, but it was clean—and empty. We'd been asked to train over the summer: Did that mean I still had twenty-four-hour access? One day I went into the city a few hours before my shift, stopping first at the athletic facility, and I discovered that my code still worked.

The next day, I raced back to the gym after work, praying that the maintenance staff were still there, cleaning the building. I keyed my way in, opening the door gingerly and tiptoeing through. My heart in my throat, knowing how exposed I was under the entrance's bright lights, I held my breath until I reached the swinging door that led to the women's locker rooms.

That door was easier to open silently—first just a peek. Once the hallway seemed clear, I raced down it, passing the soccer and volleyball rooms, thinking, every time, Please, don't let anyone be at the end of this hallway, mopping. Or: Is that someone coming?

I imagined what someone might ask me, upon discovery. *What are you doing?* they would say. *Please don't let anybody know,* I would beg.

I always waited a second when I got to the women's track door, listening for voices before swiping my card to access the locker room. That was where I slept for the month, on the cushioned chair mounted on the wall.

By the time I heard that inner door click shut behind me, it was usually late, and I was tired from a long shift. I'd head straight into the shower with my plastic shower caddy, peel off my waitressing uniform, wash it out, and leave it in the locker room to dry. When I awoke the next morning, I'd swap it out with the one I'd washed two nights before. I tossed my underwear in with the team laundry, knowing that it would come back clean in a few days' time.

The locker room was a nice space, and clean, but I was not a fan of being in the dark alone. I slept uneasily, knowing that, however unlikely, someone could come in.

Still, I tried to stay positive: I was training, a bit, on my time off. The job was a good one—one that I would keep until graduation. Many mornings, before it was time for me to go to work, I was able to take long, leisurely walks through the city—walks I kept up even when I moved out of the locker room and into my friend's apartment. It gave me quiet time to think about what all this maneuvering was for: a chance to grow into a great artist who could one day "cut it" in New York City. A life beyond all the struggle, in which I was settled on my creative path, ready to dare the world to look at me.

Chapter 9

Nigeria gained its independence in 1960, when my mother was nineteen years old and a student at the brand-new University of Nigeria in Nsukka. Her college was founded by Nnamdi Azikiwe, one of the most well-known Nigerian nationalists, who would go on to become the first president of the independent nation.

"Complete ownership of one's own place and identity." That was independence, according to my mother. "Incorporation, rather than exclusion from government, and being able to decide for oneself how the country is meant to be run."

For oneself. To come of age in a new republic was personal. The way she spoke of it was urgent and recent and felt different from my own history class conversations.

"It was probably the biggest thing that ever happened in Nigeria" was the way my Uncle David described it to me. He was just six at the time of independence, so his memories are of marching bands and streets lined with schoolchildren waving the green-and-white Nigerian flag.

English language and literature had long been the focus of all formal education, but now Nigerian students began studying in their native languages. The novel *Things Fall Apart* by Chinua Achebe, published just a few years earlier, was declared by one critic to have "inaugurated the modern African novel." For the very first time, a worldwide audience read—and celebrated—the story of an Igbo family and village. The book is still considered today to be among the greatest. With it, Nigerian people assumed the international stage; their stories held just as much value as the Western ones my mother and her classmates were tasked to know.

As an American kid raised with the stars and stripes, I associated independence with "bombs bursting in air," but there was no warfare reflected in this chapter of Nigerian history. I have watched the 1960 footage of that first flag hoisting at a racecourse in Lagos, as the British flag lowered, and wondered about the moment they passed each other. I have read that Martin Luther King Jr. was there as a witness. What, really, had changed at that stroke of midnight?

Celebrations lined the streets again a few years later when Nigeria officially became a republic and the "Great Zik," as he was known, became president.

At the time, my mother's life was flourishing. She was still in college, active in sports, and surrounded by friends—fellow young people bubbling with the expected promise of the future. In her circle were women and men, some classmates and some on other campuses. In her journals she writes about Chris Ohaegbulam, who played cricket. "We always connect during West African University games and vacations," she wrote.

During these years, my mother fell in love. The man she fell for gave her a record player, she told me. Every few weeks, after he had saved up a little bit of money, he would buy a record, and then he would ride his bicycle to Nsukka to give it to her. Together, they would sit outside and listen.

She loved him, but she couldn't marry him: He was Roman Catholic, and she was Anglican, and at that time, stuff like that mattered. Still, she loved him desperately, and he loved her desperately and wanted to marry her so desperately. They drifted apart, but she carried, for years, the idea of what might have been.

By the mid-1960s, my mother had graduated and was working as a teacher. My grandfather Egwuenu was well-established in his career, managing a big railway station farther up the rail line—about six hundred miles north of Obosi—in a Hausaland city called Kano. An interstate station, Kano's was one of the oldest and largest—an ideal last stop for my grandfather on the road to retirement. "At that time, my father was waiting for his gold watch," my mother told me.

My grandmother continued to trade fabrics and look after her two youngest daughters, Oby and Uju. As there were no longer so many mouths to feed, my mother's two beloved little sisters were not sent away to study or stay with relatives. Growing up watching my grandmother in the kitchen, these two aunties wound up being the best cooks in the family.

During the first few years of the republic, Nigeria's political parties remained divided by ethnicity as well as the geographical lines of its people's ancestral lands—Igbo people in the southeast, Hausa people in the north, and Yoruba people in the west. In each region, people feared that the tribe in power would hoard resources for their supporters at the expense of those in the minority. Violence broke out when the next elections were held; many citizens disputed the results and questioned the nation's democratic system.

Political tension seeped into the words and actions of everyday people. The long-held Igbo stereotypes of success and wealth were now threaded with suspicion at best, and often much worse, suggesting that our people keep all our money to ourselves. Sadly, the neighborly cultural exchange that my Igbo family had long enjoyed among Hausa people in the north was becoming rarer and even risky.

In 1966, a group of several military officers, most of them Igbo, attempted to overthrow the government. With the stated aim of rooting out corruption, the Igbo rebels killed twenty-two people—including the prime minister. Ultimately the coup was unsuccessful, and the military took control of the country. They were led by the commanding officer of the Nigerian government, who also happened to be an Igbo man. The shared ancestry of both the group stirring up trouble and the man who rose to power in its wake only fueled the rumors that the Igbo people conspired to "dominate" the other people of Nigeria and all the regions.

The attempted coup set off a wave of violence against people like my grandfather, who had come north to work. As many as one hundred thousand easterners were hunted down and murdered in these pogroms. Revenge killings in the southeast, targeting Northerners, also became more common. The military governor of the Eastern Region, Lieutenant Colonel Ojukwu, urged the speedy return of all Igbos living in the north and west.

My grandfather was in no hurry to leave his life in Kano. My grandmother refused to join the wave of women and children fleeing, regardless of the danger, as she was convinced that her husband's generosity could put his own life at risk. She imagined that, left to his own devices, he might prioritize supplies and even his own safety for his employees.

"If I leave, your father won't come home alive" was the way my mother remembers hearing the explanation.

The violence continued to escalate, and my grandmother finally took the youngest girls—my aunties Nkem, Oby, and Uju—and returned to Obosi, where the rest of the family had gathered.

In Kano, my grandfather heard a knock at his door late one night; he opened it to find one of his Hausa neighbors. Speaking in a hushed and rushed voice, the neighbor told my grandfather of plans being made, for the following day, to massacre the Igbo in the town. He'd come straight over from the community meeting, the neighbor said. My grandfather had no choice but to leave immediately.

Traditional Islamic dress, such as turbans and veils, are common in the north. As such clothing also makes helpful disguises, the neighbor lent my grandfather some fabric. He then escorted him through the winding streets of the city, so he wouldn't be caught before reaching the railway station.

Still enveloped, my grandfather boarded the next train and arrived safely home, thank God; he lingered at the station in Enugu afterward to help guide the following train. When the car doors opened on that train, every passenger, all of them Igbo, had been hacked to death with a machete.

When I asked my Uncle David, my father's brother, about the war, he said, "I didn't understand the implications of it all. I only knew what I saw at the Enugu railway station: people maimed in all kinds of ways. It was horrible."

It was, and still is, unimaginable. After months of such pogroms, the answer to the question of whether Igbo people could ever be safe in a unified Nigeria seemed clear.

. . .

MY FATHER WAS WORKING as a teacher in Enugu at this time; he and the rest of his siblings—including Uncle David, still just a teenager—attended pro-secession demonstrations.

"Everyone was huge on separation," my Aunty Ifey told me. "These pogroms, these massacres, were killing us."

In May 1967, Ojukwu established the Republic of Biafra, named for the bay in the Atlantic Ocean off Igboland's southern coast. This split shattered the dream of a united Nigeria for its people as well as for the British government. Rich in oil, Biafra was Nigeria's most valuable region; production had increased significantly since initial discoveries were made in the mid-1950s.

In retaliation for the secession, the new head of Nigeria's federal military government divided Nigeria into new states, including three in Biafra; they also created a new currency, which rendered Biafran reserves useless. Creating a tight blockade around Biafra, the Nigerian army stopped exports and squeezed out shipments of all kinds. Then, they began their advance.

They attacked first in Nsukka, the site of my mother's alma mater. When they came to Onitsha, so close to Obosi, my mother's family prepared to flee. Terrified of what soldiers might discover, my grandmother took all the family's papers and most of their photographs, burning them in a bonfire that Uncle Bertie built in the compound. They packed all that they could, loaded into Uncle Bertie's Jeep, and drove fifty miles south, to Imo State, where they stayed with a cousin.

Whenever conversations with my mother wandered into this passage and we took a few steps in, I hit a wall. My mother was typically such a talker, so I couldn't help but wonder what in the world could be behind all her silence.

The rest of the family politely fielded my questions about the war and then quickly changed the subject.

"If she were a man, your mother would have been fighting in the war," my Uncle Ifeanyi once told me.

When another opportunity presented itself, I pressed my mother for more, to give context to my uncle's words. "I used to drive and do trades with people," my mother said.

"With people?" I asked. "What does that mean?"

"People who wanted information," she said, "to find out what was happening."

The Biafra-Nigeria war waged on for two and a half years. "A colossal loss," as Uncle Ifeayani described it.

While I didn't get much detail from my mother's family, what I gathered is far more than what I got from my father, who never discussed the war—not once.

The truth is that I don't need all the details to understand that the war forever changed the trajectory of my family's life. I could never speak about the shades of war, but I can imagine that when so much is lost, survival is the only victory.

That is the way my mother chose to describe the war to me.

"In our family, we were lucky," she said. "We didn't lose anybody."

Chapter 10

T he first time I arrived in New York City on my own, I knew
    I was home. Stepping off the $15 bus in Chinatown, weaving
my way through the puddles and crowds on Canal Street over to
the subway station, I was so inspired that I wrote a song:

Thanks for the date last night New York City
I had a marvelous time
and I loved the part when you took my hand
and we danced and you sang me your rhyme.
Have you been all alone
or am I just the first one tonight
I've been waiting for someone like this
Just one kiss
From Mr. Right.

The energy I felt there was everything I loved about my high
school trips to the art house cinema in Brookline. Here, I believed,

I could create the kind of bohemian life that made space for art. It could be just as Mike and I had experienced it in a coffee shop near Coolidge Corner Theatre, surrounded by other cinefiles trying to unpack what we had all just seen on screen.

I was not totally new to NYC. I'd been there to visit relatives. I'd also spent some time toward the end of college going to open casting calls—a theater industry term for an audition that's open to the public. Simi was already there, working as an intern in the music industry, and I'd been able to crash with her.

In addition to being brilliant and driven, Simi was passionate about music. She began volunteering at our local radio station back in high school and had now landed a summer position at a record label. Simi was, by far, one of my most "established" friends: working at Urban Outfitters, living on peanut butter sandwiches and scrambled eggs, and sleeping on someone's pull-out couch in northern Manhattan. We'd become even closer over the years: Each of us was doing something so out of the box in the eyes of our immigrant parents, who'd raised us to do something "respectable."

"Can I stay over?" I'd asked, telling her about the open call for a production of *My Fair Lady*. "I'll come late and leave early."

"Stay for two days," she'd insisted. "Come, get ready, orient yourself, and then take the time you need for the audition."

That's Simi: Even as she's pushing and struggling herself, she's cheering you on.

I hadn't gotten the part, but the visit did step up the conversation with my family about my returning after graduation. It all fell into place: I'd stay with Aunty Rachel's daughter, my cousin Obioma. If I needed money, I could file scans, notes, and other paperwork at Aunty Rachel's office.

Just as soon as the lease ran out on my apartment in Boston, I packed up my clothes and headshots, caught the Chinatown bus, and headed for Obioma's apartment in Sunnyside, Queens, to begin my new life.

My Aunty Rachel was tall and slender, with a small, narrow nose and a very bright smile. She was rational, measured, super smart, and very successful: an obstetrics and gynecologist nurse at Roosevelt Hospital, on the west side of Manhattan. She was my father's cousin, but more than that she was my mother's best friend. Now, she could also be my mother's eyes and ears.

Aunty Rachel was completely supportive of my goals, if also a little curious how this whole thing was going to shake out. "This one, my Uzo, I always thought, lawyer, lawyer, lawyer"—this was Aunty Rachel's favorite line.

And that was the subtext for many years: I love you and support you, but . . . why are you doing this?

"Lawyer." Her voice is unmistakable: caramel-y, in the throat, with a little lilt to it. "Hel-lo!" she'd say, in a singsongy way. She drew words out sometimes, especially on "ridiculous"—one of her favorites—as "ridicool-ussss." She never said goodbye on the phone, only "bye for now."

While Aunty Rachel wasn't as loud as some, she had power over her volume. Like my mom, she could hold on to her confidence. Sometimes, if you asked her how she was doing, she'd respond, all calm and collected, by quoting the fourth chapter of Philippians: "I have a peace that surpasses all understanding."

She did for me what Ike had done for me in London and what, before that, my mother had done for Ike, Chudi, Uncle David: She helped me find my feet. In those early years, Aunty Rachel truly played the role of a godmother, giving me not just a place to live but also a place to go and something to do. She taught me to classify ultrasounds and other test results and forms, giving me a far wider window into childbirth than I'd bargained for. She paid me well—too well. I'd walk out of her office with what felt like so much money—$60, $80. Enough to cover the train, my cell phone, and a few groceries besides.

Really, Aunty Rachel was also my first agent. She hired me to sing for her daughter Tochi's wedding. If anyone she knew needed entertainment, for any event, it was, "My niece, my goddaughter, she can do it." One of her friend's daughters got married, and I took the subway all the way to the end of the line to sing for a crowd of people I didn't know. Years later, on her recommendation, I would perform at the Abyssinian Baptist Church, a gorgeous, Gothic cathedral in Harlem.

Her daughter Obioma was about my brother Rich's age. She lived in a beautiful and open two-bedroom apartment. One bedroom she shared with me; in the other was Obioma's roommate, Linda, and Linda's boyfriend, Gabe. Linda and Gabe were Obioma's age too: On the far side of their twenties, close to thirty, and very truly grown-up in a way that I simply wasn't. They showed me every kindness, from the space that Obioma made for me in her full-size bed to the dinners and late-night conversations we shared.

This Sunnyside apartment was the headquarters for making all my dreams come true. I just loved it: There was a living room big enough for an entertainment center and two three-seater couches arranged in an L, with an end table in between. Room for a dining table too. True luxuries in New York City, when you're starting out with nothing.

There were three other apartments in our small building, each one filled with people who went off to work or school in the mornings. This meant that on weekdays, from about 8:30 in the morning to dinnertime, the whole place was mine. Or almost mine, figuring in Linda's orange, white-pawed cat, Jack. The only other person around was the elderly woman who lived next door with her two grown children, but we never saw her.

Each day I awoke just as Obioma and the others were heading off to work. The first thing I'd say to myself was, Decide now. Then I'd get up and go for a run, down the tree-lined stretch of row houses and apartments on Forty-Ninth Street to Skillman Avenue, past little shops, laundromats, dollar stores, and nail salons, all the way over to the snarls of traffic around Queens Plaza. Heading onto the narrow footpath of the Queensboro Bridge, I'd push all the way up the steep approach to the first pillar. It's just a hill, I'd say to myself, over my dread and the sound of the N train. Just a hill.

From the top, I'd turn around, run the two miles home, and make breakfast: two egg whites and a half yolk, a splash of milk, two slices of turkey bacon, twenty-one blueberries. It was light, fortifying, and kept my weight in check. I'd fill my oversize mug with green tea and take it over to the computer for what I called my "morning calisthenics." First I'd scour the industry websites for open casting calls; then I'd study the print editions of *Playbill*, *Backstage*, and other trade magazines, cover to cover, as well as the classifieds in *The Village Voice*, circling and ripping out ads and jotting down details into my notebook.

After I'd cross-checked the list, I'd begin stuffing envelopes: Return to the computer and customize my stock submission letter and adjust the quotes and reviews of my past shows. Print it out. Find a headshot and résumé, stick it all in the envelope. Print out the label and get the stamps, crossing my fingers that I had some left from my mother's most recent care package.

"Decide now." This was my reminder: I'd chosen something that didn't guarantee that better life my parents sought with their sacrifice. I needed to do everything in my power to pursue every avenue, to make sure that promise was fulfilled.

What I wanted was to do it all: singing, starring, acting, directing. I wanted to perform at the Met and be a mainstay at the ballet, while pursuing all these high art and experimental projects at the same time.

What I needed to do was make rent so that, as the saying goes, if all else fails, my hands—and not my mom—would feed me. I began calling up restaurants, leaving messages inquiring about openings for server positions. When I didn't hear back, and I didn't, I walked by and dropped off a résumé.

One day a "concert performance venue" on the Lower East Side returned my call and asked me to audition. I prepared my musical theater pieces—something up-tempo as well as a ballad—and walked into the place wearing what I called my "cool" musical theater getup: my college roommate Alana's blue track jacket with white stripes up the side, zipped over a cream-and-pink A-line skirt that hit just above the knee with tall, slouchy sheepskin boots.

"I'm here for an audition," I told the hostess, who was standing behind a podium and wearing a black bustier.

"Oh yes," she said. "Follow me." She turned around to lead me wherever I was going, her large-hole fishnet stockings pouring into her knee-high, high-heeled boots, the rest of her hanging out of a G-string, as plain as day.

Where was I?

I settled into a banquette at a low cocktail table—one of several in the small, empty back room, which had a U-shaped stage with a curtain on the back. I sat alone for a few minutes, and then a man walked in, super skinny and pale-faced, with white-blond hair long enough to be coiffed. He looked like a goth version of the emcee in the musical *Cabaret*—androgynous, with the same sort of slinky way about him. All he was missing was the character's lipstick.

I climbed up onto the stage and sang both of the pieces I'd prepared for him. Then, once I'd finished, I stood there and watched him fold one long leg neatly over the other, very relaxed. His crossed foot dangled near his other ankle as he studied me. I was used to people looking at me during auditions, but there was something unnerving about the way he was taking me in, as though I were an object—not a person.

He offered me the job and noted my hesitation. "Do you know what we do here?" he asked. I think he used the word "burlesque" after that, but at the time, as I heard "performances" and "entertainment," all I could think of were the words "strip club"—a place I had never been.

"Like . . . naked?" I asked him.

"No, topless," he said. "How do you feel about that?"

"I . . ." I began. "I don't know if I think that's something that I feel comfortable with."

They made a lot of money, he told me, implying that the same would be true for me.

"No, I can't do that," I said. I wasn't going to do that. I happily returned to filing.

Eventually, my college friend Mary Ellen helped me land a job waiting tables at City Lobster and Crab Company, a restaurant on the edge of Manhattan's Theater District. Decent pay and enough flexibility in the schedule that I could still audition as much as I wanted to—or, to be more accurate, to work as little as I needed to. By that point, I'd figured out, to the penny, how much I'd need to survive. I had no interest in working one second beyond that.

Still so new to the city, I welcomed the routine and built-in friends a restaurant provided. Most of my fellow servers were also in the theater world. There was Matt, whom I once ran into at an audition, and Denise from Pittsburgh. There was Susan, a tiny blonde with glasses, inseparable from Ceci, a brassy, ballsy Texas firecracker who'd arrived in New York for an adventure, with no plans to stay. Some of the others were older, and they felt so much older: There was the woman from the Midwest, with a worn look and dyed-black hair, who was waiting tables full-time while her husband gave acting a shot. And Jim, a slim man with big glasses and sandy-colored straight hair, another actor, who worked most days at the restaurant and auditioned on the side.

This will not be me, I thought so many nights, as I took the walk down Broadway to the subway after my shift. What I wanted—needed—was to wake up in the morning, every day, to go to work and do what I loved.

I knew it'd be the hardest thing I'd ever try to do in my life, and that I'd likely miss out on some things—personal, financial— in order to get there. Still, all that work was worth it to me, if it ensured I didn't come up empty-handed.

"Decide now." I didn't want to be an artist who tried. I wanted to be an artist who did.

LINDA AND GABE had a baby, so for a little while, in the Queens apartment, we were five. Then the little family moved out, and Obioma soon followed, having taken a job in Virginia. Luckily

Chi-Chi graduated around this time. She moved into Linda's room, and we picked up right where we left off.

I continued to audition, wearing the weight of rejections more heavily. Gone were the highs I'd felt that first summer in the city, when I was just trying on the experience before returning to college. Then, life as an actor was an experiment. If I'd had the great fortune to be cast in a play—which I hadn't—I would have needed to leave the show in the middle, to return to school. Now, as I put myself out there again and again and came back with nothing, I began to worry.

I need to get to the next best thing: This was all I could think of as I lugged my dance bag through the city, warmed up in the stairwells, and lingered in the hallways post-audition to see if I'd made it to the next round. There had to be other possibilities, other connections. I spent my tips on musical theater and on-camera classes, twenty minutes of rehearsal space, a refill of headshots at Reproductions. I borrowed stacks of scores and soundtracks from the performing arts library at Lincoln Center. I listened to them on my commute home from the restaurant, first on the subway and then as I walked home past the rolled-down security gates. It was so late that only the bodegas were open.

I spent so much of my twenties this way: headphones cranked up and one foot in front of the other, traveling for miles, clearing my head, saving on subway fare. Sometimes I would have a conversation with God, and by the time I got to my destination, I'd have some things sorted out.

I often felt lonely. I had plenty of friends, but very few of them, and none of my siblings, were considering—no, hoping for—an opportunity to work for free. Some were in competitive fields with low starting salaries, like Chi-Chi, who worked in advertising, but they still had ladders to climb and some confidence that, in time, they would be rewarded. Even my younger brother, Junior, who was considering a career in professional hockey, had a degree in criminal justice and the idea of business school to fall back on.

Give me a training plan, a script, or a piece of furniture to put together, and not one corner of the manual will be missed. Now I had only my morning calisthenics and the list of contacts from the BU theater program's industry showcase, which didn't guarantee me anything.

"You know what I wish?" Baron said one day, as we walked together through my neighborhood. "I wish, sometimes, that we could just go back to high school drama club."

"What do you mean?" I asked.

"We were so green then," he said. "They call us green, living here in New York, but we're not green in the same way as when you're green in high school."

Baron and I often talked about work. He was reaching for similar goals, and, at that time, more than any other friend, he was achieving them. While still in college, he'd landed a prestigious internship that had led to an audition for and a role in Regina Taylor's new Broadway play, *Drowning Crow*.

I understood very well what he was saying. Back in high school, theater was about the costumes and the parents sewing them. The kids in the band and orchestra playing in the pit. There were high stakes, as we waited in our lunchrooms for the cast list to go up. The heart palpitations of that urgent question, as our eyeballs or fingers moved down the list: am-I-the-lead-am-I-the-lead-am-I-the-lead?

Once that news had settled, however, it was just about those three performances, or six if we were lucky. Then it was about the craft—that pure love, and the feeling that comes with pure love.

Now the joy of creation was more complicated. The love was still there, just as strong, but it commingled with so many other things that we didn't love, like rent and health insurance payments. No longer were we living just for landing the role but for all these other markers of success, like finding an agent; landing a job that qualified us for a union membership and health benefits; landing a role on Broadway; landing a commercial, a television spot, a film. It was all about the next thing: What was the next thing?

Baron's success was an inspiration to me and to a lot of our friends; we knew how talented he was and how hard he'd worked to achieve it. I had never known anyone who was on Broadway, let alone originating a part, let alone playing alongside Alfre Woodard, a fellow Boston University grad. She was a kind of icon in the College of Fine Arts, especially among students of color—a living example of someone who'd walked the same halls and emerged with her dreams.

I truly did not envy the pressure he felt at that moment. As we walked, we tried to remind ourselves of where we both had been just a few years earlier, and to imagine how much those truly green kids would now envy us.

Baron invited me and our friend Chinasa to come to *Drowning Crow*'s opening night. Having lived through his rehearsal experience together, we were beyond thrilled to celebrate. Chinasa and I dressed at my apartment, going all out: My red heels matched the red-and-white thin-striped pantsuit I'd bought for the occasion. It was the first article of clothing I'd ever had professionally tailored, at the dry cleaner downstairs—a few key tucks so I could wear the blazer without even a camisole underneath. We were so chic, so fierce, we thought, walking up to the theater, mingling with the crowd, bumping into all the well-known actors we knew we'd see at the after-party.

Never had I been in the midst of such extravagance—so many people taking pictures, a real red carpet. The lights were bright enough to make us feel, standing at night on a city street, as though we were inside the most exclusive, well-lit room. The people surrounding us seemed somehow to stand taller than most people; they were better dressed and more turned out.

Hearing the photographers call out names of artists I knew, I imagined what it might feel like to be known for my work. Mingling among them afterward, I knew I had been brought into a club I was not a part of yet. This whole world did exist: These prominent talents, the best of the best, were just hanging out, catching up among themselves.

This was the height, I thought, cradling my wineglass and trying not to stare: Creating work that had something to say, that inspired. Work that created this kind of atmosphere for aspiration, and, most importantly, that was respected by my peers.

That whole night I wished, more than anything, that I was known too.

Chapter 11

I t's a known theater," I told my mother breathlessly over the phone.

An impossible-to-miss, red-and-white painted, off-off-Broadway house in the East Village called Theater for the New City. There, I'd perform in my very first professional production, a musical called *Pyrates! The CourtShip Chronicles*. While I'm still unclear on the exclamation point, *Pyrates!* offered a role that I'd play four times a week—for free, yes, but also for the better part of a month!

She was the first call I made. "Really? Well done," she exclaimed, after I'd relayed all the details. I could tell she was super proud.

I was cast again, not long after that, in another musical, called *Love According to Luc*. This was something called an Equity show-case, a production that could be done without a contract, meant to highlight new talent. This time I was paid—$75 for subway fare.

During the audition process, I became friendly with the casting director, Judy Bowman. Judy also came to our rehearsals from time to time. One day, I got up the courage to ask her: "Do you know of any agents I can reach out to, who might want to come to the showcase?"

"Sure," she said. "I can invite a few of my friends."

"Thank you so much!" I said. "Who are they? Can I walk head-shots over to their offices?"

"I'll call," she said, defusing my eagerness. "We'll see what happens."

Back then, I didn't know what I didn't know, which is that many would consider someone like me asking Judy for a favor to be too forward a request. Thank God for my innocence. To my amazement, all of the agents Judy had called came to see *Luc*; they all reached out afterward to schedule meetings. I was interested in two of them.

I sat in the office of the first agent, thrilled to hear that she was interested in working with me. "We think you're fantastic," she said. We spoke for a while longer, the conversation flowing easily, until she asked, in a sort of conspiratorial way, "So what are we doing with your gap? Are we keeping it?"

I froze. That question, as if we both had gaps in our teeth. As if we were sitting not in a Midtown Manhattan office, a big one with an assistant out front but at a sleepover, dyeing our hair, you guys, with the stuff we got at Hot Topic. Are we getting tattoos or no?

"We're keeping it," I told her.

My answer would have been different if the agent had caught me back in high school, when I was begging for "perfect" teeth. With time, I'd further warmed to the idea of my beautiful smile. Having someone in my corner so clearly ready to make "perfection" happen helped me decide that I couldn't work with her.

The other agent had a smaller office—a room, really, with a big window opposite the front door and a chair in front of it where the client was meant to sit. Two desks faced each free wall; from one, Judy Boals had turned her chair around to face me. A white woman with a blunt bob cut, Judy had a soft voice, but one that suggested a kind of quiet toughness. I liked her instantly.

I took my seat, and, squinting slightly through her round glasses, Judy launched into a familiar spiel. "We think you're great," she began. Then, during a natural lull in the conversation, I could feel a hesitation. Here we go, I thought.

"So, what do you think about my gap?" I asked her, leaning in a little. "Do you think I need to . . ." I brought my right hand up to my mouth, pinching my thumb and forefinger together a few times.

"Oh no, no, I love it," Judy said, surprised. "I think it's great."

I signed with Judy, and I loved working with her. As much as she helped me in my career, she also helped me understand that in such a partnership, I needed someone with whom I could be entirely myself.

I wish I could say that this was the end of my hesitation around my smile. At one point years later, after I had made the difficult decision to move on to a bigger agency, I worked with a manager who raised the issue again.

For a while I tried a kind of middle ground: My friend Alana's dentist father made me a prosthesis I could pop in and out, as if I were on *Toddlers & Tiaras*. I wound up hating it—both the way it affected my speech and what it represented.

Ultimately, I tossed it, and that manager too.

MY MOTHER MADE REGULAR TRIPS down to Queens to check on her children living in the big city. After dropping her bags, she always walked directly to our kitchen and opened the fridge. "Where is your food?" she asked on her very first visit, when I was still living with Obioma.

"Oh, you know, I don't buy a lot," I told her. I had been there just a few months at that point. "If I work in the morning, they give us breakfast. If I work in the afternoon, there's a shift meal, and that gets me through."

For me, this was a point of pride: Fresh to the game, I was making it work on my own. But my mother saw something else. She'd sniffed around a bit more, approvingly unearthing a piece of salmon in the freezer. Other than a half bag of frozen vegetables and some rice, there wasn't much more to find.

The next morning, while out walking, I realized that she was turning toward the grocery store. As we walked through the sliding doors, she said, "Get whatever you want."

"Anything?" I asked. I knew that in those days she didn't have much money to spare.

"Anything," she insisted. I stood awkwardly a few steps behind her at the deli counter, watching her order a pound of turkey for the turkey and cheese sandwiches I loved so much. "Is that enough?" she asked me. Hearing that need for reassurance in her voice, I knew: My mother may not have seemed afraid in the way she spoke or moved, but she was concerned about the choices I'd made.

I followed her through the narrow aisles. Anything I said I wanted, she pulled two from the shelf. Two loaves; put one in the freezer. On her way out of town, she handed me a wad of cash.

From then on, whenever she drove down for the weekend, it was with a cooler of Nigerian food. She'd put half in the freezer and then stock the fridge. "Defrost just a little bit, so it lasts," she'd say.

Peppers and basil from her garden and still-quite-green tomatoes: "Put them on the windowsill; in a week they'll be red."

This was the ritual: My mother came to fill my kitchen, and then we went shopping together. A few days before she left each time, she'd take me back to the store to buy ingredients so we could cook together, and we did. That way she knew I'd eat well in the first few days of her absence, and even longer, as we'd put my leftovers in the freezer stock. She also opened an account at a bank nearby, so she could transfer money if I was coming up short.

On one of these visits, my mother organized what she called a "cooking session." We began discussing it over the phone beforehand, as her plan was to go through a wide range of dishes—not just basic red stew, but several of the more time-consuming dishes that we didn't eat every day.

That meant several varieties of soup, as well as satisfying akara, fritters made of black-eyed peas. It also meant Nigerian snacks—chin-chin and puff puff, flash-fried pastry that you'd see at an Igbo wedding or another kind of party. It was usually found on a plastic or Styrofoam plate, in the middle of a paper tablecloth–covered round table.

My mother watched as we kneaded the dough, rolled it out, cut it, and prepared to fry it.

Chi-Chi brought out a journal and a pen, trying to remember the ratios. "Mom, on the sugar, would you say that was a half cup?"

"When have you ever seen me put in a measuring cup?" asked my mother.

"I'm just trying to make sure I get it exactly right," said Chi-Chi.

I didn't cook with spoons, cups, or timers. I really took my mother's direction on that—to keep watch, feeling the dough come together between my fingers. Wary of overworking it, I called her over to the counter. "Now?" I asked, still kneading.

Looking over my shoulder, she took a small hunk and pressed it with her thumb into the crook of her forefinger. "Another thirty seconds," she said. She turned to look at Chi-Chi: "And that oil better be really, really hot."

I was an eager student, truly wanting to get perfectly right some of the recipes expected of a "good Igbo woman and wife." I might not have admitted it at the time, but this was the ideal I kept in mind for myself, to correspond with the vision of the Naija man I believed was right for me. My chin-chin couldn't be too crunchy, like the kind we always seemed to have when we were young kids: round, yes, but almost rock-hard. (As we got older, and people had more time and money to buy higher-quality ingredients, I'd come to understand that the best chin-chin had a kind of softness—almost like a shortbread, with that same slightly sweet finish.) It couldn't be greasy, as I knew it would be if I left it in the oil too long.

So many Nigerian recipes require a kind of balanced hand, a sharpening of the eyes. I began to apply this logic to all the soups: not just for onugbu soup, made from bitter leaf, but also the ones made from ogbono seeds or the one thickened with ground egusi seeds, both from the seeds of local fruit.

The first time I cooked a big batch of Nigerian food on my own, I brought some to my Aunty Daisy, who lived in Brooklyn. I didn't stay to share it with her, but the next day she called. I picked up the phone and heard, "Whoa!" She sounded surprised. "You know how to make this on your own?"

"Wife" talk aside, all this cooking effort was not just to land a husband, but to elicit this kind of reaction.

For Nigerians bringing up their children in America, the expectation is that some things will be lost along the way. Much was—and is—lost, and yet I wanted my relations to be proud. I wanted them to see not only that I was trying, but that I could.

I was cast in a show in Boston a few years later, and the producers rented an apartment for me in the heart of the city. Now, if I might be so bold, I would say that around this time, I had perfected red stew—and was eager to make it. So I invited my mother to dinner.

After tasting it for the first time, she looked at me. "You made this?" she asked.

"Yes," I said.

"It's delicious," she said.

"Really?"

"Delicious," she repeated. I felt so proud.

MY CAREER WAS PROGRESSING, but the speed was slow, the lack of good news dispiriting. It was clear that my voice, which had been so praised in college, was not resonating in New York's theater world. I went into one audition for a soprano lead, similar to the role of Eliza in *My Fair Lady*, with sixteen bars of one of her songs from the musical: "I Could Have Danced All Night."

"That was beautiful," said the artistic director. "Do you have anything else?"

"Anything else," I repeated flatly.

"Anything slower and, like, R&B?"

I didn't have anything else, I told him. I wasn't auditioning for a role as a gospel singer in *The Wiz*, I thought. Together we went through my entire book, trying to find something that he wanted to hear that I could actually sing. You can guess how this story ended.

Over time, I grew accustomed to these saucer-eyed reactions from people sitting in judgment behind the table. I didn't expect that to come out of you! Most casting directors either wanted to hear something super low, warm, and mothery, or they wanted to hear what's called a high upper belt, something more like Jennifer Holliday, who had originated the role of Effie in *Dreamgirls*. I had a big voice, but I couldn't shout from the rafters. I didn't know how.

Once again, I wondered if I'd erred in pursuing opera instead of musical theater.

I still wanted to believe it was possible to have a career spanning both—a career like operatic soprano and Broadway superstar Audra McDonald's. When I looked in the mirror and heard myself sing, I remembered all that she had accomplished.

As inspired and hopeful as I'd been by Audra's range and rise, I'd come to understand that she was the exception. I'd thought space had been created—that the rules had changed—but here was space for only one.

I began to practice at night, trying to use my voice in another way. Like any other instrument, I could push it, but when I did, it was difficult and even painful sometimes to get the right tone.

My natural voice has an open sound, round and high in the head. Shifting it lower to fit the musical theater realm required a new focus and much more effort from my chest and throat. I rehearsed until my body was tense, my throat scratchy and strained.

Claudia, I knew, could help.

One of my former vocal performance professors, Claudia Catania, had become after college a kind of confidante and counsel for (lucky) me and a few of my classmates. She understood my voice forward and backward and knew how to manipulate sound.

I'd been to her Upper West Side apartment many times over the years, to seek her feedback on pieces I was preparing for auditions. For a lesson, she left the door of her apartment perched slightly open for the students to give themselves entry; her walls were lined with photos from her appearances with the Metropolitan Opera and on Broadway. In addition to all the rugs and beautiful lamps, she had a real piano in her apartment—an unimaginable fortune.

I didn't have the money to pay Claudia for voice lessons or reimburse her for studio space and accompanist time, and she knew it. If the topic arose, she'd brush it off or say, "You'll get to it one day."

I sang, and Claudia stopped me along the way, giving notes, breaking down sections and transitions. She understood very well what it took to broaden a range. She also understood my career dilemma. It wasn't simply that they didn't like my voice; they didn't want my voice. They didn't think it was what I was supposed to be.

MY MOTHER had her own context for my career milestones. When I was cast in a performance of *The Jungle Book*, I was able to work enough hours to qualify for what is known as an Equity card— proof of membership in the Actors' Equity Association, which guaranteed salary and benefits.

I may have been working at a theater she'd never heard of, but there was steady pay and health insurance. This, my mother understood.

If my first real show was *Pyrates!*, then my first big show was *Abyssinia*. A gospel musical about a girl who is able to heal a town with her voice, it played at the Goodspeed Opera House, a historic theater in Connecticut, about halfway between New York and Boston. With *Abyssinia*, I was able to quit my day job; I could sublet my apartment and live on what I made.

Abyssinia was one of the first shows I'd been a part of that had an all-Black cast. By this point, I was working with actors who were well-established in the industry, many of whom seemed to know one another. I knew no one, and I didn't like that.

In these early days, I sat in rehearsal, taking stock, thinking, OK, Kelly, Shannon, Lisa . . . we four are around the same stage in our careers . . . Still, as much as I was hoping to find friends in that production, I wasn't so sure that I'd get along with Lisa, who had breezed in late to our first rehearsal without even acknowledging the time. We are not late in the theater. The time called is the time; even three minutes matters.

This person is difficult, I concluded, one eye clocking Lisa's all-white outfit. She could be a problem.

Abyssinia was written up in major newspapers; it attracted attention from producers and went on to play at Boston's Shubert Theatre. It also led to an audition for Regina Taylor's gospel musical *Crowns*, in 2006. When I was cast, I was able to reach another milestone: I was able to fly my mother in from Boston to the Denver Center for the Performing Arts to see me in the show.

"You don't have to . . ." my mother said, when I told her about the plane ticket. I'm so glad I insisted. She loved the show, which is set in a Black church and filled with gospel music. Afterward, I took her for dinner at a steakhouse. She couldn't stop talking about the size of her baked potato.

One day I saw the news that a play called *Coram Boy*, about an eighteenth-century orphanage, was coming from London's National Theatre to Broadway. Reading about the role of Toby, an orphan boy, I told myself: I'm going to do that part.

During the audition, I could feel the casting director, Laura Stanczyk, rooting for me. Seeing her nod encouraged me to lean into the choices I had brought into the room—to believe that my instincts for the role were correct.

I was called back for another audition. I sat in the waiting room, listening for my name. After welcoming in the next actor, Laura walked in and sat down next to me. "You're back with us!" she said with excitement. "You were so great."

By the final rounds, when I was reading lines with one of the show's leads, I felt so free. I was just playing, really, tumbling around, feeling bold enough to allow the character I wanted to come through to do so without interruption. Laura helped me believe that I could be more than other people's expectations. There's no question that her recognition gave me the confidence to land the part.

When I shared the news with my mother, she was proud but still cautious. Her front-row seat to all the challenges of my chosen industry had made it even more clear: These roles were not destinations but occasions. I could take dream roles like this, and the run—and the money—could end early. I could go back to the other theaters that didn't pay as much. But the opposite could also happen, and I tried to emphasize that.

She was looking for security, I knew; in her mind, the security was not there yet.

I felt that I had found what I was looking for—that a prayer had been answered.

The view from the stage in Broadway's Imperial Theatre was the same as it had been in rehearsals, but the feeling on opening night was completely different. If there is such a thing as a good heart attack, that was what I felt: my heart bursting with gratitude. Finally, I was part of the tribe.

Chapter 12

I no longer had to skimp as much on subway fare, but I still seized every opportunity, when I'd leave a performance, to walk as far as I could through the city before jumping on the train. It still felt soothing and grounding. Never fresh, the air in Midtown was filled with energy and effort, with so many people going to and from work. After inhabiting someone else all day, I welcomed the chance to flow out of the theater and into the world, back into my own thoughts, plans, goals.

One summer night in 2008 started like so many others: slip-on sneakers; a steady pace; a backpack slung over my shoulder; a head full of monologues, gossip, and plans for the next day. I hadn't even brought my phone to my college friend Marissa's place—just my wallet and my dog-eared copy of *The Complete Works of Shakespeare*. It was 11:00, just about the limit of what I thought was safe for a young woman walking by herself on the better-lit streets of Astoria, Queens.

Our night had been about as nerdy as it got, and I was dressed for it in a bright red T-shirt that read "Switzerland," and my yellow backpack that read, "Jamaica." My hair was still short in those days—clipped close to my head, as it had been for *Coram Boy.*

My mind was working through the monologues that Marissa and I had been rehearsing for upcoming auditions. That was what I was thinking of—the cadences and their nuance—as I headed back to Sunnyside, about a mile and a half away. Committing words to memory was made easier by my forward motion; I was in a groove when I heard the sound of screeching tires.

I turned around as a brown Lincoln Town Car pulled a U-turn and headed back in my direction. The driver was a middle-aged white man with sandy-colored hair and a mustache. He was wearing a short-sleeved white button-down.

I had time to notice all this because he slowed down to look at me through his open window. His head even turned back, his gaze lingering for a moment before he hit the gas and was gone. That was weird, I thought for a moment, but I moved on, continuing my walk down Steinway Street. As I got closer to home, I decided to turn down Forty-Eighth Street, a two-way street, bigger and better-lit than my own, Forty-Ninth.

"Freeze!"

My hands flew open for a moment, out of instinct. I saw two men coming at me.

The first thought I had, clear as day: I am going to be raped.

Then: Oh my God. Should I run?

Muscle memory from track took over as I wheeled my shoulders around and started to take off down the street; then I heard someone, faint in the background, shout, "Police!"

What?

"Identification, now!" The two men who'd been running toward me were on me, left and right. Just as I stopped, a car pulled up alongside us: the same Lincoln from Steinway, with the same man in the front. My eyes darted back and forth: all these men were white with brown hair. The one standing with me was stocky and the second heavyset, wearing a Dallas Cowboys jersey. Not a police uniform in sight. And this same strange mustached man in the car.

"Wait," I said. "Why are you wearing regular clothes? How do I know you're police?"

One of the men on the street reached into his shirt. He fished out one of those metal chains with a police badge on the end.

My wits snapped back as I put it together: These men had been following me.

"You could have gotten that badge at Party City, for all I know," I said, buying time. "How do I know that's real?"

They exchanged a look. "We're police," scoffed Cowboys Guy.

For about twenty minutes, these men had been following me. My mind raced with the realization. "Why?" I asked.

"We had a call come in," said the man in the Lincoln. Someone fitting my description, he said. "Vandalizing a wall."

For the first time in my life, I understood perfectly that a police officer could lie. These men certainly did not just happen upon me. They'd been following me—stalking me—observing me as I did nothing wrong.

"Someone fitting my description," I challenged.

Yes, they responded.

"Someone else is walking around with a red T-shirt that says 'Switzerland' and a yellow backpack that says 'Jamaica'?" I asked. "That is the description that you had?"

"I don't know. We were told you match the description," said the third guy. "ID."

I did not want them to see my fear. I did not want to make any kind of sudden move. "I am not going to give you my identification," I said carefully. "There is nothing right now distinguishing you as police. And I am not going to reach into my backpack because I don't know what you're going to do."

A kind of calm deliberation had taken hold of me. Surveying the lonely block, I told them: "This is what's going to happen. We are going to pull over a car, and we are going to ask them to call the police. The police will come, and then we are going to handle this situation."

The men watched in silence as I began to move toward the street. It was an excruciating ballet. "OK," I said again. "Now I am going to step into the street and hail a car."

I saw a yellow cab sailing down the avenue, and I stretched out my arm as far as I could. The car slowed to a stop, and a man who looked to be of South Asian descent rolled down the window.

"These men are pulling me over," I explained in a low, steady voice, still sensing their eyes on me. "They stopped and jumped on me and said they're police, but I don't know if they really are."

What happened next, I'll never forget: The man looked in my eyes and saw exactly what was needed. We were seven years out from 9/11 at that point, and people of color were being stopped and frisked with a startling regularity, and for no reason at all, in New York City. "Can you call the police for me?" I said, our eyes still locked.

"YES," the man told me. He dialed, then handed his phone through the window.

"There are men here," I said, after hearing the voice of the 911 dispatcher. "They stopped me. I thought they were rapists. I thought they would kill me. I'm afraid to leave."

The dispatcher told me to ask for their badge number, so I did.

"I'm not giving you that," said one.

"Are you refusing to give me the badge number?" I asked the man, making sure to hold the phone receiver up to my mouth as I walked slowly to the front of the car. "They're in a Lincoln Town Car," I told the dispatcher, reading off the license plate number.

We waited there, the five of us, the cabdriver included. We stood in the middle of Forty-Eighth Street, in the middle of the night, to await a uniformed police officer.

BEFORE THAT MOMENT, I still had trust in the police. Sort of.

There were good police where I grew up. Fine police, who came to our school and taught us about safety.

But then again, those police had stopped Uncle David and Chudi one afternoon, in broad daylight, when they were out taking a walk near our house. It had been Chudi's very first day in the United States; my family had picked him up at Boston's Logan Airport and driven him back to our home in the suburbs, where newborn Chi-Chi had arrived just a few days prior.

David and Chudi: two young men, college students at the time, visiting their aunty for a rare home-cooked meal. Walking off their dinner, as anyone might on a warm day. They returned to our home confused and a little shaken.

Suspicious walking. It didn't even make sense. What exactly defines a suspicious walk?

Back when I was a kid, the big commotion in our neighborhood was the block party that happened every summer down at the end of the cul-de-sac, near the Callahans'. The Browns' pool party had cars lined up the block, and never once did we see the police driving by to check out why. Ours were the only ones clocked by the neighbors, the cops slowly passing by, back and forth.

Now there I was, grown and living in another city, a block and a half away from my own apartment, waiting for an NYPD car to pull up. Just as was true for the rest of my family, I did not have the equal right to walk around anonymously. These men saw me, and they had attached whatever they wanted to the seeing.

FINALLY, A MAN IN UNIFORM ARRIVED. He stepped out of his cruiser and confirmed that the men surrounding me were police.

"OK," I told him, "I'm going to get you my wallet now." I still moved slowly, handing over my license.

I watched him return to his police car so he could run my ID through his computer. I knew that nothing was going to happen. I have never in my life stolen even a glass of milk.

After a few minutes, he came back and handed me the license.

"Ma'am, we're sorry," he said. "We just had a call with your description come in." I was free to go, he said.

I couldn't help myself. I needed them to know. "I know that's not true," I said through the lump in my throat, "because I remember seeing you"—I pointed to the Lincoln—"on Steinway, and you have to have been following me since then." I summoned all the courage I could. "That's not true," I repeated. "I will be filing a police report tomorrow."

I walked away, my face still hot with anger and humiliation. I remembered my initial impulse to run. Thank God I hadn't run.

Still, I walked home quickly, feeling as though my life were in jeopardy.

So many people think, as they read the news, Oh, the police shot him, but he was fleeing; he was running. But how clear did they make it, before they started to race at that person, that they were police officers in plain clothes?

Let's assume that we're talking about good police. That a person matches a description. Let's be charitable, even, and say that I matched the description that night. Still: They had all the information; I had none. Neither had Rich, when the police had stopped him as a kid, outside Friendly's, where he'd just finished his very first shift scooping ice cream. He had been waiting for my mom to pick him up, and somebody had ducked into a phone booth to report that a Black man was outside the restaurant, dealing drugs.

Every single day Rich worked that job, the police had shown up like this. Every day.

By the time I made it back to my apartment that night, it was nearly one o'clock in the morning. I immediately called my mother. As soon as I heard her voice, I burst into tears.

Some of it was a letdown from fear and the effort it had taken to stand there, publicly shamed, stripped of dignity and fighting off tears. Some of it was a familiar hurt: Those men had already decided who I was, based on I'm not even sure what. Those people, watching Uncle David, watching Rich, watching me, looking for us to be "that person." At what point in our lives were we stamped as "that person"?

Though I cried, I hadn't called my mother to talk about any of that. I had called because I was proud. "I really am Nonyem Aduba's daughter," I told her. Pulling myself together, I explained the way I'd handled every part of her in that terrifying, enraging confrontation.

I told her that from the beginning, I was 100 percent clear with those plainclothes cops that the whole story they were concocting was bullshit, and that I wasn't going to be sold on bullshit. I was a grown woman, solid in my power, and we were going to sort it out, right there on the street. My level stare, deep into the eyes of those men, was my way of saying, You mean to tell me that I am the suspicious one?

I know the fighter that I am, and that's because I know the fighter who taught me how to fight.

When my mother had learned that the police had stopped Uncle David and Chudi, she immediately jumped in her car and drove down to the Medfield police station. "We live in this neighborhood," she'd told them. "I don't want to ever hear again that any relation of mine had been stopped because someone said that there were suspicious people in the neighborhood."

This is the clarity of thought I brought to Forty-Eighth Street and the message I wanted to send to those cops: It's going to be on the books somewhere that we had an issue.

Uzo Aduba said she had an issue.

ONE NIGHT I prepared some Nigerian food for a new friend from a show's production team. Standing next to me by my stove, the new friend said, "I have to ask you a question."

"Sure," I said.

"Now, I don't know if this is going to sound dumb or not . . ."

Now, I knew, from hearing this setup many times in my life, that the question wasn't going to be a good one.

"Does any of your family, you know, who still lives in Nigeria . . ." She paused. "Do they live in huts?" she asked.

My eyes widened so much I could feel them moving backward in space. "A hut?" I asked, feeling my hand close around the spoon.

By this point, of course, I'd been to Nigeria many times; I'd been to South Africa. A hut? That felt foreign and far away to me, as foreign as men in powdered wigs and breeches, walking around with snuffboxes.

For some reason, I still hesitated before telling her no.

This wasn't a twenty-two-year-old graduate student. This was an accomplished woman in her thirties, walking around, thinking that Nigerian architecture had not progressed past the nineteenth century. Her question seemed to me as absurd as asking if people in America still lived like the people in Colonial Williamsburg, which I'd visited in the eighth grade as part of a history lesson.

I knew she wasn't trying to be offensive. She was asking the question because my apartment, our relationship, felt safe. For so many years I was deeply invested in creating that feeling of safety— wanting to educate, in some way. Instead of feeling bad, I worked doubly hard to make sure the questioner didn't feel bad. I knew she wasn't trying to make me feel bad.

"I'll ask my mother," I told her. I didn't want to answer definitively without checking in with someone who had lived in Nigeria for an extended period of time.

"Mommy," I began, the next time we spoke. "I'm not asking this question for myself, but I also didn't want to say categorically no . . ."

When I finished, my mother asked me to repeat the story. "A hut?" she asked, the guttural "h" registering her own bemusement.

"That's the word she used," I said, laughing.

"Stupid girl," said my mother.

She had prepared me to recognize and challenge the most obvious forms of racism, which, sadly, often came from people in positions of authority. Far more dangerous and lethal were these more subverted forms—assumptions and gentle challenges that nudged me back into old behaviors, questioning what I knew to be true.

Softening, my mother told me that she'd learned about people living in tents in the very early 1900s. "But I haven't even seen a hut," she said, "since way, way, way back when I was small." Even then, she said, it was not the way Western people thought of huts or showed them on television. "They carve the clay around, so it's done smooth, almost like concrete. You can sit on it with a white dress, and you would still be clean."

The next time I saw my friend, I told her that I had asked my mother, and that she did not know a single person who lived in a hut. In our lives, hers and mine, I promised, there was more money passing through the hands of more Nigerians than we will ever see. "People in cars, plural, with homes, plural," I told her. "Even if I'm going to my father's place, which is very rural, it's still not a hut. And that's a rural place."

As insistent as I was, I still felt some pity mixed in with my frustration. Maybe the only version of Africa this woman knew was a *National Geographic* or a television ad, begging viewers to sponsor a poor African child for 20 cents a day. If that was all I knew—the distended stomach and the flies on the face—I'd probably think people were living in huts too. Could her thinking really be so different from my cousins in Nigeria watching VH1's *The Fabulous Life* and assuming that everyone in America had a Bentley?

Then I remembered the day in elementary school when my

social studies teacher had rolled in the television cart so we could watch a video about "Africa." The cassette she had pushed into the VCR was some kind of documentary, zeroing in on a tribe in the most remote of villages, likely somewhere in East Africa. The camera, probing and curious, had lingered on the young women, many of whom wore lip plates—a sight I found disorienting and exotic, though not nearly as disorienting as their bare chests.

Topless women! The whole thing had felt so disrespectful as I sat among my snickering classmates. I'd sensed their eyes on me and felt shame rise. The video did not capture the Africa I knew; it was just as foreign-seeming, to me, as it was to the rest of the class laughing at the women on the screen. I thought of the embarrassment I felt whenever my mom came downstairs to ask me a question, and I'd have to tolerate the feedback of whatever silly friend exclaiming, "Your mom's accent is so thick! What did she say?" How many kids in that social studies class had told me, over the years, that my father was hard to understand?

Sitting there in class, I'd wondered if the next time my classmates heard my parents' accents, they'd think about these tribal women. Was that what they thought? That before my mother or father or aunts or cousins came to America, this was how they carried themselves?

I came home from school crying, and my mother, who had seen enough television, sighed and shook her head. "All they will show you, the British, is how Africans are nothing," she said. "You know colonial masters. What can you say?"

She did not want such fears to color my concept of being in America. "You have to sort out and respond to them, when it happens," she'd told me that day. "And then you have to move on."

Now, there we were, however many years later, talking about

huts. The question did not seem to be about the materials used to make my family's homes—about whether we used wood or stucco. It was an assumption about a lifestyle. How many times had I been met with quizzical or even shocked expressions when I'd said that Nigeria was my favorite place?

I can't capture how hurtful it is to describe a country where all your family is proudly from to someone who can't imagine its value. How can people who have never been to such an incredible land instantly doubt the complex beauty found there, viewing it as nothing more than backward, simple, or a place unworthy of desire?

I'd considered saying some of this, but the energy I'd been using to explain myself since age five had been exhausted. It was much easier to let this comment and so-called friendship fall aside.

AS MY CIRCLE OF FRIENDS in New York began to widen, I found that more of the women in it were Black. Many were Nigerian American, Nigerian, or otherwise of African descent. It was a sisterhood I was so grateful to find. Very few were artists by training; even those I'd met through the theater had first pursued a different kind of career. My friend Adepero was premed; my friend Idara had attended business school. Lisa had studied broadcast journalism, graduating with the highest honors.

While I have said that I'd written Lisa off by the end of our first *Abyssinia* rehearsal, I think that was actually the only day of my life that I didn't like her.

Lisa is beautiful—one of the most beautiful women I have ever seen. She's chocolate—dark chocolate. Darker than me. She's slim yet very strong, with a grace to her musculature that reveals her dancer's training. Given that, it seems funny to say that she stumbled into this business, but she did—as I'd learned the first time we had an actual conversation. Sitting next to her on the couch in our rehearsal room, I saw how open she was—how smart and insightful. Lisa was equal parts intellectual and fun.

She was generous too, encouraging people who weren't dancers to dance and not making them feel as if they were the world's worst dancer.

Pragmatic and linear in her thinking, Lisa was excellent with money. While we were working together on *Abyssinia*, she bought an apartment in a brand-new building in Harlem. She was the first artist I knew who had done such a thing.

"I've always wanted to own property," I told Lisa one day on a break from rehearsal, as she shared the latest update from her real estate agent. I paid close attention to her process, asking questions and even taking notes. She lent me all her books covering budgeting, accounting, and financial literacy.

This was security to me: a home that I had control over and a mortgage that I could afford without worry. A place where my mother could come and stay for as long as she wanted.

I grew even closer with my cousin Nwamaka, the daughter of my Aunty Daisy. We had spent so many years together as kids, bonding because we were forced to be polite. Now that we were adults, it was clear that we had a lot in common.

Nwamaka's older sister Ifey tipped us off to an event called Naija Happy Hour, which happened once a month, invitation only. Once we walked in, I understood: If they'd opened up the happy hour to the entire Nigerian community in the tristate area, the whole world would show up.

Naija Happy Hour was set up by two Nigerian American women who wanted to find husbands. With that goal in mind, they threw a party, inviting the suitors they wanted, whom I wanted—young, well-educated professional men—to come after work and have a drink.

It was always a very elegant setup, rotating to different restaurants, bars, or lounges in Manhattan. A place to stop by on your way home before settling in for the night.

My friends made all sorts of work connections there, but as one of only a few artists, I wasn't helped along those lines. My closet didn't hold the business casual, office-to-drinks fare the event required, so I bought a few things that wound up coming in handy later, when I was auditioning for secretary-type roles.

Naija Happy Hour was the source of countless first dates. While out to dinner with one of the men I'd met, I mentioned that I was an actress. His reaction, which would be echoed by others in similar moments, lacked seriousness. He addressed my career as if I were talking about a hobby.

Another mixer that started soon after, Nollywood USA, was less buttoned-up and more of a party. The meet-ups always took place on a weekend, starting and ending late, as is the Nigerians' wont. Instead of restaurants and bars, we're talking bars and clubs, with people handing out flyers promoting other West African events. This wasn't about exchanging business cards; you were there to let your hair down.

At these events I met people in a way that felt natural—a setup I didn't even know I was longing for. Decor and menus aside, the nights out weren't so different from the house parties that my parents had when they were young, or the Igbo meetings, when I'd see them thriving as actual adults, among people like themselves.

My parents and their friends grooved to high-life music; for us it was early-day Afrobeats and hip-hop—a familiar mix that really moved me. In New York, I connected with my community—this crop of first-gen Africans who shared an understanding of what it felt like to have a foot in both places. For some, that meant growing up in an all-Black community with parents sending them to an all-white private school. Others had attended mostly Black high schools and then predominantly white universities.

My new friends sounded like me, with cultures like my own and an understanding of code-switching on the same frequency as my own, regardless of whether they grew up in deep Brooklyn or the Midwest. Black American culture was not our born-into culture, and yet it was our culture. The colorful mix of all our histories and currencies—from places known and unknown—was Black culture. I may not have caught every reference made by Onyi's Bronx-born roommates or the other girls at the track invitational, but now, as adults, none of the distinctions mattered.

IN THE WEEKS AND DAYS before an audition, I read as much as I could about the show and researched the period or part of the world in which it was set. Then I dove deep into the script, doing a lot of subtextual writing of each line—replacing each of my character's statements with what I believed she meant to say. When I could, I wrote down three new lines for each one written, drilling a bit deeper each time.

If my character asked, "What time is it?" I'd replace that phrase with what it was that I thought she really wanted, which was to ask, "Can we leave?" Maybe that really meant, though, "Want to fuck?" or, at its core, "I need to be loved."

My professor Jim Spruill taught me to go beyond what characters said to what they meant, and even further, to what they wanted. So did another acting professor, Bill Young. Still another, Jon Lipsky, taught me about dreamscaping, which meant putting down the script and all my notes and then waiting, sometimes weeks, for inspiration. Even if what I imagined for the role felt off-kilter, like it might not fit, some part of the idea endured and enlivened the role.

For one audition in particular I had prepared extensively; as I listened for my name to be called, I kept my eyes low, my head clear.

"Hey, are you sizing people up?" asked my friend sitting next to me, who was also waiting.

"No," I said. "I don't know if it's for better or worse, but I'm really not thinking about anybody else."

I bristled once when another friend mistook my drive for jealousy. Of course I'd felt an ache when looking at someone else's success and wondering why it hadn't happened for me. But the expression she'd seen on my face was focused: If I was up against her for a part, and I'd shown up at the audition, trust and believe that I was booking it.

That had to be my mindset, just as it had been on the ice and the track. Before each audition, I still felt as I did in college, when Bruce had me look in the mirror and said, over my shoulder, "This is the person you're racing."

During ensemble rehearsals, I often remembered the way my track coaches talked about relays: If the goal was getting the baton around the track the fastest, it didn't matter how fast you sprinted. You were done if you failed to smoothly pass the baton into the next girl's hand. It didn't matter if I wanted to come into a scene with a hot intensity if what ultimately flowed better was my coming in quietly.

The only difference I saw between the entertainment industry and sport was that in sport, no matter how fierce the competition, you had to say "good game" when it was over. You left it all on the rink or the track, and then you humbled yourself and acknowledged that you were done with that part. "Good game." You could be devastated and still want the other girl to succeed.

The New York theater world often made us feel like crabs, scrambling and clawing as if only one could get out of the barrel. The industry relied on this. So long as people compared themselves to one another, the many who didn't feel good enough would tolerate bad behavior or take less than they deserved.

Actors have the experience of really needing everyone to like us. But for some, once they've won you over, they really don't care anymore. They've received the validation they've sought, and the box is checked. Continuing to talk to these people as if they were real friends, I was disappointed, even wounded. Oh, I realized: This was not about friendship? Then I'm not really sure what we are doing, and, in the meantime, I'm not sure of the point of any of those moments that had come before.

When my relationships with castmates went south, I didn't feel challenged by maintaining our chemistry onstage. That part was easy. Far more difficult was the offstage acting now required to keep us getting back up there, together, for every performance.

When I began working on a new musical called *Venice*, I approached new people from a neutral position, without any responsibility to be extra. I couldn't be "on" with someone, and certainly not with everyone, until I actually knew them.

This is why I don't remember meeting my friend Angela, or even our first conversation. I just remember that one day, on a break from rehearsal, we went out for lunch and hit it off.

From Kansas City, Kansas, Angela was unapologetically country. She was a top Spelman grad, and yet because of her downhome Midwestern accent ("Eekers!" she'd say), people made assumptions. She was entirely content with that—a clarity to which I was drawn. Angela didn't adjust the way she spoke in order to convince someone of her intelligence. In her mind, there was no point wasting her time doing so—trying to operate on their level—when they were too foolish to understand what she'd said.

Angela was also fiercely real with others, straight with the truth even if there was a sugary coating to it. This was part of what made her so funny.

One day, we were standing together near a piano as someone tried out a new song for us. "Happy to listen," Angela had said sweetly before they'd begun. She used the same tone for praise immediately after and hesitated to provide more detail. "Just give us a little time to sleep on it," she said.

We walked out, and as soon as the doors on the elevator we'd stepped into had closed, she turned to me and said, "What'd you think about it?"

"I don't know if that was good or not?" I said.

She met my eyes as she nodded. Then, in her honeyed voice, she said, "It sounds a little homemade."

I almost died laughing when she said that. Somehow knowing exactly what she meant, I was still cracking up, shaking my head, when she continued. "You know," she said. "It's the difference between buying your cake at the store and the one your mama made.

"It's cake," she went on, smiling with a nod and a shrug as I wiped away tears, nodding in full agreement. "But it's not the cake you get from the store."

Angela and I called our shared dressing room Suite 100 because we knew that we'd be direct with each other, for both of our benefits. When *Venice* moved to Los Angeles, I stayed in Angela's apartment. Later, when she was in New York for a show, she stayed in mine.

We watched TV together and went out dancing. We also drilled lines together, worked through our choreography, and rehearsed the vocals for the ensemble pieces. We scrutinized each other's audition videos and gave performance notes—costume notes as well. "I love the performance," I said to her after she'd closed up her laptop. "But you need to think about whether that skirt reads too young."

She came to me for advice during a particularly tough spell, and I raised the issue again: "I don't think they're feeling the way you talk or dress," I said. "They don't see you the way I see you. They have a real, strong opinion about who you are, and the way you're presenting yourself is not serving you."

I saw the hurt first in her forehead. "I know," I said, "it's not right, but you asked me how to be cast. That is something that would help, if it's just about getting the job."

When she got up to leave soon after, I felt terrible—a feeling that only grew over the following days. How could I suggest that she change? How could I push on her the exact piece of advice that I'd worked so hard to ignore? My mind flashed back to my earliest days in the business and my own indignation. You want me to change my what? My smile? But my critique was even more fundamental.

I'd advised Angela to tamp down her urban-country dialect—her own Black American experience—in the name of auditioning for "the great American theater." I'd suggested she dim the part of her that I most admired, that was most special, and that she owned with such command and power. Every time I thought about it, my stomach hurt.

I'm just so glad she didn't listen. The special fairy dust that she possessed would sprinkle over the whole world eventually.

"Be good to women," my mother constantly ministered to her children. When I think of the ideal friendship, what I imagine is my mother standing with my Aunty Rachel at a Naija event. I see Aunty Rachel tying my mom's skirt so she looks her best, then turning her around to admire the view.

The only way to get anything accomplished in this life, I knew, was to surround myself with women.

Chapter 13

I didn't dream about settling down with a Nigerian American man to make my parents happy; I knew they were more open-minded than that. When my cousin Chudi fell in love with Robin, a white, Jewish woman, my mother had played an important, mediating role in the broader family conversation. In response to some initial misgivings about such a difference in culture and faith, my mother had supported and even encouraged the match. "Who cares?" she'd told the skeptics. "He loves her."

Still, as I was getting to be of "marrying age," the idea that I might not need to explain so much of my background to someone else became more and more attractive. My ideal partner understood and embraced the parts of me that were entirely American but also entirely Nigerian.

To that end, on my petty list of what I was looking for in a man: Igbo heritage, and either born in Nigeria and Westernized or first-gen. He had to have a good job that made good money . . . to like sports but not be obsessed. He had to be a great dresser, to love to travel . . . all these things that did not matter.

As my twenties became my thirties, my joke was that the Department of Sanitation should cut me a check for the number of garbage men I'd dated. I was completely distracted by one of them during a visit to Onyi in Blacksburg, Virginia, where Joseph, my brother-in-law, was teaching at Virginia Tech.

It was late summer, and Matthew, my oldest nephew, was still an infant, his car seat strapped tightly into one of the bucket seats of Onyi's Honda Odyssey. As my sister drove us along the two-lane highway threading through the rolling hills back to her house, I sat in her passenger seat, eyes fixed on my phone, trying to formulate yet another text message to this guy I'd been dating . . . on and off. OK, this guy I'd been chasing, trying to win over, knowing full well that I was diminishing myself in the process.

We were arguing over something small—his lack of response to my earlier text message. It was the latest in a series of other bad signs. I knew that I wasn't being considered, and yet that was all that I wanted. I wanted to be loved. I was still trying to convince him to love me, taking scraps, compromising.

I thought back to previous relationships that had been just as terrible—moments when I'd not just bent over backward but into a full backbend, hands on the ground, having contorted myself as much as humanly possible. This was not the first time I'd let myself be used, my needs made small.

In any other part of my life, this kind of behavior would never have been tolerated. I would stand up for myself, even if I wasn't sure of myself. That is what felt so terrifying about this moment— these feelings, that text. I understood that I was doing what I was doing because I didn't feel I was worth more.

Uzo, you need to be careful here, I told myself. You have a weakness for men; your mother does too. If you're not careful, you're going to find yourself in some of these situations that she has found herself in.

My mother put up with a lot that she shouldn't have. I can't remember exactly when I began having that thought, though it was probably in my teens. I could not understand her seemingly endless capacity to forgive. When I had been upset with somebody, and I had felt that the relationship was done, it was done.

In my mother's marriage to my father, I observed a relationship between two people, born of a certain time, where one of them— my mother—had been raised with a primary example of a very progressive marriage. When my parents had their disagreements, my mother wasn't going to be docile or submissive. I saw the challenges that could create in a marriage. Particularly one in which one partner, my father, had been brought up in a very different way.

There were a lot of other things in there, in my parents' marriage, but in those moments, that was what I saw playing out. My father had many great qualities; he was also a complicated man.

My mother and I didn't talk much about relationships—certainly not hers, and not my own, either. In my culture, you didn't date; you got married. The person you brought to meet your parents was the person you'd chosen. Otherwise, it was your friend—friend, never boyfriend.

The only time I had ever brought a name into this sphere was the first time I'd dated an Igbo man. He wasn't the first Nigerian man, but it was the first time that I thought the relationship had potential. While I never questioned that my parents would approve of whomever I chose, I knew too that it would be a little extra if I could marry an Igbo man.

I instantly regretted telling my mother; for so long, every time we were on the phone, she would ask, "How is Eze? How are things with Eze?" I hadn't the heart to tell her how brief the relationship had been. Her hopes were pinned.

The single piece of relationship advice that my mother did give, to all her children, was about communication. "You have to be with someone you can talk with," she told us. "Someone who can tell you the truth and who you can tell the truth to."

A more common refrain, which applied very well here, was, "I just want you to be happy."

There are so many lessons that parents teach by doing. Some of what they do, we see, and then we think, I do not want a life like that.

It was often hard for my mother, with my father. There were moments when I'd ask myself why she didn't leave. She had her reasons, I knew, and I'd only grow to understand more. My mother had such a big heart and desire to help—and that ability to forgive that I just didn't possess.

By this point in my life, Onyi was less of a parental figure and more of a confidante. We'd discussed our parents' marriage, of course, and our own relationships too. I told her about my current frustrations, and then our conversation dropped off. I fixed my gaze on the center of her front windshield, trying to focus on her neighborhood's tree-lined sidewalks and whatever song was playing on her satellite radio. I resisted the urge to look down at my phone again. You need to be careful, I repeated in my head.

Later that day, from Onyi's spare bedroom, I texted every one of the men I'd dated, minus one, to tell them that they'd hurt me and I hadn't deserved it. I didn't expect a response; I just needed to take ownership of those situations. I needed them to know.

To my surprise, each one either called back or sent a message along the lines of "I know and I'm sorry." Those responses not only confirmed that I was not crazy, as at times I'd been led to believe, but also that I hadn't deserved the treatment I'd received.

One thing nagged at me as I fired off the messages. I had dated one good man, one who had wanted to treat me well, and I'd kicked him away. He was an actor, so good-looking—soap-opera good-looking—that when he'd told me he was interested, I was bashful. You can date supermodels, I'd thought at the time. What can you possibly see in me?

Feeling like a fraud, I treated him like garbage. If he wanted to get together on a Friday, I had too much hair washing to do that night. Games, games, period. End of story.

Was I only going to clean up my side of the street? I picked up my phone and texted him an apology. I knew how it felt, and I didn't want to do it again. He wrote me back, acknowledging the games, mentioning the word "childish," and telling me it was all good.

In time, I would significantly distill my view of what I wanted in a partner, shaking out the trappings of a so-called good match. It really wasn't so complicated: I wanted a good man who wanted to show me the world.

That didn't mean I wanted someone who had the money to buy plane tickets to exotic places—that, I thought, I could do on my own, in time. I wanted someone who would open up my eyes to something essential that was completely his own.

That was something I prayed for, for a really long time.

WHILE WORKING ON a show in Los Angeles, I began seeing someone new. Right away, our connection was different. It was the first romantic relationship I'd been in where I didn't have to guess if someone loved me. I knew he did. He saw all of me—and found all of me beautiful. He also taught me that love didn't have to be hard.

I still gave away far more than I should have. I also came to learn, through that experience, that someone could love you and not respect you.

He called me one night, soon after we finished our performance of *Venice*. Angela and I were in her Mustang, heading back to her apartment; she'd pulled into a gas station on the way and was at the pump when I answered the phone.

"Where are you?" he asked. "Are you alone?"

"I'm in Angela's car," I said. "Why?"

"Call me when you get home."

"What's wrong?" I asked. "Is everything OK?"

"Yes. Just—when you're back, call me."

"I think he's going to break up with me," I told Angela when we hung up.

"WHAT?" Angela shouted, in one of her typically big reactions. "HUH? No, girl. That man loves you."

The week before, he'd sent me flowers—something I'd long wished a boyfriend would do. "The way he's behaving . . . it doesn't sound like it," I said. I knew that whatever was wrong didn't have to do with him; it had to do with us.

The first thing he asked me when I called back was the same: "Are you alone? I need to tell you something." When he said that he couldn't come to California to visit as planned, I was almost thrilled, imagining scheduling troubles, money difficulties. "I get it," I told him. "Don't worry."

Then he said, "There's something else." After a brief pause: "I no longer wish to be in a relationship with you." I tried pressing him for clarity. He didn't give a reason—not that I think any would have satisfied. Space, he said, or something like that.

"OK, well, take care," I said, and we hung up.

I called him back seconds later. Anger first: "I'm not going to let you do this!" I screamed before hanging up.

However long later, I called him back again, sobbing. "Why are you doing this?"

He didn't change his position. Still, as the weeks went by, he continued answering my calls and reaching out as well. For a while after, we had a cat-and-mouse game. With each interaction, I had to sew my heart back together.

I now understood that something that could last forever would not, and it kicked my legs out from under me. I had been nicked countless times before, by so many little relationships. I'd long ignored signs I hadn't wanted to see: his lack of interest in meeting my parents, for example. Still, now that something close to the real thing had come along, then left, my belief system was devastated. I felt disposable, my feelings thrown away so easily.

If I didn't trust men before, I really didn't now. After so many years of that feeling, I began to wonder: Am I jaded? Hardened? I hated the sound of both of those words. Still, I knew I'd built walls around myself; I didn't want to have anything else taken from me.

My new wry self-deprecation told the outside world that I felt sorry for the man who would come into my life who was serious. With my friends, I would laugh: "It's going to be really hard for him to get through."

Jokes aside, I knew I would rather be alone than get half of what I deserved.

. . .

WHEN WE WERE IN OUR late twenties, living together in Sunnyside, our friends joked that Chi-Chi and I were "almost twins." The other joke was that I was her "wife," cooking in my downtime and greeting her in the evenings upon her return from work in Manhattan. We spent weekends together: lazy Saturday mornings after Friday nights out with her friends. Lazy Sunday nights too, binge-watching the latest on HBO or true crime on MSNBC while getting ourselves together for the week ahead. When I was cast in a show in San Diego, Chi-Chi visited me there, and we turned it into a little vacation. I tried to counsel her through the beginning of a new relationship and the end of a job, as well as a flurry of studying for the GRE, required for graduate school admission. In the end, she decided she'd spend the year traveling instead.

I was sitting outside with Chi-Chi one day when our mother called. She was going to New Jersey to stay at Onyi's, she said. "For a while."

I knew that she and my father were going through a particularly tough time. I could tell by her voice that she'd had enough. Every person hits a point where they know that they have had more than their fill; they're stuffed.

My mother was born into a culture that says: You get married, you stay married. Her religion says: You get married, you stay married. She was overwhelmed by the idea of starting over at age seventy—emotionally, logistically, and culturally. She had been through that once, in her thirties, after the sudden death of her first husband.

She would stay married, and yet, upon her retirement, she could also leave. Onyi had invited her to stay through Mother's Day, and then to celebrate my niece Gabriella's birthday, on June 28. Her plan was to return to Massachusetts for a long-scheduled knee-replacement surgery, but it didn't wind up that way. The Saturday before Gabriella's birthday, at her party, my mother tripped over a step, fell, and wound up breaking her leg in three places.

As the break was the same leg meant for surgery, she decided to go ahead and have the knee replaced while they set her leg. Staying for all that, as well as for the recovery and rehab, wound up being the perfect excuse to not go back.

God has a devilish way of working, I think. He had to sit my mother down. She had to be away long enough to know that everything would be OK.

CHI-CHI AND I WENT TO NIGERIA. It was the first time we had been there together in more than twenty years and the first time that we made our own travel arrangements. My father was on our flight too, though our paths diverged at the airport. He had his own agenda, and he trusted us to find our way.

When we were young there, our parents had put the fear of God in us, reminding us of the many ways that Nigeria was so different from America. Most of our family dynamics we understood through our parents' vantage. Now we'd see for ourselves.

We decided to go southeast first, as most Nigerians return to their ancestral villages during holidays. There was a huge New Year's celebration at my father's childhood home in Achi.

No longer were we huddled in the corners with the rest of the cousins, whispering about "boyfriends." Now we were out front by the fire, fully immersed in the stories about work or school and the gossip over family drama.

"Why aren't you married?" The aunties couldn't help poking at Chi-Chi and me, even as their own single daughters rolled their eyes and laughed.

Chi-Chi and I were not yet of the age to safely ignore "helpful" suggestions. "Why don't you go and find something a little longer to wear?" whispered Aunty Mercy, my father's sister, a few nights later. Any minute, the elders were due to come over to her house in Enugu, the area's largest city.

My gray paisley sleeveless dress with a tie waist hit just above my knee—conservative by American twentysomething standards. Still, I ran to my suitcase to fish out a longer one.

IT TOOK A WHILE for both Chi-Chi and me to acclimate to our independence in Nigeria—to let go of that deeply ingrained sense of insecurity. The more we went out, the more we realized: No, the driver our family called to take us across Lagos to Uncle Bertie's house would not have a friend who would stop the car, grab us, and charge our family ransom for our safe return.

"Are you sure?" I asked my mother's younger sister, my Aunty Nkem.

"It's fine," she said, handing me a wad of bills. "He knows the address. It shouldn't cost much more than this."

But then, just as we were walking out the front door, my Aunty Ifey called out: "Put your purse between your legs. They can reach in—and fast."

Shortly thereafter, we learned how to call our own cars, and then Chi-Chi and I were everywhere—out for lunch and to the mall, hitting up a bowling alley, meeting our cousins for dinner and karaoke, or dancing. I began to understand that Nigeria was not just my home but a place I could live.

"How do you know these people you're going to meet?" asked Uncle Bertie when he heard we were going to meet our friends Ayo, Tunde, and Temi.

He was so relaxed in asking, just information-gathering. His eyes shone; you could see that he had been a fun guy, in his younger days.

"We know them from New York," I told him, adding that they now had good jobs in finance there in Lagos.

"OK," he said with a smile.

When we walked into the party, the first thing we saw was a huge, all-white pool, surrounded by beach chairs and cabanas. There were hundreds of people our age, all impeccably dressed. Cars, plural, as I'd said to my friend who'd asked me about huts—in brands of the highest end, some that I'd never even heard of. It felt like a film set in Miami, as posh as anything we'd ever seen in New York City. The first floor was set up as a cocktail lounge—Naija Happy Hour on steroids. The cocktails flowed; as the DJ took over, the dancing party rivaled Nollywood USA too.

We rode home with our friends, making it through the checkpoints a little tipsy. When we returned to the house, we found Uncle Bertie sitting in the exact same place, still reading his paper, fully awake.

I would have to visit a few more times before he and my aunty would wait up in their own room, television on, to hear the key in the lock.

Chapter 14

Known in the industry as the "actor's medium," theater builds into its schedule four weeks of rehearsal strictly for our discovery—for development and invention and creativity. This is when I wrestle with the ins and outs of the character I want to play, trying on different approaches and reactions. I consider how my character fits into the story our entire team is trying to tell. I listen, beginning first with the director.

Inspired by the Gospel of St. Matthew, *Godspell*'s script is quite loose, written in a way that leaves room for each director and cast to find their own path in. The idea Danny Goldstein had for his original production of the musical, which played at New Jersey's Paper Mill Playhouse in 2006, was to portray life just as it was in our moment.

The play is often grounded in the hippie counterculture movement of the early 1970s, but we came onstage for every performance in our street clothes, as ourselves. For the first time ever, I was asked to wear my hair natural, and I did, in an Afro. As the show opened, we discovered one another onstage, as if we were strangers meeting by chance. We noticed the audience and decided, together, to put on a show. Pulling out various costumes, each of us disappeared into a kind of funhouse-mirror version of ourselves.

The audience observed us onstage getting to know one another, as we batted around ideas for illustrating Jesus's parables. "Oh, I know the story," one of us would say, starting out, until another came in along the way, saying, "No, no, this is how it goes." Once she fumbled, the third person would pick up the story, telling it well, teaching it to the whole group.

That was the setup: Each one of us took our turns; we tried, erred, and compromised, all with the goal of spreading the Word. Only through working together like this did our characters realize that we too were learning all the lessons Jesus taught—namely, that God is Love.

Five years later, I was cast in *Godspell*'s Broadway revival, as was my friend from the original production, Telly Leung. We were each used to being "the one" in a production; now we were the majority. Telly, like me, was first-gen, with Chinese-born parents. George Salazar, a buoyant, bright star who was half Latino and half Filipino, was thrilled to be in a production with another Filipino actor, Anna Maria Perez de Tagle, whose mother brought us home-cooked Filipino food to the Circle in the Square Theatre each weekend.

For one of the parables, Anna Maria spoke in Tagalog, a Filipino language, while I spoke in Igbo and Telly in Chinese. I could feel the pride onstage. The parts of ourselves that we went home to be could be alive throughout.

I shared with my Black castmates a kind of shorthand centered around gospel music. We hadn't all grown up in the same church, but music was key to each of our artistic and spiritual evolutions.

Celisse Henderson, vivacious, with caramel-colored skin and a beautiful, thick Afro, brought into rehearsal some kind of crazy riff. "Oh, you're giving us Clark Sisters!" I heard over my shoulder—it was the voice of Wallace Smith, a gifted actor with years of Christian-contemporary songwriting experience under his belt.

"Yes!" said Celisse, laughing. "Just warming up for praise and worship."

I chimed in, grateful to be among peers who understood the music's power—the gifts of tones low, smooth, and velvety as well as higher-pitched riffs and runs. Hearing Celisse inspired me to try on a few of Karen Clark Sheard's runs as well. This led to a conversation about Mahalia Jackson; that brought us to Sam Cooke and early Marvin Gaye.

Just as I had, Celisse had grown up with two sisters. She was raised in a very religious home, surrounded by sacred music. She and I often shared passages and sermons, trying to encourage each other to stay inspired, grateful, faithful. We traded recordings that we could load onto our iPods for our commutes or our downtime.

One day, we sat on the phone together, repeating the words of a prayer she'd taught me. A simple one: "I surrender. I leave this in your hands."

God and I had many private conversations in the apartment Chi-Chi and I shared. I brought Him my doubts. Sometimes my prayers were long. I stood in silence by our small kitchen window, watching the tree beyond the fire escape, waiting for a sign.

As *Godspell*'s run came to an end, Celisse's prayer, I surrender, echoed through my head. Chi-Chi and I were breaking our lease, as she wanted to live with a boyfriend. "A boyfriend you won't even wind up with," I'd pointed out cattily if accurately.

I wanted to keep on as we were, with our standing Sunday-night dates and our easy routine all the while. Finishing the half bottle of wine Chi-Chi left in the fridge, knowing I'd replace it the next day. Playfully accusing me of taking her favorite blazer or the last slice of turkey. Getting her take on the man I was dating.

The harder I dug in my heels, the more I was admitting to myself and the world that I wanted to stand still.

"Your parents didn't leave Nigeria for you to just be standing still, Uzo," Uncle David once told me.

One night, I overheard one of my *Godspell* castmates say that she was moving and I jumped on the opportunity: a first-floor, below-market one-bedroom, one-bathroom apartment in Astoria, about a thirty-minute commute to the Theater District. A "railroad," meaning that the rooms were all in one line, with the front door into the kitchen at the center.

I put in the kitchen a small, fold-up counter that fit a single bar-stool. I lovingly painted the living room a deep aubergine, and I moved in a cream-colored couch with a pull-out bed, a real-real big deal, handed down from Hunter Parrish, another *Godspell* castmate.

Across from the couch hung the flat-screen television, a huge point of pride, purchased with my paycheck from the show. I painted the bedroom a two-tone green—a sea-foamy color and a deep ivy color.

It wasn't fancy, but it had everything I needed: my own bathroom, even if it was tiny as hell; an air-conditioning unit on the fire-escape window; and, best of all, a private outdoor space big enough for a table and four chairs and a chiminea. During the warm weather, it was a place to drink tea with my sister, when she came to visit.

. . .

ONE EARLY SUMMER DAY, when buzz from the most recent Tony Awards was still in the air, Wallace leaned over as we were warming up for a performance. "Are you going in for *Pippin?*" he asked.

I hadn't heard about the musical's Broadway revival. They were seeing both men and women for the Leading Player, Wallace said. He was going out for the part.

This is my job, I thought. I had the context and the experience. I knew how fun the part was and that it was a part that I could naturally sing. The more I thought about the possibility, the more connections I saw: *Pippin*'s composer, Stephen Schwartz, had also composed *Godspell.* The director of the new production was also someone I knew, and with whom I had a strong working relationship.

I believed that this was my time to lead—to really be seen—on Broadway. I knew this show, I loved this show, and I had ideas: I wanted to play the Leading Player as a man. I saw real opportunity, and real freedom, in a role where I could show power without using my sexuality. Existing onstage as a woman I wanted all the big, bold, bad forces too.

I reached the casting agency only to learn that auditions were almost over.

I appeared in the doorway of my agents' office soon after, and I immediately caught the eye of one of them. "Let me guess: It's about *Pippin,*" he said. "Sorry we didn't call you earlier."

"I'm frustrated," I told him. Where did they see me in all this? Or did they see me?

My audition went well, and after, we went around, around, around with callbacks. I allowed myself moments to think, I'm getting this part. I felt excitement rise in my chest as I imagined the future: After *Godspell* closed, I would do the *Pippin* workshop that summer in Boston, and then, in December, we'd open on Broadway. I would be seen in a show with real staying power. I would be paid well.

Some evenings Wallace and I sat together on the phone, encouraging each other, praying, testifying about whatever small miracles had happened by that point. After we learned that the producers wanted a woman for the part, Wallace still encouraged me. "Girl, it happens at the most unexpected times," he told me.

Not only did I not get the job; of the finalists, I came in last.

The disappointment I felt was deep—similar to what I'd experienced many years earlier, when I was just starting out, after the casting for *The Color Purple* musical on Broadway. How could everyone tell me my whole life that I look like Whoopi Goldberg, and then, when I turned up, I was not right for the part?

"I don't understand how we got here," I told my agents, after hearing the *Pippin* news. "How could there be someone else?"

One night, Telly and I were out for a drink after the show. "I don't know what I'm doing next," I told him. "I don't know how I'm going to get to the next thing."

I wasn't typically this open at work, but Telly and I had known each other for six years, since the original production of *Godspell*. He immediately understood.

An incredible artist and a true joy to be around, Telly has one of the most pristine, perfect voices I've ever heard. He too was waiting for his moment in the sun. "Let me ask my manager to come back to the show to check you out," he offered.

A "Hollywood" manager: This, to me, was a big deal. While an agent is essential, finding you work, getting you from job to job, a Hollywood manager was someone who would look at my entire career.

Telly's manager, Joan Sittenfield, came to see the show the next time she was in town. We met up for coffee afterward, in a Starbucks on the Upper West Side, about a mile and a half from the theater. Over the chaos of the busy café, I tried to put my feelings into words—my desire to push myself, to do more and to be given the opportunity to do more.

"I wish I had a more flowery way to say it," I said. "I just don't know how to get to the next level. I don't know what I need or how to get it. I need help."

The honesty and openness of that critical word, the vulnerability, even if I didn't like it, allowed people in. It took this kind of asking to encourage people to think: What tools do I have?

"Have you ever thought about doing film and television?" Joan asked.

"Not really," I lied.

In my heart, I knew that was my first dream. The previous fall, I'd taken my first on-camera acting class. Still, it felt foolish to dream it out loud or admit it to Joan.

The theater was an island of misfit toys where I thought I could exist safely. Even if there weren't people who looked exactly like me, there were enough who, like me, didn't fit into any box. The field for film and television, for people who looked anything like me, was so barren. It felt like a place I'd be so supremely rejected.

With a few exceptions, the roles for Black women played on TV were the maid, the police chief, or some other asexual dispensary of information with no life. They were functional: "We've run the tests in the lab." Their job was to say, "The body was found three feet from the door. It was a forced entry." They gave the information, assisting the "real" stars in getting from plot point A to B.

Who is this girl? I often wondered, as I watched those characters on my own television. I had never known her.

Other than Denzel Washington's, the acting careers I admired most belonged to white women or white men. Meryl Streep. Julia Roberts. So many Black women with clearly exceptional talent were hamstrung by the system. They were larger than life when given the opportunity to explore their possibility. Still, most of the time, they were made small.

"Think about giving TV a chance," Joan said. "I think you could make a real go at it."

I wonder: If Joan had come from anywhere other than Los Angeles, would I have believed her? There was something about that fact that made me think that she must be telling the truth. I could sense that she believed in me, so I decided that I'd work with her. If she could see me, I thought, then someone else might be able to see me too.

Chapter 15

W hen I was a child and our family took a road trip to visit Aunty Azuka in New Jersey, this was how it worked: We would leave the house playing whatever radio station we kids wanted. Once we had driven out of the station's range and the static overtook the music, my mother and her leather case of cassette tapes would have command.

The playlist varied over the years. There were the classics, chief among them Motown's very well-loved *25 #1 Hits from 25 Years*. Often a new mixtape made by my Aunty Oby would follow, and always, always, Simon and Garfunkel's greatest hits.

"The Boxer," by Simon and Garfunkel, was my mother's very favorite song. When it came on, without fail, she was there for every word—swaying her head, pointing her finger up to the top of the car as punctuation, singing, "I am leaving, I am leaving, but the fighter still remains."

"I am leaving, I am leaving . . ." My mother was singing about her own life, in that bit; even as a child, I could tell. These are the moments that we realize that our parents were once young people who had interests beyond our soccer games.

When "The Boxer" was first released on the album *Bridge Over Troubled Water*, my mother had been rebuilding her life after the war. For a while, she'd returned to education, taking a job as the vice principal of a girls' secondary school, teaching English literature. But her new friends—members of the foreign press and international aid workers—urged her to leave Nigeria. "Because of what we saw in the war, they felt I might be killed," she told me.

By then, in the early 1970s, my Uncle Adazie, her eldest brother, lived in London. Going there was not possible, however, given the British support of Nigeria's federal government. Sweden, on the other hand, was not involved in the war, and so the journalists found a place for her to stay in the suburbs of Stockholm. They set her up on job interview after job interview, and one of their friends chauffeured my mother back and forth in her brand-new Volvo.

"Taking me around and around, with that record, Simon and Garfunkel," my mother told me. "We were playing it in the car, driving all over the place."

She wrote letters home, detailing her first impressions of snow. She compared it to feathers: "You know, if you hit a truck full of chickens with your car? The way the feathers float down? That is snow."

Thanks to her friend with the Volvo, she was able to see some of her idols from the records; she saw Miriam Makeba in concert. She saw contemporary films in beautiful cinemas, something she hadn't experienced in Nigeria since long before the war, when one of my uncles brought back *The Sound of Music* and played it on a borrowed projector.

My mother lived for five years in Sweden, making a living

importing and selling traditional West African crafts—an industry that always picked up around Christmastime. She became known
for explaining the use of these baskets, trinkets, and other instruments. She had three very, very good friends, as she explained, and
they stayed in touch for a while, until, as she said, "everything
scattered."

You see, as all this was happening, my mother's family had begun
a conversation with a prominent local family about their son. My
mother had met him, briefly, before the war, but he'd moved to
the US on a scholarship.

When they asked for my mother's hand and the match was made,
my mother moved from Sweden to Montreal, to teach English to
the two young boys in a French-speaking West African family.
They lived in a suburb called Saint-Bruno-de-Montarville, with
snow so high that they had to tunnel out.

"It was just so nice seeing someone who knew and spoke my
language, even if we weren't from the same place," she told me. "I
was so grateful. Everybody I connected with could put me somewhere that was meaningful."

My mother and her first husband were married at Montreal's
Notre-Dame Basilica. The few people my mother did know all
came and stood up for her, sending my mother off to her new life
in South Kent, Connecticut, where her now-husband worked as a
minister.

Now, she thought, the most promising part of her life would
begin.

Chapter 16

Shifting my focus from theater to television and film filled me with uncertainty. While life in the theater was hardly easy money, the work had become steady.

My new manager took a hard line, however: "No more auditions, and we are entertaining no direct offers," she said. (Never mind that I'd never had a direct offer—a job that someone asked me to do.) Still, I agreed to audition only for film and television roles. That summer, I went to more auditions than I had in my entire life.

Figuring that I had several months of savings to lean on before I'd need to start looking for a day job, I budgeted accordingly. But somehow, I'd overestimated my savings. I watched my bank account deplete as I went on what must have been a hundred auditions or more, hearing "no, no, no."

I had planned on a fresh start, but I hadn't expected at this stage to be catapulted back to my earliest days in New York, living as I had before I'd built my way in, show after show. Back then, accepting help from my mother had felt embarrassing, even burdensome. Now, having made my own ends meet for so long, I felt that I couldn't ask again.

My agent called one day to say she had spoken to the artistic director of the Kansas City Rep, where the musical *Venice* had first been staged. They were casting for their production of *Pippin*, she said. They wanted me for Leading Player.

My first direct offer. The first part I'd ever loved. My heart sank.

"You'd wanted to do this," my agent reminded me.

"I have to pass," I said, echoing the new manager, using this industry pleasantry for "no," hardly believing my own words.

I had wanted it, but I hadn't wanted it this way, I reminded myself. I tried not to think of the possibility before me, the joy in the music, the flexibility of the role.

I continued to audition for months, working with casting directors who had met me numerous times, who had heard me speak, whose job it was to suss out who I was and to put me in the right boxes—who were now calling me in for the 'hood kid. The no-nonsense single mom with a teenager. The sassy whatever-the-hell.

I wanted to grab them and say, You have seen me. Multiple times. If you stop for one second to hear my voice, actually hear it, you will have all the information you need to know that I'm not right for this part. If you took in how I dressed and listened to the regionalism in my speech, you could tell that I am not right for this part. I cannot produce this person—the only person you want me to play.

If I had twenty parts to try, a range of pitches, say, to swing at, then I'd probably hit the ball four or five times, when I was up at bat. Give me twenty of the same option, which I can't do, and I'm going to strike out a lot.

That euphemism for rejection, "We're going another way," sounded to me like it had never truly gone my way.

"Just keep at it," my mother said. "I've never heard of nothing coming from hard work."

As usual, my mother was constantly praying for me and over me. So many days we would sit together on the phone, our heads bowed in silence—a shared feeling, a focused breath. If I were out walking while talking with her, I'd find a place to sit, even if it was on a park bench. One of my favorites was on the tiny triangle of grass underneath the elevated train tracks near my apartment.

"What's going to happen?" I asked her while sitting there one day, surrounded by screeches and honks.

"Well, just have faith that everything is going to work out," she said. "Everything's going to be OK." Then she prayed over me for so long—so, so long. I don't know if she sensed I needed that much prayer, that much time, to calm down, but I did.

"Remember, when you were in the third grade, your teacher could hear that you could sing, and she pulled you up to that stage," she said. "And you had to sing in front of everyone. And even though you were nervous, you found your courage. And everyone was . . . Don't you remember in the sixth grade, where you never sang a song, and then who was that music teacher? Mr. Hershey—"

"Hersee, Mom. Mr. Hersee," I said, shaking my head.

"—who told you to get the music, 'I Will Always Love You,' from that thing I love, Whitney Houston. And you came, and everyone was . . .

"So you have something special," she concluded. "So people, they see you. There is something—I don't know what . . . They want something that you have. So you have to be patient. So let's pray."

Finally, I received my first callback; it was for a job that I liked.

As I ran the lines, I let myself hope. It almost broke me to learn they were going in a different direction.

Then came my second direct offer—a request for me to reprise in New York a role I'd played—and loved—in Boston. I called my manager and told her I thought I should take it.

"We're passing," she said.

A few weeks later, the script for the pilot of *Orange Is the New Black* arrived in my mailbox. I was auditioning for the part of Janae Watson, a former track star turned inmate in the fictional Litchfield Penitentiary.

From the moment I pulled the manuscript from the envelope and began reading, I was sold. The story was so bright and vivid, like a 3D castle in a children's pop-up book. The princesses—watched over by prison guards—were so colorful, rising off the pages. Even though it was a story about mass incarceration, *Orange* was not about crime and punishment. There was little shared about what brought a character to this place and more about the person herself.

Wow, I thought, when I finished it. I'd love to be a part of something like that.

THE DAY OF MY *Orange Is the New Black* audition was steamy. Before I left home, I twisted my still-wet hair into Bantu knots atop my head so it would stay fresh.

I had two other calls that day, before and after *Orange*, and I knew I wouldn't have time to take the subway back to Queens in between. I texted Lisa to see if I could camp out at her air-conditioned apartment in Harlem. When I arrived there after the first audition, I was thrilled that she was home waiting for me. I lost track of time as we rehearsed lines, then shot up with realization, dropping my phone in my bag and running for the door.

"Your hair?" Lisa asked.

"I don't need to be done-up for prison," I told her.

To me, Janae was a girl who had the potential to run herself out of her circumstances but lost her way. Other than her track prowess and an arrest, the script and description didn't offer me much in the way of her circumstances, but based on my own experiences with track teammates and competitors, I could imagine.

The casting director, Jen Euston, had me read the scene twice, gently suggesting, the second time, that I do it without yelling "Fuck!"

When I finished, she said, "That was really good."

"Aw, thanks," I said, gathering my things. My mind was already on other meetings and auditions.

Even by my standards, this was an exceptionally busy time. Each day was a math equation based on the timing of buses and trains, the number of subway rides I had left on my Metrocard, and my willingness to carry a bagged lunch, multiple outfits, a drawer's worth of makeup, and whatever else the next call required.

I'd sit in waiting rooms, surrounded by people fixated on the same goal, trying to ignore the nagging questions as they arose: Is this my life? Is this enough?

BEFORE LEAVING, I squeezed in an audition for a television series called *Blue Bloods*. As I prepared, I flipped back through my email to the surrender prayer Celisse had sent me. God, I leave this in your hands, I repeated to myself. I called my manager to share an idea I had for the audition. "I think it can be funny," I told her. "I think I can get it."

But when I arrived for the audition, it was immediately clear that I was in the wrong place. So I doubled back to the subway and showed up twenty-five minutes late. By the time I arrived, I was sweating.

Standing in front of the huge industrial fan in the building's lobby, I explained my situation to another actor waiting there. "I'm just going to cool down for a minute before I sign in," I told her. I often used this delaying tactic to buy myself an extra ten minutes and catch my breath.

Just then, the casting director walked out. "Who's next?"

"I think she is," this other actor said.

I looked over at her. "You just heard me say—"

"I think she's next," she said again. "I think her appointment is before mine."

"OK, yep, coming," I said, glaring at the girl.

I walked into the room and saw a long table with six chairs on one side. On the other side, a single chair faced the table, as if before a firing squad.

I sat down to deliver my lines, and I got a laugh at the line I'd changed. They asked me to read it again. The energy was good in the room in a way that I'd never experienced before in a film and TV audition. I could feel their interest.

That went really great, I thought on my way out. They really liked what you did. It was a great audition, Uzo. But you're not going to get that job because you were late.

I could feel my blood turn to ice, the tears coming up as I pushed out the door to the street. It wasn't a loud or wailing cry, but it still consumed me.

The universe is trying to tell you that this is not for you. You keep trying to make something happen for you that is not for you. I couldn't stop the thoughts long enough to sober up and wipe off my face. The world I'd been holding together suddenly fell apart. If this dream, this goal, was not true, then what else wasn't? By the time the G train pulled into the subway station and I walked on, I didn't know what to believe at all.

They've been trying to tell you by who you see on those screens, they've tried to tell you by flat-out rejecting you, and you're not listening. This was what I thought, all the way into Queens, from the G to the E at Court Square, to the R at Queensboro Plaza, to the N out to my apartment in Astoria. I had never been that person on the subway before: the one whose eye everybody is trying to avoid. The one you look away from, not knowing if she's crazy or if there is even anything you can do to help.

While on the N, I looked up. I saw a young guy in the two-seater across from me, wearing all black, with black Sambas, trying not to watch as I cried.

I dropped my head, pulled out my phone, and pulled up the surrender prayer. I hadn't really been saying the words earlier in the week; this time I was really saying them.

"Dear God, my desire, my priority, is inner peace. I want the experience of love. I don't know what would bring that to me. I leave the results of this situation and every situation in Your hands. I trust Your will. May Your will be done. Amen."

I repeated it, and my heart broke even further. I knew what I was going to do next: I was going to quit. I may have said it or wondered about it before, but never in my time living in New York had I ever truly considered quitting. I had 100 percent doubted, 100 percent questioned, 100 percent sobbed. I had 100 percent felt unsure and 100 percent felt lost, but I had never quit before.

That was what I did on September 14, 2012: I quit. I'm done, I said to myself a few times, believing it instantly. I'm trying to do something that is not for me, as You have already articulated, God. It hurt my heart so much.

My parents always thought that I would make a good lawyer. Lord, if You can figure out a way for me to go to school and become a lawyer, I will go. I will go.

My resolve built but did not lessen my sadness. Even if I did become a lawyer, and everyone on the street looking at me would think that I was successful, I would still know that I'd failed.

It wasn't the system that was frustrating me, I told myself; it was that I was trying to fit my square peg into a round hole. That was not for you. There is a square peg hole, called law school, that you are resisting. That resistance isn't the world. It's you trying to take something that's not for you. Thinking along these lines, I felt better: I was going to be living my life on purpose.

That was how the rest of my life would start: I'd text Chi-Chi, inviting her over for dinner. I would grab a bottle of wine as I walked home from the subway station, and we'd order sushi from the place we liked. Then, on Monday, I'd call my manager and agent and tell them that I was out.

I resolved that from that moment on, I would do what I was there to do, and I would be successful. Ultimately, my success in law, or another field, might even give me what I thought acting was going to give me. The things we dreamed of, I knew, were sometimes symbols of a deeper prayer. I had always thought of the arts as a kind of service industry; I wanted to be of service. Maybe

I'd go and become a pro bono defense attorney. Maybe I'd change some kind of legislation down the road.

I followed through on the first steps of my plan, uncorking the wine and waiting for Chi-Chi and our food to arrive. I flipped on the television, scrolling to find the saved episodes of *Oprah's Master Class*, a series of in-depth interviews with acclaimed artists, leaders, and other public figures. I hadn't yet watched the episodes featuring Jane Fonda or Lorne Michaels, the creator of *Saturday Night Live*. For some reason, I put on Lorne Michaels.

In the early days of *Saturday Night Live*, in 1975, there was a sketch that the network hated, called "Bee Hospital." In it, a bunch of father bees buzzed around a waiting room to find out if their newborns were queens or drones. The network had wanted to cut the bees, Michaels said; he'd refused. For the rest of that first season, the cast kept popping up in bee costumes.

Master Class was shot in a confessional style, which meant that I was seeing Michaels on a stool, in front of a gray backdrop, looking directly at the camera. From time to time we heard a voice-over and saw his words of inspiration flash across the screen.

As he was saying something along the lines of "If I could just keep the faith . . ." the words became an image. "Keep the Faith." I read them, left to right, across the screen. His image faded into what I can only describe as a kind of lemonade ad: oranges and purples and reds in the sky, big, fluffy clouds. A field and a stately tree with a swing gently rocking. On one side of the frame was a house with an open window, curtains blowing through. A pie on the window-sill . . . and that phrase, "Keep the Faith," across the screen.

Oh, I really like that, I thought. It would be the perfect thing to post on the Twitter account I had started, along with my castmates, at the beginning of *Godspell*. I decided that when the episode finished, I'd rewind it, take a picture, and tweet it. As soon as I had that thought—tweet it—my phone, on the coffee table, began to ring.

I picked it up and saw the number of my agent, probably calling to share my manager's annoyance about my late arrival to the *Blue Bloods* casting. Though I'd planned to wait until Monday to quit, this was as good a time as any. "Hello," I said.

"Hi, we have Joan on the phone too." This had never happened to me: Both my agent and manager on the phone? This must be bad, I thought.

"Oh, hey—hi," I said.

"What are you doing?" asked Joan.

"I'm at home, sitting on the couch," I said.

"Mm-hmm," she said, and then she said the weirdest thing: "Everything's OK, you're not fired."

I wasn't fired? Could agents even fire their clients?

"Do you remember that audition you went on a few weeks ago, for *Orange Is the New Black*?" my agent asked.

"I remember," I said.

"Do you remember the part you auditioned for?"

"The track star," I said. "I remember."

"Well, you didn't get it."

OK, so now agents were calling actors to say when they didn't get jobs? It really was time to get out.

"But they'd like to offer you another part. The role of Crazy Eyes."

"Are you joking?" I think I asked that several times.

They weren't. It was two episodes, possibly three.

First I screamed; then I burst into tears, a combination of relief and elation. "To tell you the honest truth," I said, "I was going to call you Monday and tell you that I was quitting—that I was out."

"Well, now you don't have to be out," Joan said.

I truly could not believe it. "God is good!" I hung up the phone, jumped up and down, and paced from bedroom to living room, filled with joy. A few minutes later, the sushi arrived, then Chi-Chi, and we ate, drank, and talked together late into the night.

Some say that when you're close to your dream, the devil tempts you. I'd made a pact to not take any theater auditions, even as the auditions—the offers—were coming. In my doubt, I was just seconds away from giving it all up forever. Still, I'd kept the faith. For weeks, I was elated. In my heart was a lightness; there was a rightness in my career too. After all that, I landed the role on *Blue Bloods* as well.

One night I went home remembering that I'd never taken that picture from the Lorne Michaels episode. That's exactly what I need to say to the world, I thought. Keep the Faith.

I put on the DVR and started fast-forwarding, then rewinding, looking for that part and finding nothing. I must be going too fast, I thought; instead of watching at four times the speed, I went down to twice the speed. Still, I didn't see it. Finally, I decided to watch the whole thing again, to be sure. I watched and watched. The first season, the bees, all of it, but no image. It was just not there.

I saw that image. I've seen God work in my life. I know it sounds crazy, made up, embellished, when I tell this story. But I know what I saw.

Chapter 17

During my first few months of work on *Orange Is the New Black*, I thought back to what my friend Baron had said to me in college about missing the intense camaraderie of high school drama: That feeling of being so green, with such stars in your eyes, was exactly what I had walking onto the set at Kaufman Astoria Studios.

I was very nervous to begin. While theater is typically generous with its rehearsal time, television allows only one or two official run-throughs on set before filming begins. These rehearsals are for the director and crew, who will start and stop the actors to cue cameras and adjust lighting and set pieces. How would I do, I wondered, walking into a scene with such little idea of what the other person is going to do and say? What if their idea doesn't work with my plans and I have to adjust?

Many of my castmates were theater actors with a similar amount of professional television experience—maybe a bit part here or there and not much more. I knew a few of them. We had a cast of about sixty (I believe I started off season 1 as number fifty-three); throughout the season, many of us would be featured. Our shared understanding of the meaningful opportunities ahead impacted the way we went to work, I think. I felt just pure, pure excitement, every day, from everyone.

I had worked with Black actors in the past, and even with all-Black casts, but *Orange* was one of the first wholly inclusive shows on television. While *Godspell* had diversity from a race perspective, now I was playing alongside almost any identity I could think of, from male to female to trans to Black to Latin to gay to straight to white to abled and disabled. All these people, from every socioeconomic background, were not only represented but normalized as a presence on that show.

The studio couldn't find enough dressing rooms to accommodate our outsize cast. (*Sesame Street* was filmed at the same location, but puppets don't need to change their clothes!) The leads and major guest stars quickly filled up what is known as the "first team" hallway. The rest of us used another communal area, off another hallway—an open-space green room connected to a conference room where we could dress.

We sat in that open area amid bags strewn around the room. We studied lines and waited for our scenes, just as we had back when we were theater kids. The number of new faces crowded in, playing cards and killing time together, all gave it the feel of a college dorm.

We didn't know what we didn't have—the relative space and privacy of a smaller cast, for example, or the pressures of a larger role. All we knew were these chill, easy, fun moments, which created the bond, I think, that you can feel on that screen.

There would come a point, in later seasons, when I would understand my character, Suzanne, just as much as I would if I'd had those weeks of theater rehearsals. For now, I was just learning the gymnastics of her insides: what got her there, what kept her there, what kept her going.

Suzanne was introduced in the second episode. When I'd first read the script, a picture had flashed in my head, a voice. The writer, Marco Ramirez, described her as being "innocent like a child, except that children aren't scary." That innocence, in my mind, was the beautiful key to who Suzanne was—and into how her actions could be misinterpreted.

I spent that whole first season experimenting, information gathering. Through Suzanne, I expressed behaviors that I wasn't aware I'd filed away while people-watching. People like to compare actors to the characters they play, but the only qualities of Suzanne's that were mine were the biting of nails and that desperate place of loving—like the inside of my heart being worn on the outside.

When I walked from my Queens apartment to the set, I tried to get into the character's frame of mind, slowing down my breathing and clearing my head. I was so accustomed to the immediate feedback of a live theater audience that I struggled with the silence on set, as we began filming. In my head, I knew that the people watching me couldn't laugh; it would ruin what they call "the take." Still, in the moment, I couldn't help feeling like all the silence meant I'd bombed.

Over time, I developed a different tuning of the ear; I could feel the crew around me, and even in their quiet, I knew when they were connecting with what we were doing. It was a subtle tension, but when I am working, my senses are heightened, as if my peripheral vision extends in all directions. I can feel a smirk on a cameraman's face, an uncomfortable shifting of weight offstage, or the satisfaction of a director in the moment of silence after the scene ends and before they call "cut."

I began to feel life inside the camera itself—a box made of metal and glass. When the camera operator moved closer, I felt the audience and their line of understanding—as if they were studying me. It's a kind of dance: Your partner leans in, and suddenly things become very intimate.

Orange had its first team, and yet, just as was true in a human body with eyes and a brain, there was no single star—or organ—that could carry the story. There were simply too many vital links necessary for the thing to work. It took every arm on the relay team to get the baton around the track.

What we lacked in official rehearsal time my castmates and I gained in hair and makeup. If more than one of us was in a chair, we could rehearse our lines together. This turned out to be the very best place for such a thing. As actors, we still had to play with what we had—the seat, the space, even the brushes in our faces. With all these distractions, our knowledge of the material had to be even tighter.

This last-minute work of figuring out how to make the thing sing helped the Ghetto Dorm (the name for the Black characters' housing unit on the show) understand and know how to be in service to one another. Some of the back-and-forth banter you see on-screen has that kind of musicality, dance, and flexibility that you have in a Black hair salon.

By the time we got to our "cell" on set, we already had the pace and the ping-pong down.

SEEING *ORANGE* FOR THE FIRST TIME, I thought, Uzo, you're doing too much. You're doing *three* much. I often don't know how to judge my performance, as I'm harsher than any critic could be. I once had a castmate tell me that my "eyeballs were broken."

Angela, sitting on the other end of my couch, looked at me, shaking her head with closed eyes and saying, "I don't even know. I can't even believe that's you."

"Are you serious?" I asked.

"The way you are moving . . . I see you, and I know that's you, but no one who knows you would ever think that's you," she said. She paused for a moment to think. "I do hear your laugh in there sometimes?"

Chi-Chi had a similar reaction. "This is crazy, to me, that you're playing this role," she said when we next spoke. "People ask, 'Is she like that?' and it's, 'Not at all, not at all.'"

The show was a huge success at a time when video streaming services like Netflix were just beginning to offer original content. Unlike in network television, where viewers get to know characters slowly during weekly episodes across weeks and months, there were now people who binged the entire thirteen-hour season over the course of a weekend. This thrust our work—and even my likeness—into the world in a much different way, even before we'd had a chance to promote it on nationally televised talk shows, in magazines, or even on billboards.

My initial three-episode deal was extended; *Orange* went on for a second season and then many more, changing my life in ways that I could have never imagined.

When it comes to recognition, my instinct is typically not to share, for fear of excitement coming across as braggadocio. I certainly didn't mind standing outside a theater's stage door, receiving people's compliments and thanking them for attending my show. But being spotted at the grocery store was something new. I didn't like those kinds of surprises.

A woman delivering takeout saw me in my bathrobe, at my

front door, and her jaw dropped. A few minutes later, as I was eating, I saw a text message; she still had my number, and she wanted me to know that she was a fan.

During our European press tour, one of my castmates and I were leaving an interview when the security guard told us to wait. "There are fans outside," he said. "We'll bring the vans around."

"Fans?" I asked. "How?"

He ignored the question and leaned into the logistics, reiterating that he'd bring us out through a side entrance. "We'll pull the van onto the sidewalk, and you'll jump in."

"Are there a lot of people out there?" I asked again.

"Yes," he said. But how many people could it possibly be? Ten?

It turned out to be more than fifty, possibly closer to a hundred people, mostly teenagers. As we drove off, they began chasing us. The state they were in was truly scary: They were running into traffic, banging on our car. I banged back on the window at one point: "You are going to be hit by a car!" I shouted. God forbid someone was injured—or worse.

Many followed us all the way to our hotel. We lost them as we pulled into the underground garage and rode up a back elevator.

AT THE PREMIERE of *Drowning Crow*, I had had such a strong desire to be known. I didn't want *this* kind of attention, though, just as I didn't want special treatment at a club or to be overly served in any way. I'd also been in the industry long enough to understand the dangers of becoming too intoxicated by fame. You get to the goal, and you are immediately thinking about the next goal. You are enticed, even encouraged, to do whatever it takes to get there.

"Remember, Uzo. All you have is your name," my mother told

me when I'd first left home. The advice was about living right in my daily life, but I also think she saw certain realities of my chosen field that I couldn't in the moment. I knew how my family carried themselves publicly. Now that my name was being carried further than I think anyone in my family could have ever imagined, it became even more important to me to protect it.

Orange Is the New Black and my own work playing Suzanne were recognized widely, winning Emmy, Screen Actors Guild, and Critics Choice Awards; Golden Globe nominations; and many other honors.

I wish I would have known how to celebrate it.

"My gosh, mate, you'll have to tell me all about it," wrote one of my old friends from college in an out-of-the-blue email. "What's it like, being famous?"

"You know me for real," I replied. "I don't want to talk about this. Let's just talk about . . . real life."

I didn't want to question whether people I knew perceived me differently—people who knew me better than any stranger who had once read a magazine or watched an interview. New friendships also began to feel more challenging, as I developed a sense— right or wrong, real or imagined—that an acquaintance might know something about me. I had to figure out if they did or not, and if they did, how much. How much of what they knew mattered to them?

I started to be a bit guarded: Why are you reaching out?

I didn't know how to talk about any of this with my friends, many of whom were actors. It felt somehow impolite to speak of success in this hard business, where everything can feel like a rejection. When we spoke, I focused instead on the challenges of the work. This apprehension often caused me to diminish what was happening in my career without thinking—a nervous reaction, out of a desire to not make anyone else feel bad.

I also felt conflicted about how my career success fit into the bigger picture of my life. I imagine that many artists dream of being on a big stage, whether that's a stadium, a museum, a bestseller list, or Broadway. When we imagine success defined in this way, we attach to it so many other kinds of fulfillment. I suppose I did expect some kind of sweeping change, but if anything, the recognition made me that much more keenly aware of how much I had stayed the same.

I was certainly blessed: For the first time in my life, I didn't have to worry about making rent. I felt that I could say no to projects that I knew wouldn't serve me and be all right, from professional and financial perspectives. I could buy that fancy camera I wanted, but I still lived modestly. I was still single, still wondering what came next.

My family typically reserves excitement for when we know that something's going to happen. So I hesitated to share good news or look too far ahead. I could hear my father's advice echoing in my head: "Stay humble."

Chapter 18

Onyi called one day, in the fall of 2016. We caught up about work and her kids, and as the conversation turned toward our mother, my sister said, "I need a break. I mean, we need a break."

I imagine that there is a trust required, on both sides, for a mother to begin to lean on her children. While Onyi had been a caregiver from the time that Chi-Chi, Junior, and I came along, at this stage of her life, now she also had a home, family, and career of her own. While my mother contributed to the household in many ways, the shift in roles was clear.

My mother had happily handed over the holidays several years earlier, once Onyi had the space to host. My mother still pitched in, chopping lettuce for a salad that one of us would later assemble. But she would no longer fuss over a turkey.

She welcomed the passing of the baton, in that sense. Thank God she was too old to shovel snow. No more mowing, raking, scraping off the grill. My mother was happy just to sit there and preside. Still, the transition—as well as the loss of her life in

Medfield after more than thirty years—was not easy. She still spoke with my Aunty Azuka every day, and she loved her Zumba and computer classes at the senior center, but she missed her life. There were no more weekend runs to the bank or stops at Shaw's grocery store to pick up some sugar cookies as a treat. No more dropping by the Swansons' or checking in with Lillian to see what her week was like.

While still fearless in many ways, my mother was now in her seventies, and some of her boldness had been reined in. Driving at night, or on the highway, no longer felt like a wise choice. Giving my brother her car made sense, practically speaking, but the hand-off also represented a finished chapter.

I hung up with Onyi and immediately called my mother with an invitation. I knew that she loved the energy of Queens and that one of the strengths of living in such a place was that she didn't need to get around by car. She arrived a week before Thanksgiving and stayed on through New Year's.

When I was on set, she often took long walks, organizing her-self with an errand to the grocery store or the laundromat or both, in an effort to "be useful." She pulled out the rickety granny cart she'd bought for me when I'd first arrived in New York. Other times she'd walk for two or even three miles, stopping at park benches along the way to rest and people-watch. I'd come home to find a full cart at the bottom of the stairs. I'd hoist it up, unpack it, and start making dinner.

My mother came to work with me one day, as we were filming the second episode of the second season. The director, Michael Trim, who was a friend, invited her back to watch with him in the "vil-lage" of video monitors and listen in on headphones.

That day, we were filming a scene in which we are playing a

game, with one inmate standing by the clock, calling "Time!" At one point, I am the one to yell; from there, the scene changes into a flashback.

The camera operators set up again and again, closing their coverage on me, right by the clock. "Time!" I yelled, on the last take we did, and then I heard the voice of my mother.

"Cut!"

"Oh my gosh!" I doubled over, laughing.

AFTER THAT, my mother decided it was time for her to watch the series. I taught her how to use my TV, pausing and rewinding so she could get all the nuance. While the show was a whole new world for her, she loved it. I always found that funny; I definitely did not think that she would.

Even though she didn't know my industry at all, my mother knew all the roles; she was deeply fascinated learning how all the pieces fit together. She knew every person supporting me directly, even if she couldn't keep their names straight. I could always celebrate freely with her, speak breathlessly about possibilities, feel my excitement rise alongside her own.

THERE IS A FESTIVAL in Obosi called "*Ito Ogbo*," which means "eighty." Families from all over the town and its surrounding villages gather to celebrate all the loved ones who had reached this milestone age.

This centuries-old tradition began with families pooling their resources to buy and then slaughter a single cow to mark the occasion. The meat was then prepared and shared with the entire village, who all came out for a weekend-long celebration. After that, each eighty-year-old received the new title of *Ogbueshi*, for a man, or *Ogbueshi Nwanyi*, for a woman, meaning "killer of cow." As elders of the community, they were then free from taxes and other obligations. Their only role, from then on, would be to serve as wise counsel.

The idea of *Ito Ogbo* is significant on its own, and even more so because the celebration happens only once every three years. If your eightieth birthday does not fall within a certain window, then you must wait for the next one. For example, my mother's father, Egwuenu, was seventy-nine in the year of *Ito Ogbo*; he passed away the month before the next celebration. My grandmother lived only into her early seventies, so she didn't make it. Neither had my mother's immediate biological older sister, Ifeoma.

In a place where, even today, the average life expectancy is just shy of fifty-five, everyone anticipates *Ito Ogbo* with excitement and cautious optimism. As we all know, nothing is guaranteed at that stage of life. Every message or mention about the event begins, "With God's grace . . ."

Ito Ogbo, my mother explained, is an event like none other. It's a huge party thrown by your children—a kind of funeral that you're alive to see happen. *This*, your loved ones are saying, is how you will be celebrated when you are gone. It starts with the cow, a sign of prosperity in our culture. (As Chudi once said, "Once you get to be that age, there has to be a cow involved.") For three days, there are grills going, tents in people's yards, and fireworks. A loose, chill, relaxed party, with many hundreds of visitors coming to visit, bearing gifts.

Everyone comes through at some point. Even people who can't make it on Friday night or Saturday will pop in, even if just for two minutes, to see and be seen, to pay respects as if to say, of all that will follow: "Know that I will be there on the day."

My mother's sister Adora turned eighty while she was staying with me. The year of her *Ito Ogbo*, that March, would mark fifteen since my mother had last returned to Nigeria. "We'll go together," I told her. We'd never been in Nigeria together. I'd been working nonstop and was already planning to use my upcoming time off to travel.

Though excited by the prospect, my mother was also nervous: Her knees were bad, and she was concerned about how difficult it would be to move from place to place.

"Mommy, I have it figured out," I insisted.

She'd had a hand in organizing my last trip with Chi-Chi: When I'd asked for our family's contact information, I'd received an email with a long, painstakingly organized list. This time I was the one to make the plans, arranging the flights, airport transfers, and schedules.

Only after I walked my mother through the itinerary—this car here, that flight there, all the preparations and accommodations, west to east, east to west—did she begin to relax.

As I'd worked my way back down my mother's list, letting our relatives know of our plans, I felt, for the first time, like more than the fragile, precious "egg" doted over by my uncles and aunties. I felt like a daughter—and that felt even more special. A "super-egg," as my Uncle Ifeanyi had once joked.

I knew now that it was a joy for them to host, as much as it was for us to be hosted. This *ikune* is a kind of code: If something is offered, you take it, regardless of how much you already have. The beauty of receiving in this way is knowing that you, one day, will give too.

We arrived in Nigeria and stayed first in Lagos with my Uncle Bertie and Aunty Elo. Every morning my aunty and I took a walk, to enjoy the city before the full hustle and bustle broke over the quiet. Later, over a traditional Nigerian breakfast, I'd listen as they reminisced with my mother about moments and people still left from their younger days. Their eyes danced as they discussed this party, this cricket tournament, or that holiday.

In the evenings, I went out with my cousins and friends. One threw a party for me at her art gallery. Another night several of us met at a rooftop bar, mingling, taking in the view of the skyline, the lagoon, and the sweep of the Third Mainland Bridge. When I returned home after midnight, my mother, aunty, and uncle were still upstairs, carrying on.

We learned that my Uncle Adazie and Aunty Bunmi were also traveling home to Obosi around the same time, so I called them to coordinate flights for Uncle Bertie and Aunty Elo and my mother and me. Business class, I told Uncle Adazie, adding that they were welcome to share the car I'd arranged to take us from the airport to the village.

It was a proud moment for me, seeing my mother, surrounded by her siblings, traveling in style on this Air Peace flight. I knew how their story began. As grown-up as I was, Uncle Adazie nevertheless insisted that we ride in his car, with armed escort. I would always be their daughter and their niece; culturally, he was still the one to look out for me.

When we arrived in Obosi, the sense of occasion and celebration was immediately clear; huge banners emblazoned with the honorees' photos hung from the rooftops. We stopped by Aunty Adora's house first. "Nno, welcome home," she said, hugging my mother. Then she turned to me. "Thank you for bringing my sister to me," she said.

During the days, we sat together at Aunty Adora's, catching up, greeting visitors. Chudi, her son, was there; it was the first time in decades that all the children were together in one place. Together we looked through old family photos, including some from my mother's first marriage—most of which I'd never seen.

In the evenings, my mother and I stayed, along with Chudi, at the home of Uncle Adazie and Aunty Bunmi. Here too I saw my elders transported back into their youth, with my mother in the role of little sister.

Having followed my career with pride and concern, my family understood that my work had received a new level of attention. During the first few seasons of *Orange*, relatives and even their friends had sent messages. I knew many of them had not seen the show—Nigeria is a pretty conservative country. Still, they'd noticed: *She is being honored for her acting.*

This Nigerian pride—to our betterment and sometimes to our detriment—carries a high bar for success. When someone is doing something that's being celebrated, we're very glad to claim that success as one of our own, as if Chinua Achebe or Chimamanda Ngozi Adichie were our own grandfather or sister.

Many outside our family felt a similar kinship toward my Uncle Adazie, who, in a single generation, had done something extraordinary in both politics and diplomacy as the Commonwealth's secretary-general. Newspapers the world over had carried stories of his work as well as photos of him working and walking alongside his friend Nelson Mandela. There was a road in Obosi named after my uncle; he was showered with attention everywhere we went.

The respect and the space he was given, and the way he held it, was a real touchstone for me. It reminded me not only that I had an opportunity by which I had to do right, but I had a blueprint as well.

While I could always feel my mother's pride, even when she was quiet, she did not stay quiet in Obosi! "My sister had that voice," she reminded old friends as she received them. "Adazie, you saw it when she was young. Uzo, you had it—everyone knew."

On Friday, the day before the public ceremony, I stood with my mother in a receiving line, helping to accept gifts for Aunty Adora and distribute the ones she'd wanted to extend to her guests. "Ah, you are the one who won the Emmy," said one man, after greeting Aunty Adora and sharing his congratulations.

"Yes," I said, feeling heat rise in my cheeks.

"I saw your picture," he said. "Oh, you're doing great!"

"Thank you," I said.

"Hey, Uzo, do you mind getting me a beer?" Chudi interrupted.

I turned my attention away, meeting Chudi's eyes. He nodded his head back with a faint smile, eyebrows raised, as if to say, *Oh yes, younger cousin, the rest of us are all still living our lives here.*

Uncle Adazie led us in the breaking of the sacred kola nut, my favorite Igbo tradition—the highest respect you can offer to a person. The practice is a ritual, combining the fruit of the tropical kola tree with peanut butter and pepper. At its heart, though, it's a prayer to the ancestors as old as we are, as a people. We all crowded into the room to ask God to bless the event, Aunty Adora, her children, her grandchildren, her siblings, all the way down.

A while later, a side conversation that I was a part of turned to another Igbo tradition—*omugwo*, the practice of caring for a mother after the birth of her child. After Onyi's eldest was born, my mother stayed with them for a few months. When the other two came along, the time shortened progressively to a month, then two weeks. By the time Junior's Ada was born, my mother was seventy-four and even further from the experience of caring for a child of any age. She visited with them for a week, but she didn't clean or night nurse—she was too tired.

"Will you do it for me and Chi-Chi?" I now asked my mother.

"Yes," she said, "but I'm not going to be doing it *that* way, exactly."

"Exactly," I told her, reminding her that I would have nannies and a housekeeper.

"Then I will be delegating," my mother said. "I'll tell them it's time to feed the child, change the diaper, start cooking."

From the other side of the couch, she raised her arm and pointed, first left, then right, as if she were watching two people intently— staring them down. "This is me, sitting here, watching you treat my grandchild," she said. Then she pointed two fingers back toward her face. "You think this comes from Crazy Eyes?"

I laughed.

"This is my *omugwo*," my mother said, once again pointing to the imaginary help. "I'll be delegating."

THE MORNING of the *Ito Ogbo* ceremony dawns, and the family and close friends of the honorees walk over to a big field with high bleachers. Each member of the audience holds a thick program, with every one of the celebrated elders listed in it, as if it were a yearbook.

The king and queen of Obosi enter, followed by all the chiefs, wearing red caps that vary, depending on the level of their chieftaincy; others wear big hats. Meanwhile, on the edge of town, the entire eighty-year-old set for that year gathers together, each one wearing the mutually agreed-upon outfit, all in the same orange color. They walk for miles, parading toward the center of town as people cheer them on. They make their way up to their rightful place in the field, where they sit on beautiful, carved, throne-like chairs, watching this whole spectacle.

The hour-long ceremony includes an Anglican prayer and the blessing of the kola nuts. Each one of the people being honored receives their own cap, one of these so-called cow-killer caps; in this case, it is the same bright orange, beaded, with a kind of coral-colored, stone-encrusted tassel.

Amid the food and the loads of dancing, the toasting of these lives, all I could think was how amazing it was that this people, my people, had this ceremony.

I love that with advanced age comes a title giving people a status that, by law, must be respected. Most of all, I love celebrating these lives while they are still here—the significance of their contribution reflected in the ways we celebrate. We instinctively gather for weddings, christenings, and other events focused on the promise of the future.

Now I understand that it is just as important to focus on the past.

MY MOTHER AND I RETURNED to the US a few days after the ceremony, but for months after (six months!), whenever I called to see how she was doing, she would say, "Zozo, I'm still not back from Nigeria."

I began to pray for an opportunity to work in Nigeria—to have the experience of living in this true home that I had not yet known. Each time I traveled there, it had been for a short stay, as the guest of someone else. At some point, I vowed, I'd return to my own place.

I called my cousin Chubi, the eldest of my Uncle Ifeanyi's children, to talk about fixing up our grandfather's house. "It has to be tip-top for my mother's *Ito Ogbo*," I told him. "We have to start planning now, getting organized."

It could take years of planning, according to Chudi. Coordinating logistical elements, getting someone on the ground. The tent, the music, the caterer—especially the caterer. All those elements would book up far in advance.

I told my mother that I was saving my money. She would be the first of the house of Egwuenu. I wanted everyone—all the grandchildren, even—to be there, at the same time, having the same experience that I'd had. They too were an essential part of this story.

I felt like I would be making good on a kind of long-ago promise. It was as Maya Angelou once wrote: "Your passage has been paid for." I wanted my mother to see the fullness of her life through this important and prized event. I wanted her to have the opportunity to sit in her own throne of sorts and have people come to visit with her. To celebrate her. To share with her just how much she meant to everyone. She had more than earned it.

Here was my opportunity to acknowledge that cost paid on my behalf, long before I was even an idea.

Part III

Uzo . . . amaka.

—*Nonyem Aduba*

Chapter 19

Orange Is the New Black's production team generously gave us about a year-and-a-half notice that, after seven seasons, the show would come to an end. During this time, I really wondered: What was coming next?

I loved the comfort of knowing that, through Suzanne's character, I would be able to work on interesting stories. Still, most artists don't get into this nomadic life to be in one place forever, and I was ready to say goodbye. I wanted to play other notes on the keyboard and explore other stories and ways of storytelling. I didn't want to be pigeonholed: Without six months of a year committed to Orange, I'd be freed up to pursue other opportunities.

As we began filming the final season, reality set in. Then my manager retired, and I began working with someone new, Eric Kranzler. I could tell right away that he was easygoing—that he had a good heart and a great gut.

"What are you looking for?" he asked, as we first sat down for lunch together in the quiet lobby of a beautiful Beverly Hills hotel.

Where to begin?

"I don't want to stay Crazy Eyes forever," I said.

"Got it," he said. "What else?"

"I brought a list," I told him.

We all know that a person who is strong also has moments of vulnerability. I no longer wished for the lives of my characters to be so perfectly stereotyped as "strong" that they warranted no time or explanation on-camera. I was aching for the opportunity to be soft in the way that I can be soft.

I heard myself speaking, but what I was thinking was, *I am giving you this roster of things that I want, but the truth of the matter, and the thing I am leaving out, is that I actually don't know how to do it.* I wanted more than the next job—more, even, than to take my career to the next level, if it meant the next level of playing whatever role of a strong Black woman that the system had carved out for me.

I have worked with amazing managers, but Eric Kranzler—whom I call by his last name—has a piece of my heart. He wanted the world to see me the way I saw myself. Before I knew it, he was in every part of my work and every part of my life. I found that I could be my whole self with him, without question or fear of judgment.

Most importantly, Kranzler taught me patience: Good work, respectable work, quality work is what we sign up for, and it will come.

ON MY WAY home from a girls' trip through Europe, I stopped in Boston. Crowley picked me up at the airport and drove me to Medfield, where I was to be inducted into the Medfield High School Hall of Excellence.

Now, for the first time, I *did* feel that I could celebrate the fruits of my efforts. I'd always wanted to travel the world; now I had the means. I'd never before gone abroad with girlfriends, but I'd just returned from laughing my way through France, Italy, and Spain with Angela and my cousin Nwamaka. Now there I was, riding shotgun with Crowley, one of my oldest friends, racing past the familiar street signs, coming home.

The Hall of Excellence ceremony was an all-school event and open to the public. I walked into the auditorium and saw the teachers and neighbors I love so dearly, the Swansons and the Browns. My old teachers, Ms. Featherman, of course, and my beloved French teacher, Madame Sharack.

Standing in this familiar place, I remembered so vividly who I was back then and who all these names and faces were to me. When you feel alone, you can so easily spot the people who are on your side. A lot of my crossroads had to do with these people who were educators going far beyond "I'm here to teach you math."

Still, as I milled around, preparing to take the stage, I felt a little uncomfortable.

"Do you remember me?" one of my former teachers asked.

"Of course I remember!" I said, startled. "How could I forget?" She had met me when I was five and had known me until I turned eighteen.

Growing up in Medfield had been uncomfortable at times, but if I belonged anywhere, it was to this community. Despite our challenges, this place raised me to be proud. Period. The people in that room with me were among those who'd most helped me understand what might be possible for me, out in the world.

Some believe that people in the public eye create personas, removing themselves from their hometown and their past. I wondered if that was what others saw. Was I no longer the same person I imagined myself to be?

While writing my speech on the plane, I'd struggled to say something important about myself. I decided to use the time I'd been given to celebrate my teachers.

"I could say I was the sole architect, but that's not really the truth," I told the audience of students, adding that, at this point in my life, there were many builders and contractors. "I think it's important to highlight them," I said, naming each one of the teachers and handing them a small gift.

"The people who can lift you up are the ones sitting among you," I said. "If you're paying attention—if they're paying attention—they can directly impact your life."

After the event, Crowley joined me onstage, as students surrounded all the honorees for pictures and autographs. I noticed that one student hung back—a Black girl whom I'd noticed earlier in my presentation. She was one of only two Black girls in the audience.

It became clear in the chaos that I wouldn't have time to get to everyone. I gestured to the girl and motioned for her to come forward. "Come up for a picture," I said.

I didn't know her, but I knew her better than any of the others. I knew it was impossible that she was unaware of being an "only" in that crowd. I wondered how that fact had shaped her every moment, movement; how close in step her experience was to my own. I met her on the stage, creating space in a room and a place where there was often very little.

Maybe I was the one and only example of a speaker who reflected back her own story. Maybe that was not the case. If I had even an opportunity to play that role, then I wouldn't—and she wouldn't—be deterred.

Yes, she stood out. There and then, that very fact would get her to the front of the line.

ONE NIGHT, while I was in Los Angeles on a film shoot, I got a call from my younger cousin, who is also called Onyi—the daughter of my Aunty Ngozi and Uncle Uzol. "I'm engaged!" she said.

I asked her about how she met her fiancé and about their plans, and after she caught me up, she said, "Cuz, you're going to meet someone; don't worry."

"I know, we'll see," I said evenly.

"Really. Enjoy this time you have now, being single," she said.

"What do you mean?"

The benefits of singlehood didn't get the attention they deserved, my cousin told me. "We always romanticize marriage," she said, "but for the rest of my life, I don't get to just go anywhere, jump out of a plane, without thinking of someone else.

"Enjoy it," she continued. "It's going to happen."

I was initially irked, but the conversation stayed with me. I was often so focused on what I lacked, both in my career and my personal life, that I didn't give enough thought to what I had.

Why had I been so eager to give myself away to men who did not value me? Why didn't they value me? Had I somehow invited or entertained that behavior?

One night, after a long day of filming, I sat in bed, phone in hand, and searched, "Why am I still single?" A flood of articles rushed in.

I can't say why the "Ten Reasons Why" headline caught my eye. I clicked, thinking to myself, OK, I'm going to read this, and then I'm going to be really honest and open with myself about what might be in here.

I made it about halfway down the list and then tossed my phone onto the bed. Uzo, you do that, I told myself, feeling tears rise. You guard yourself so well. What had never registered previously is that I dated out of desperation—even if it was a thread of desperation. Instead of enjoying myself, I had always carried the hope and intention of something more. My insecurities, my hopes of being "picked," kept me clinging to the relationships, praying that they would validate me.

"No, you really are so beautiful," I had always told my mother. I remembered my disbelief as a child, watching her take in her reflection in her bathroom mirror and hearing her say the opposite. How could she have thought anything but the truth?

I put down the lists and resolved to walk into the summer with a different outlook. Rather than finding forever, I would experiment: I would date without expectation. I would say in the moment whatever I was thinking and feeling; I would say yes only when I meant it. I wouldn't bend and contort myself into whatever woman I thought he wanted, whomever he was.

Doing this could free me up to learn about what *I* wanted, so I could know when the right person came along.

Now, I KNOW how this is going to sound: I was single for so long that, for me, it was always, "Go fuck yourself with your 'you just know.'"

But you really do. The way Robert moved was so distinct from the way any other guy in my life had moved. The space that he was prepared to occupy was just different.

We owe our relationship, in part, to the fact that Lisa, my friend from *Abyssinia*, celebrates her birthday for the entire month of July. This is not an exaggeration: Each year she puts out an itinerary, which always includes, at the very least, a beach day and a picnic. That July, however, I would be on a film set; Angela would be away as well. So we tossed out dates over text messages until we landed on one, June 28, when we'd all be in New York to celebrate.

"Cool!" Lisa responded. "There is this young Black professionals mixer that night."

In a separate thread, Angela and I exchanged rolling-eyed emojis. We'd clearly meant dinner, not networking; still, for Lisa, we agreed to go.

That night, Angela, who was staying with me at the time, surveyed my sweatpants and insisted that I change into something nicer. "I thought you wanted to meet somebody?"

"I do?" I said sarcastically.

"Then you've got to put a little effort into it," Angela said.

We met up with Lisa on a hotel rooftop in Midtown Manhattan, walked to the bar, and ordered a drink. We waited. No one appeared to offer to buy us the next round or make small talk— the baseline for any thirtysomething single gal like me, especially as a fan of *Girlfriends* or *Sex and the City*.

Feeling some kind of way that no one had approached us, Angela attempted some dating feng shui, arranging us in more "noticeable" locations, to no avail.

I felt too out of practice to even think of other ways to turn this

Titanic around. I didn't even want to. So I waited until I felt enough time had passed, and then I mentioned that I'd heard about another party in Brooklyn. "I'll call us a car," I said.

"We're not leaving till someone talks to us," Angela said. "You see that table of guys over there? They're going to talk to us."

"What?" Lisa and I were terrified.

"We're going to walk past them," Angela said, "and they're going to stop us on the way to the bathroom."

They absolutely did not stop us. We made it all the way to our destination, where Angela nodded at each of our reflections: "Now we're going to go up to them and introduce ourselves," she said.

With eyes rolling, Lisa and I swung back through the door after Angela, following her as she retraced the path back past the table; this time, she walked straight up to one of the men sitting there. "Hi, I'm Angie," she said, extending her hand.

"I'm Maxwell," he said. The others looked up.

I felt sick in the moment, standing there with my two beautiful friends. Those old high school fears, still following me: What if two of these men decide to pick up my friends, and I'll just be hanging out, with nobody wanting me?

Continuing her round of introductions, Angela shook Robert's hand. After that, he stood—the only one to do so—and walked directly over to me.

"Hi," I said. "Uzo."

He told me that he didn't really know the others at the table; the friend he'd planned to meet there had canceled at the last minute. He complimented the gap in my teeth, and he pointed out his own. He reached for my elbow—his touch soft, warm, welcoming.

When the other men got up to leave, I realized that we had

been talking for an hour. One of them walked in front of us, and Robert said to him, "I'll call you later."

There was his out, I realized. I liked him; I wanted to be generous. "You can go be with your friends if you want to," I said.

"No, I'm fine here," Robert said.

We found a table nearby, sat down, and continued for another hour. When I looked up to find Angela and Lisa, they were sitting at the bar top, heads in their hands.

"Now I have to go," I told Robert.

He asked for my number. While I typically said no, I paused for a half second. Just give it to him, I told myself, remembering my resolution to say yes without expectation. So I gave it to him.

On the way to the next party, I told Angela and Lisa that Robert was a filmmaker. We had actually met once before; he was the director of production for a video interview I'd done for a magazine. Hearing about his career definitely sparked my interest: Never in the countless Black or African-oriented mixers I had attended had I encountered another person in the entertainment industry.

Late that evening, as I was getting ready for bed, I saw a message from an unfamiliar number: "Hey, Uzo, it's Robert. I want to see you again."

Not "We should hang out sometime." Not "If it's cool, we can chill one day when we both have a minute." But "I want to see you again." The clarity I'd prayed for.

OUR FIRST DATE had a rough start. Earlier in the day I'd gone to the beach with Onyi and her family, who were in town visiting for the Fourth of July. I was wearing a weave at the time, my own hair tightly braided underneath; I styled it for the date before we left for Rockaway Beach, so I'd be ready to go quickly. At one point in the day, though, Onyi's last born, Michael, was knocked down by a wave, losing his footing. I dove after him instinctively, soaking my head.

As soon as I arrived home, I texted Robert: "Can we push dinner back an hour?" When the hair would not straighten or dry, I begged for more time. Finally, I gave up and jumped in a taxi, only to discover, looking at traffic, that I'd be delayed again.

"Don't worry," he replied to the most recent update. "Get here safely. Thanks for letting me know."

I was two hours late by the time I arrived at the restaurant, and Robert had been sitting there for far too long. The owner came over with a menu and recognized me. She was a kind of *Orange Is the New Black* superfan, wanting to know about my castmates, the next season.

"I'm sorry, I know I'm interrupting . . ." she said, coming back with another question just minutes after taking our order.

It was the first time in my life that anything of this nature had happened, and the experience was about as unwelcome as I might have imagined. By this point, my conversation with Robert had dipped below the surface. He listened intently, asked thoughtful questions, and seemed to really want answers. I shared confidences about parts and pieces of my life I'd never shared, and I did so because *he* shared—something I'd never really experienced.

When the owner's interruptions came, and they did, continuing past the first course all the way to dessert, Robert just sat there, watching my awkward attempts to deflect attention.

"I don't know how to help you," he said quietly at one point, brows raised, as the woman walked away.

I shrugged my shoulders.

"Does this happen all the time?" he asked.

"This has never happened," I said.

I told him that I was still working out what it meant to be a "public person," as my friends in the industry called it. I'd wanted to be an artist, after all, but the kind who is recognized for my work—not recognized on the street. I understood that I couldn't control public attention or confine it to moments when I was on a red carpet. In those moments? Keep it coming. That is where we're playing the game, where we're in the clothes, and I'm one thousand percent, Hey, look at me.

What was not comfortable, I told Robert, was the idea that my real life could become anyone else's theater or entertainment. My *work* was public; anything else that people reacted to was just a projection.

After dinner, we took a walk and wound up sitting and talking in a courtyard near the West Side Highway. "What are you looking for?" Robert asked. "Short-term, long-term relationship?"

"I don't know," I said. "But I'm looking for the real thing."

"What kind of man are you looking for?" he asked.

I told him the truth—that I was looking for someone thoughtful, who was good. Someone respectful and considerate, and a few other qualities as well. I laid bare what I felt, and Robert listened. He thanked me for sharing.

After a brief pause, I asked, "What kind of woman are you looking for?"

"I don't know," Robert said.

When I asked him what kind of relationship he wanted, he had the same answer.

"If you don't know what you're looking for," I told him, "then I don't think you're looking for me."

. . .

ON OUR SECOND DATE, Robert met me in Brooklyn's Prospect Park, at an outdoor food festival I'd wanted to explore. After popping in and out of several food stalls, we carried our lunch around the lake to the steps of the boathouse. This time I was dressed casually, wearing a simple wrap dress, my glasses, and sneakers.

I was not trying to impress him. I didn't want to get on that roller coaster, thinking that my job was to win someone over who was not going to meet me where I wanted to be.

Sitting with our takeout containers, we talked at length about my recent travels—to Nigeria for *Ito Ogbo* and many other adventures beyond that. I'd recently been to Antarctica, which was the first time I'd traveled anywhere by myself.

"I needed to take a break and some time," I told Robert, when he'd asked why I'd gone. Holding my phone, I flipped through the photos I'd taken with my new digital camera. He complimented them, and knowing his line of work, I was bashful. "They're all in autofocus," I said. "I barely know how to use it."

Halfway through another story, about my safari in East Africa, I felt Robert staring at me in a different way. "What?" I asked.

"You've got me rethinking my whole situation," he said.

"OK," I said flatly.

"You know, I was listening to what you were saying and . . . That thing you talked about the other day. I want you to know that I'm serious."

"OK," I said again.

"No," Robert said, "I need you to hear me. I'm serious." The way his eyes locked onto mine, I knew that he was.

That was the beginning. When I was home, he wanted to get

together; when I was away, on set, he wanted to talk. We spoke for hours over the phone or by video. When I came home, he took the subway all the way down from Washington Heights, in the northern part of Manhattan, to my apartment in Brooklyn.

"I want to make you a priority," he told me. I had never been any other man's priority.

We can't predict blessings, and Robert is a walking blessing. He helped me let go of certain stories I had carried for a long time. I'd long felt that there was a big cost to love, but he helped me feel that I was worthy of all my dreams—not just the ones about work, but all of them.

He did come up against a lot of resistance, as my instinct was to question his motivations and, at times, to push him away. He was patient, though. As we got to know each other, I appreciated that patience more and more.

One Friday afternoon, he came to my place holding his camera—a DSLR, like my own. "I'm going to teach you how to shoot," he said.

"Are you joking?"

"No," he said. "Go get your camera; I'll teach you how to use it."

For hours, Robert explained stoppage and the functions, the light meter and all the numbers. Once I had the basics, we took a walk together, cameras in hand, capturing everything we saw. We continued for an hour, all the way down to the Brooklyn Museum, which had opened its doors for a "First Saturday" party with music and dancing.

Finding a quiet corner, we swapped cameras to study each other's work. I stopped on one of his photos of me. I looked and looked again, and then I put down the camera and leaned closer. "I don't know how to describe it," I said. "I feel like you see me the way I see myself."

Sometimes, when I'd see photos of myself, I didn't recognize the person looking back at me. Robert *saw* me, and in so doing, he reminded me of who I really was.

When my mother heard me describe Robert as "a good man," she didn't ask for more details, as this was, truly, what she wanted for me.

I hosted Thanksgiving for my family that year; I invited Robert to dinner, and I asked him to bring his mother and brother as well.

He helped me with preparations early in the week, and on Wednesday, as my mother made the trip over from New Jersey, he went back to his apartment uptown, to give us some space.

As we set the tables, I felt a nervous twinge, remembering past boyfriends who'd shied away from meeting my family. I wondered whether, once gone, Robert would invent a reason to avoid coming back. But he did turn up the next evening holding two bouquets of flowers—one for his mom and one for mine.

"You know how to do it," I said into his shoulder, as we walked through the entryway and into the party already underway.

The group had gathered in the kitchen, as usual, mostly talking and drinking as I was prepping and cooking. My cousin Chubi and his partner, who had come in from Chicago, were chatting with Chi-Chi and Onyi, who were mixing drinks, pouring heavy. My brother-in-law Josch offered Robert a drink, but Robert just stood there, a little on the outside, holding a glass of water.

"Can I get you anything?" Onyi asked him.

"No, no," Robert said.

"I've got this," I told him a few minutes later, gesturing to the stove. "Go socialize. Have a drink. Why aren't you drinking?"

"Your mom is here," he said. "I need to have all my wits about me when I'm talking with her. I don't want to say or do anything crazy."

Oh, I realized then. You're nervous.

By the time Robert met my mother, he had heard countless stories about her: a strong lady, a big talker, as I am, who is not afraid—at all—to ask whatever question she wants to ask. As I've said, he is also an excellent listener, which meant that when they did start talking, she had a captive audience.

They sat down in the living room while my prep continued. As we began to pass the hors d'oeuvres, I realized that my mother was still talking his ear off. I leaned over to him. "You don't have to sit there, if you're done listening."

"No, I like what we're talking about," he said. "I like your mom." So it continued, for two hours, through dinner and beyond, talking until whatever happened next.

Seeing that, I knew that my life would be different.

Robert was the first man who truly gave to me, and he keeps giving. One of the best things he says is, "I'm not going anywhere," even if he's going into another room.

Right there in my every day, I could feel his unconditional love for me—a feeling I had only ever known from a sibling or parent. Experiencing this love from a place of choice felt like freedom. In that free feeling, I could breathe.

Chapter 20

K ranzler called with good news: An offer had come in for a role in a new limited television series, *Mrs. America*—a true story about the movement to ratify the Equal Rights Amendment in the 1970s.

I was asked to play the part of Shirley Chisolm, the first Black woman to be elected to Congress, in 1968—an essential part of the story. "My fighting Shirley Chisholm," as my mother had called her, when I was an elementary school kid in search of a social studies hero.

I was excited by every aspect of the opportunity. Like *Orange*, *Mrs. America* had a predominantly female cast and deep cultural relevance. I had hoped that at some point I might get one of those things again, and there I had both of them. We would film the series in Toronto; I flew there for camera tests. I returned home to Robert, only to leave him a few days later for Los Angeles, where I was the maid of honor in the wedding of my *Godspell* castmate Anna Maria. For the first time in my life, it felt like every corner was filled with something joyful to celebrate, and I could not have been more grateful.

The beautiful ceremony was held at the Cathedral of Our Lady of the Angels, and after, we returned to the hotel for the reception. On my way to the cocktail hour, I ducked into a side room to get my handbag. I pulled out my phone, surprised to see a text from Onyi. My heart froze and then immediately started beating rapidly. In shock, I read the text again, my mind refusing to entirely process what had been written. I had to slow the message down in my head. Our mother was in the hospital, it read. "They found a mass on her pancreas."

Without another thought, I walked straight out of the event and back to my hotel room to grab my things.

From there, I called Chi-Chi, who, three time zones ahead, was out late, at a party. "Did you see Onyi's text?" I asked, when she answered.

"I'm out right now," she said. "I'll look at it later."

"Chi-Chi, look at it now," I said.

"OK?"

"I'm coming home right now," I said. "You need to go to New Jersey right now to be with them."

"I'm *out*, Uzo. Let's talk later," she said, hanging up.

A minute later, as I was feverishly packing, Chi-Chi called me back in tears. "She's going to be fine," I told her, understanding that she'd needed her own moment to process the news. "It could be anything. Just go to New Jersey to be with Onyi." Feeling a little more settled, Chi-Chi left for the hospital.

By the time I called Robert, *I* was in tears. "I need a flight home right now," I said.

"I got you," he said. "Keep packing. I'm going online to look for flights."

A few minutes later, he called with details of my ticket, bought and paid for, on the last flight of the evening, a red-eye into Newark Airport.

By the time Anna Maria made it into her reception, I was already gone.

I sat motionless the entire cross-country flight, watching whatever I was watching, tears streaming steadily down my face as I gripped the seat handle. The woman sitting next to me, who clearly noticed, said nothing. At one point, she soundlessly extended her hand and patted my knee three times—a sympathy.

By the next morning, my mother, sisters, and I were all together in the hospital, and it seemed clear that the doctors were trying to warm us up to whatever they were going to come in and say.

We waited. For days. Doctors needed to run and analyze countless tests before they would offer any diagnosis, let alone a prognosis. We tried to remember, digest, and interpret clinical language for bodily function and complex procedures, and then we tried to forget. At one point, my mother expressed concern that her roots were showing; I fished around in my suitcase and pulled out my sleep cap.

We took naps and watched whatever we could find on TV. We ordered takeout from the fancy steakhouse in town. We waited, stared at our phones, and took turns curling up with our mother in the hospital bed.

Specialist after doctor after specialist came in, asking my mother, "Do you know why you're here?" Though she nodded along, each time she responded to the doctor's grave analysis as if it were the first time she'd heard the news.

This deeply bothered me. *Why are you now acting like you don't know what's happening?* I wanted to ask her. *What are you doing?* I could feel frustration building with no place to direct it.

As we waited, we remembered the wedding of my younger cousin Onyi, which was scheduled for the following weekend. Robert was going to come as my date—to meet my extended family and to experience some of the Igbo wedding traditions. The idea of marriage had begun to creep into our own conversations.

All those plans—next weekends, next chapters—were already far in the distance. Among so many tests and so much unknown silence, we were in an entirely new sea, just learning to swim.

My mother did not want to share what was happening; it was up to me to make up an excuse for the last-minute cancellation.

"We can't say it's a family emergency," I told my sisters, holding up my phone. "Then everyone will call to find out what happened."

We heard a knock on my mother's door: It was the hospital chaplain, who introduced herself as Mary. "Somebody wanted a prayer?" she asked.

We exchanged glances.

"No?" she asked. "Would you like a prayer?"

We shrugged. How about no cancer? Or may this not be true, please?

My mother had a different idea. She invited Mary in. With our heads bowed, my mother said, "We pray that God's will be done, and that we all might be strong enough to answer the call."

That was the ask? Not a miracle, a cure, a break? With seemingly no other choice, my sisters and I looked down at our laps and rolled with it.

On the fourth day, as we sat awaiting the oncologist, I thought back to the number of times over the past year that our mother had been nudging us to come visit her in New Jersey.

"I'm not seeing you together as much as I'd like," she'd often say when I called.

She had five children who would go to the Earth's ends for her, I'd remind her—and who all lived in different cities. Five grown and quite successful children, with different schedules and demands on our lives. It wasn't so easy, I'd say.

Then came this oncologist, saying "pancreatic cancer" and leaving. Confirming what we'd known but hoped, wished, prayed was untrue.

"So what?" I asked, turning around to where she was propped up in bed. "You want to see your children so badly that you came up with this thing?"

"We do what we must do," my mother said.

THE MOMENT WE RECEIVED the definition we wanted and the words had been pronounced, all my sisters and I wanted was to escape. Onyi stood up and left our mother's hospital room for a minute. Then she returned, and Chi-Chi walked out.

I remained in my place, phone in my lap, and looked over at my mother, who lay back as if nothing had changed. Her hands cradled her head on the pillow, and her legs splayed into a figure four, with her left ankle loosely crossed above her opposite knee. Her comfort position.

Chi-Chi returned, and I stood up. "OK," I said. "Now I need to speak to somebody." I pushed through the door that led to the hospital stairwell and lifted the phone to my face. By the time my finger found Kranzler's name, I was already sobbing.

I didn't know the man in this way, but I couldn't help my

reaction. I was supposed to leave to begin filming a new television series in six days, and my entire world had collapsed.

"You have to call the producers," I told him. "I have to be here with my mom to do this. If that can't happen, I can't do it." My character, Shirley Chisholm, led one episode but recurred throughout the season. I knew I was asking for the impossible, but there was no way I could live near the set in Toronto, as my contract stipulated; the only way I could continue was if I could fly back and forth to work from New Jersey.

Kranzler listened without speaking, until he was sure I was finished. "You know, I support you no matter what you want to do," he said. "If you want to leave the project today, we will." He'd call the producer and call me back, he said. "Just sit tight."

I was certain that the role wouldn't work out, but to be honest, I didn't care. Never had my real life—a personal crisis of this magnitude—intersected with my work.

I thanked him. Then I called Robert.

I shared the unbelievable news and then said, "There's a prayer box on my nightstand. Please—we need prayers for my mom. Go over, write something down, and put it in there."

"OK, I'm walking back to the bedroom," he said.

There was a particular marker to go with it, I told him. The paper itself needed to have a torn edge. "Write it with the torn edge side down, fold it in half, and put it in the box," I said.

When I hung up, I called Angela, then another friend, sobbing and even screaming at times.

After that, I took a few deep breaths, trying to collect myself. I had never felt so emotionally fragile. I opened the door back into the lobby and saw Joseph, my brother-in-law, standing near the nurse's desk. I froze for a second, on the precipice of a fall, as he began to walk toward me. There was nothing I could do to save myself. Still, I would try.

"She's going to be fine," I said, trying to avoid his sorrowful eyes piercing my heart and to anchor myself in some percentages or whatever odds I was sure my mother could beat. He just continued coming in for a hug, as if in slow motion. His words echoed Robert's, but his eyes said more. They weren't apologizing that my mother was sick; they were expressing regret over what was to come.

I stiffened in his embrace at first, searching for more facts, but it was useless: All the emotion that had bubbled up in the stairwell returned to the surface, flooding all the reason I'd tried to use as an anchor. This time there was no screaming, only silent tears. Instead of feeling relief or release, I sank further into a dreamlike state that would become familiar.

Fully alert, I questioned everything. I expected to wake up, to hear music, to unearth a talisman, yet I knew my reality lacked a script and camera. There would be no discovery other than two seats near a window, where we could sit and chat.

There could be no conversation other than this: Our telling one another that there were no words.

ONYI, CHI-CHI, and I decided that we'd all join my mother for her chemotherapy appointments at Robert Wood Johnson University Hospital, which was close to Onyi's house in New Jersey.

Soon after, while awaiting her first treatment, my mother and I found ourselves alone in the waiting room.

"Do you believe there is a heaven and a hell?" I asked.

"I don't know," she said, just as Chi-Chi appeared. "I think so."

"I do think we get a window into where we are going," I said. "There's a hell on Earth, I think. Maybe this is also a heaven."

I looked once again at the other people waiting in the straight-backed, pastel-colored chairs—some reading, some staring into space. Some were clearly caregivers: parents, spouses, friends. A few of the patients seemed to be alone. Alone! I could not imagine.

"Look at you here—how your life has gone," I said to my mother. "Your children, on their own feet, coming here to be with you, sitting with you, talking with you, and looking after you. These beautiful grandchildren who love you . . .

"This is what heaven looks like," I concluded, catching my sister's eye.

Upon hearing that flat word, "immunocompromised," all four of my brothers and sisters and I had gathered in my mother's apartment and cleaned the entire thing. This was my insanity: new bedding, new flatware, a new toaster oven. If there was a chance that something could kill her, then we would get rid of everything and start over. We would do the good work now, starting fresh, to salvage as many days as possible.

In our culture, and many others, caregiving is not only your responsibility; it's the highest currency. The greatest show of love is to care for a life, your life, your blood. The circle begins with a parent, who bathes you, stays up at night to breastfeed you, finds food to give you, and goes without for you.

I believe all debts are paid before we leave here. Care is the most loving and respectful offering that those who give so much can receive.

My sisters and I alternated three-day shifts caring for our mother, adjusting for our own family and work obligations as best we could. When we had tricky spots—if Chi-Chi's agency had a big meeting, for example, while I was on set—one of our brothers would drive down from Massachusetts to cover for us.

As expected, we siblings had plenty of spats, fights, and frustrations as we struggled with our new reality. Still, for my mother, our presence really was a kind of heaven. In the midst of our scrubbing and squabbling and list-making, our arranging and our preparing, she sat, beaming, as her children worked together.

Chapter 21

T he role that I stepped into was not a simple one. I knew of Shirley Chisholm, and I knew too that the world didn't really know Shirley Chisholm.

"My fighting Shirley Chisholm." Whenever the stories of famous women were told—particularly famous Black women—through art projects or essays, my mother would invoke the phrase. I hadn't really considered the depth of this description, or the story behind this "fighting," but the phrase had stood out.

Shirley Chisholm was one of my mother's heroes. As my mother was my hero, I'd insisted, as a child, that Shirley Chisholm was my hero too.

It wasn't until I was an adult reading Cornel West and Henry Louis Gates Jr.'s *The African-American Century* that I learned that Chisolm, the first Black woman in Congress, had also run for president. I had recently moved to her district, Brooklyn's Twelfth, and she was everywhere: Shirley Chisholm Post Office. Shirley Chisholm Day Care Center. There, decades earlier, she had worked her way from teacher to the halls of Congress. Knowing the limited role the world saw for her, she fought every day for all people who had been marginalized.

Through photographs, her autobiography, and other accounts, I understood just how groundbreaking her presidential run had really been. I learned that the "fighting" prefix my mother always used was one that Congresswoman Chisholm—or Shirley, as I came to know her—had given herself. She needed to be heard.

Shirley was a woman running for president—a Black woman—at a time when both of these identities were beyond what most Americans believed a president could be. She was also a Black woman who did not look, sound, or act like the Black women who were seen and celebrated in her day, such as Diahann Carroll and Lena Horne.

Her permed wig and brightly patterned suits and dresses were the armor that she wore, and nothing more frivolous than that. She knew that it didn't matter how stirring, how hopeful her speeches were. She needed people to first see her; only then could they consider her platform and point of view as they might those of her opponent, Senator George McGovern.

I fully embraced Shirley's look, but I felt differently when exploring the idea of taking on her pronounced—and often discussed—lisp. "I'm not conscious of it," she once said. "If you pay a lot of attention to it, it could give you hang-ups."

The sentence could have come out of my own mother's mouth.

My work wasn't simply a matter of "doing" Shirley; I feared that putting on the lisp might distract from her powerful words. Our audience did not know Shirley Chisholm. I wanted them to really hear what she said during a time when many—even prominent feminists—doubted that a woman of color could achieve all that she had set out to do.

I could see so much of my own belief in self, my *mother's* belief in self, in Shirley.

"I didn't get to where I am," Shirley once said, "by waiting on someone else's permission."

The woman she wanted to present to the world—a forceful, fierce, singular image—was not the whole Shirley. I watched documentary footage of her dancing. She looked so light and joyful and innocent—a young spirit.

Near the film's end, she appeared again at the Democratic National Convention in Miami to relinquish the twenty-eight delegates she'd won in the primaries to her opponent, George McGovern. I was struck by the sound she made and the way her face fell into her hands; I felt I was witnessing the collapse of a child's dreams.

Those tiny glimpses—her light steps, her childlike energy—were Shirley Chisolm. In that moment at the convention, I could see and feel the weight on her shoulders.

In every word and action, Shirley had rejected the idea that her presidential run was about identity—about being the first woman, the first Black woman. She had insisted, from the time she had kicked off her campaign, that she was not the candidate of "Black America" or the "women's movement," though she was proud of both affiliations. "I am the candidate of the people of America," she had said, knowing that her platform could and would be twisted, by others, into a race or gender agenda.

This affected the way she could approach issues that mattered most. Not only was Shirley unable to speak freely, as the other white, male candidates could. She also had to insist that her race and gender were not hurdles for her—pretending that all candidates were on equal footing on the campaign trail. She did not spend her time discussing how discrimination caused so many inequities in this country, as she seemed to know America was not ready to hear that truth.

Watching her expression, at the convention, I saw how much identity does matter in politics—and, for her, how high the cost.

How did Shirley define herself? I scribbled potential answers to this question on the plane rides back and forth, from Toronto to New York. I had my eye on the clock and the calendar more than I wished; my priority, always, was to relieve my sisters and accompany my mother to her treatment. Perhaps, in a strange way, the personal challenges that physically separated me from my *Mrs. America* castmates and from daily life on set helped to serve the material.

I didn't have this perspective at the moment; I simply felt overwhelmed. I was studying as diligently as I ever had, but I couldn't hold a line in my head. I found myself searching for words and needing to think about them in a way that was not at all familiar.

I flew in the day before we filmed my scene in *Mrs. America*'s opening episode. I hadn't had a blink of sleep for days. I faced the actor playing Shirley's husband, standing in a set designed to look like the bedroom of a hotel suite. There, inside my character, in a moment that was just hours after the Senate approved the Equal Rights Amendment, all I could say, in my head, was, My mother has cancer.

I tried to work harder. Robert came up and helped me run lines, again and again. When I wanted to quit, he was my biggest cheerleader.

It helped sometimes to look down the line of chairs in the hair and makeup trailer, reminding myself how far I'd come. If *Orange* felt like the best part of high school drama club, then this here was senior year: Each of my castmates was a force in her own right, beginning with the great Cate Blanchett, one of the show's executive producers. In those chairs were so many other women who had crushed it, repeatedly—who had been crushing it for years, even decades. Consummate professionals who still had fire for the work and who still put in the work.

This cast and crew taught me about kindness. They all knew of my mother's illness. Even those with especially heavy lifts on the show and so much going on in their lives made a point to stop, when they saw me running around like a crazy person, and ask, "How are you doing today?"

There were days when I answered honestly, but I rushed through the details, entirely avoiding my feelings. They saw me anyway.

One day I was really itching to finish so that I could accompany my mom to her treatment the following morning. In between takes I watched Coco Francini, one of our executive producers, scrambling on her laptop to find flights. "Got one," she said finally. "You'll be out of here at four o'clock."

The giants we were portraying, these second-wave feminists so focused on equal rights and workplace leadership, had produced our generation—the women now before me, behind the scenes, pivoting and managing and multitasking. Women like Coco, or her fellow executive producer Stacey Sher, who rose to the occasion when it was hard—not just when it was easy. They were the ones searching, coordinating, beyond the expected or even the imaginable.

"YOU'RE SO STRONG." During this time in my life, one phrase echoed from seemingly every corner: I heard it from my castmates, my team, my friends—even my siblings. They meant it as a compliment, I knew—one that had long been extended to my mother, now more than ever. It was a phrase, even, that my mother had used to describe me.

I began to hesitate, though, when I heard those words.

"Oh, Uzo, I don't know how you do it," said one of my friends, who was also experiencing personal challenges. "I'd be a wreck, but the way you're handling it all with such strength . . ."

"Thank you," I said.

But what I heard was: *You never feel sad about this. Your mother is never too exhausted to get out of bed.*

But I had been on the floor, multiple times, inconsolable, Robert holding me. I try not to use the word "hysterical" because of how it has been used throughout history to harm women, but I also don't think I ever really understood what it implied until I heard myself screaming and couldn't make myself stop. "You were speaking Igbo at one point," Robert said in the calm following one of my crashes. "You weren't even speaking English."

The idea of Black women's impenetrable strength—the suggestion that we don't hurt or even *feel* beyond anger or pain—brushes us off and dismisses us as if to say only, "You've got this." Shirley Chisholm tried to project this strength, even though her spirit was actually rather light.

If all we are ever told we can be is strong, then we can never have space to be the opposite.

IN 2020, the American conversation about racial injustice exploded just as the COVID-19 pandemic first took hold of the world, forcing many of us into lockdown. While Black people had long tried to explain our experience to our white friends and colleagues, it felt to me as if, for the first time, they were seeing it.

On February 23, Ahmad Arbery, a twenty-five-year-old Black man, was shot to death while jogging in his hometown—a horror that soon played out on video for the world to see. A few months later, with the murder of George Floyd at the hands of Minneapolis police, an even broader swath of Americans sat up and understood: This does not just "happen."

Nine minutes and twenty-nine seconds of a police officer kneeling on a Black man's neck: There is no possible explanation. Even if they had heard or said Black Lives Matter before, now collectively, white people were reaching for a deeper understanding.

A few months before the start of the pandemic, I'd begun working with a new therapist. I'd come to her with a goal: to learn how to say goodbye. "I don't think I know how to do this, or that I can do this," I'd told her during our first session.

At first, I'd been unsure whether we were a good fit. Our dialogue didn't always feel so easy or, at times, safe. I sometimes felt uncomfortable sharing parts of my story with people who had lived outside the Black experience, as she had. I admitted that I had tried to find a Black therapist but had been unsuccessful. "Do you have a problem being with a white therapist?" she'd asked.

"I don't think so," I'd said. "I've already had one therapist before. I think it should be fine, so long as I feel heard."

We'd had a few bumpy moments after that. I spent the bulk of one session explaining the concept of code-switching to her; in the next session, she asked if I was sure that the event I'd been describing "had really happened like that."

"I know because I was born Black—I've been Black for a really long time," I'd told her. I don't believe my therapist was aware of her second-guessing, but I was still frustrated: The only person she knew who'd had the experience was me.

After the murder of George Floyd, a different woman came to our sessions. I can't describe it in any other way. All of a sudden, subjects that I had brought up earlier in our relationship—such as my fears for my nephew, who at age thirteen was already six feet tall—found a softer and more spacious landing. The look in her eyes showed that she truly heard me.

I saw her change because the world had changed. I changed too.

I began to speak more publicly about how working in certain parts of my industry had brought me back to feelings of inadequacy I hadn't known since childhood. Both then and still, I'd stepped into the world believing that I could do anything I put my mind to—gold medalist, Supreme Court justice, you name it—and then I'd heard the world say my belief did not matter.

I had once imagined that a certain degree of success might diminish these uncertainties, but instead, it amplified them. Oh, you're saying that I can be in the film, but not in the part I want? You're saying I can be on the cover of this but not *that* magazine? Why again? Why not these clothes?

I'd been comfortable speaking about racism and discrimination in theory, but not about my personal experiences. Now, I began to open up about what it meant to see myself minimized, feel myself minimizing, as we all bought into the overly simplified way that Black women, like so many other groups, were presented. Others' ideas about me still had more power over me than my own.

I'd auditioned, unsuccessfully, for Pippin's Leading Player on Broadway, certain that my time had come. Looking back, however, there was nothing groundbreaking about considering me for parts written for a man. It *hadn't* been visionary to cast Whoopi Goldberg, in her early thirties and in the prime of her youthful beauty, as the titular role in *Jumpin' Jack Flash*.

That wasn't revolution; it was evolution. The people watching our auditions already thought of us as men.

"The women who look like me were the 'field Negroes,' out with the men," I told a colleague one day. "This is the origin of these castings that seemed groundbreaking. But I wasn't in the house; I was in the field, picking 350 pounds of cotton alongside the men and experiencing any other kind of suffering that came along with it."

Nine times out of ten, we Black women are not out there trying to be strong—at your audition, on your television, or in our real lives. This was as simple a stereotype as seeing Black kids "wiling out" instead of having a good time.

This strength that was so praised was also problematic. "Hard" is born somewhere. How exhausted does someone become when constantly convinced she isn't of any value?

Black women in my industry have always known the depth of their talent—the essence of who they are. Yet for so long, for so many, so much was unrecognized. I began looking at the youthful photos of my idols in a new way. All I could think was, shame on this business, this world, that tried to make these women feel like anything other than the queens they are.

You see her when she was young and beautiful? She looked light; she had energy. She had received wide acclaim for playing a beautiful woman. Now? You made her feel like the ugliest thing on this planet. By paying her less, you told her that she did not matter.

"I got the Oscar, I got the Emmy, I got the two Tonys, I've done Broadway, I've done off-Broadway, I've done TV, I've done film," Viola Davis once said. "I've done all of it. I have a career that's probably comparable to Meryl Streep, Julianne Moore, Sigourney Weaver. . . . People say, 'You're a Black Meryl Streep. There is no one like you.' OK, then if there's no one like me, you think I'm that, you pay me what I'm worth."

That summer, with protests in the streets and on my television, I reflected on the reasons behind my own insecurities. I remembered how I'd been received in some of my earliest auditions and the implications of that early feedback: You, girl, don't sing operatic sopranos. You, Uzo, are not "an Eliza."

Even though, in *My Fair Lady*, Eliza is supposed to be a poor street person. Isn't that my market? Aren't I supposed to be the crackhead?

Making jokes came easily. More difficult and deeply urgent was my fear of building walls around my career, just as I'd once done in my personal life. I now understood that two things could be true at the same time: I could be grateful for my success and equally aware of how much further my business has to progress.

As Shirley so rightfully pointed out, I couldn't wait for the world to change on my behalf.

"Ambition," a word from which I'd long shied away, came up often, unexpectedly, around this time. The host of a podcast, a friend, used it in such a nonchalant, beautiful way, "So what's your next ambitious goal?" she asked.

"I really love that you used that word," I replied, smiling at her image on my laptop. "I don't think I've ever heard it as a positive for a woman."

For all my childhood and most of my professional life, that word, "ambitious," and another, "competitive," felt dangerous. Now this drive felt essential.

I was no longer interested in pretending that society's perception of me capped the possibilities. I had wasted enough of my own time, in my very young days, absorbing that nonsense. Waiting for other people's acknowledgment had held me back in ways I did not ever want to experience again.

I sensed that people's ears were tuned differently, and I resolved to be even clearer with my team about the roles and projects I was interested in pursuing. If I were perceived as "strong," then I wanted to use that power in a way that actually felt good. If I couldn't, then I would empower myself to use the word "no."

"What we have to be, right now, is revolutionary in the system," I told my team. "You see a woman like myself. You see how this has played into the type of work that I've received. I hope you see the opportunity."

"Revolution," I continued, "is taking someone like me and putting her in any role and genre they'd consider right for a white woman. That is a revolutionary idea."

FROM THE FIRST FEW MOMENTS I'd sat with my sisters in my mother's hospital room, I'd sensed that we were in new territory. As her illness progressed, so did this feeling. We stared down so much that I had never imagined doing.

Onyi, Chi-Chi, and I were three grown women dealing with a crisis, and we were each finding our own ways to try to take control. Yet somewhere along the line, we—along with our brothers— tacitly agreed that the only important thing was getting this right for our mother. We doubled down, trying our best to be supportive and reassuring, even as old childhood stories and roles began to rise up. We tried to give one another breaks whenever we could or sensed that one of us needed one. We often needed one, for when we were on, we were really on.

Every time I prepared to leave my apartment in Brooklyn for my mother's place in New Jersey, I stopped first at the African market to get the ingredients I knew I needed. When I arrived, one of the first things I did was unload the groceries, breaking out all the big pots and pans to make days', weeks' worth of food.

I was grateful for the time I'd put in learning to prepare so many dishes—even if some of my attempts to satisfy my mother's cravings started out terribly. I knew my way around Nigerian cooking, but I wasn't practiced in the holiday foods for which she had a hankering. I'd never before made them away from her watchful eye.

Somehow, the spattering hot oil wouldn't be hot enough for the akara, leaving the fritters too soaked through, or it would be too hot, burning the outside while leaving a mess within.

My mother was honest. "Too much salt," she pronounced, when I delivered my first attempt to her. I pushed on, realizing that I would get the hang of it. By round four, my mother agreed.

So many little touches of mothering I'd long taken for granted began to slip away. I tried to reassure myself, as I stirred the pots on the stove: Now I could care for her in the way that she had cared for me.

Many days I felt grief-filled, sick to my stomach, doubtful, or devastated. Robert made it possible for me to get through. He minded our house and cared for our dog, Fenway, while I was in New Jersey; if I were on an extended stay there, he'd often join us, setting up his laptop on my mother's dining room table to work while she lay in front of the television. He was always checking up on her, asking what she needed, or sitting and talking with her.

If we were hosting my mother at our place, Robert knew the routine. He'd learned how to make fufu and make it well; if I were away for work, he'd pound the yams for her and serve the fufu with the soup I'd left in the refrigerator.

Whenever our conversations were lighthearted, he picked up his camera.

In one of his videos, my mother is playing Macbeth; it turns out, she still remembered the role. For Robert's benefit, we recite the soliloquies together. Her stance is confident, even in this frail state, in a chair.

Some of the passages felt especially resonant.

> Present fears
> Are less than horrible imaginings

The holidays approached. Robert and I found a gap in our work schedules and my mother's treatment schedule and planned a little getaway for the three of us. We chose New Hope, Pennsylvania, and found an inn with a well-appointed, top-floor room overlooking a beautiful farm.

By this time, my mother was using a walker. We made sure, when booking her room, that there would be no reason she needed to navigate the stairs unless she wanted to. We escorted her down those stairs to see a performance of *A Christmas Carol*—one of her favorites—at the Bucks County Playhouse. When we returned to the hotel afterward, she was on cloud nine.

Later that evening, I went to check on her and I discovered her downstairs, sitting by the woodstove and looking out the living room window.

"How'd you get over here?" I asked, sitting down to join her.

"I walked!" she said, smiling. "I just wanted to enjoy the fire."

A few months later, Robert asked my mother for my hand in marriage. Even though she had chemo brain at the time, she snapped to and managed to keep the secret under wraps.

There was a cultural way that an engagement had to happen, she told Robert. He had to ask my Uncle Ifeanyi, her immediate older brother; he would tell Robert to talk with their eldest brother, my Uncle Adazie. Robert knew my mother's opinion of him and of our future plans; he was confident that they would acknowledge that and agree.

When Robert proposed, there was no question of my answer. We were already bound to each other, having gone through many betters and too many worses. Somehow, we loved each other more on the far side of each "worse" than we had before.

I don't know why God needed me to know all that before I said yes, but He did.

Chapter 22

My mother arrived in Canada in 1972, having lived an entire lifetime since she'd first briefly encountered her now-fiancé. She'd fallen in love for the first time; she'd graduated from college. War had come, hard loss, and a passage to Sweden—a way out.

Throughout, my mother had carried her very big dreams, which included her union with this brilliant man who was going to be a minister. She'd long been excited by the prospect of going to America, marrying him, and living with him in the United States.

I have a photo of my mother in her Western wedding dress, sitting in an armchair with her hair all done up. Whose armchair, I don't know—there was no one for her, no family there. Neither do I know who was behind the camera and what they were thinking or saying to her to elicit the confident smile on her face. What I see now, as I hold it up, is a survivor: A woman who has lived the life of a thousand men and is excited to live a thousand more. A woman who knows what she wants.

For this woman in the photo, life did not turn out to be what she had imagined.

She and her new husband settled in Connecticut, and she set up a brisk business selling Avon cosmetics to other women in the area, creating deals and incentives too, just as her mother had done in Obosi's markets. She spent time in East Orange, New Jersey, at the home of her first husband's relations, who were part of a thriving Igbo community. In her new hometown, she began teaching tennis, a sport she loved, and then she became pregnant.

Shortly after Rich was born, her first husband began beating her. Rich has memories of all this, vivid memories, which are not mine to share. I can only say that after much difficulty, Onyi arrived—a blessing, with a name meaning "gift from God."

Finally, the situation became so dire that she wrote a letter home, telling her parents everything. A month or two later, she found in her mailbox a letter from her father, containing one British pound.

With that, she began planning to leave—to "run for her life," as my Aunty Ifey said later. Instead of depositing her tennis instructor salary and Avon commissions, my mother began cashing them, slowly stockpiling the money. When she felt she had enough to leave, she called Uncle Adazie in London. Travel to the UK was now possible but still seemed too risky, with my uncle's high-profile job. They schemed further.

One day, my mother's first husband came home from work to discover his wife and children were gone. He drove around all day and night not knowing they had skipped town on a plane, and that, by the time he was searching, they had reached Obosi.

Three months later, he suffered a brain aneurysm that killed him instantly. He was thirty-six, otherwise healthy, and then: gone.

In every part of the world, for good reason, questions arise if a man dies early. In a culture that does not condone divorce, when a woman has left a man who dies early, there are implications.

This is particularly true in traditional Igbo culture, where children, like women, belong to men. When a woman is widowed, she stays with her children in the home of her late husband. For a year she stays in mourning there, wearing all black, going nowhere and looking at nothing.

As my mother's late husband's body was being prepared for burial and transported back to Nigeria, she and "his" children traveled from Obosi a few hours southeast to Umuahia. As his affairs were sorted, she remained in their home, under his family's watchful eye.

It was not a comfortable place to be, as my aunties and uncles remember. Aunty Azuka came to the village to visit and saw what was happening—the insults, and even worse the accusations—and she defended my mother. Then she went back to Obosi, to update her parents and the rest of the family on the situation.

My mother feared for her children's future, knowing that there was honor—and money—at stake. Before she'd left, she'd taken the advice of my Aunty Rachel, contacting her husband's life insurance agent and claiming the funds; she held them in the US, to be leaned on later. She knew better than to hand over what was rightfully hers, from the truth on down.

One day, she discovered that Rich's and Onyi's passports were missing. Around then she heard a concerning new line of conversation: Would someone "pay" for what "had been done"?

One of the house girls came to her with the gossip: After the service, they would walk outside for the burial. Someone would take the children. Then, as they lowered the casket into the ground, they'd throw my mother in and bury her alive.

This news got back to Obosi, and so, when my mother's first

husband's family gathered for the funeral, my mother's family was right alongside. They sat quietly on their side of the church and then stood up to leave the service, one by one, my mother slipping out among them. By the time everyone walked back out into the sunshine, my mother was already on her way to Obosi.

She'd been devastated to leave Rich and Onyi; her children were her entire life. Still, she knew this was her only chance: Their father's family would do them no harm, and she needed to survive in order to get all three of them back to the United States—their home, and a place that recognized the essential role she played in their lives.

My mother received an offer for a teaching position at an Anglican girls' grammar school near Enugu, about seventy-five miles north, which she accepted. For the next two years, Rich and Onyi lived with their father's family in Umuahia.

I can share only what my mother told me, which is that she was desperate to see them. The only way was to borrow Aunty Azuka's white Volkswagen Beetle and make the two-hour drive down the Enugu-Umuahia Road. There she would wait by the fence of their school, hoping to catch a glimpse of them in the yard or grab a quick conversation during recess.

Life continued this way for a while, until the family learned of her visits, took the children out of the school, and put them in a new one. From that point, they made sure that one of their own children—or a niece or a nephew—was in a class with Rich and Onyi, to keep watch.

My mother gained the trust of the new school's headmaster, however. And, taking pity on her, he tried to help. "This woman is allowed to come in here and see her children during recess," he told the school staff. "And nobody is to discuss when she comes."

My mother took care of Rich and Onyi in ways that she could. She took some of their dirty laundry home to wash and bring back clean. Sometimes, on her way to the school, she'd stop at a nearby food stall to pick up something they could eat together.

I have a picture from these days, which my Aunty Azuka must have taken during one of these visits: my mother looking slim and content, sitting on the front bumper of the Beetle in a black, sleeveless floral-print dress, one arm around Rich and the other around Onyi.

"Onyi would cry through the whole visit, start to finish," my mother once told me. "Rich would cry too, asking so many questions: 'Why can't I come with you?'"

Behind the scenes, her siblings, both in Nigeria and abroad, were working on new passports for the children and organizing the rest of the papers besides.

"One day, when we're ready, it will be time," was my mother's reply.

Her family planned how they'd help her return to the US, but they feared they'd be overheard in a small place like Obosi, full of open windows and neighborhood gossip. So a group of them drove a few hours south, to the city of Aba, to discuss the safest path from schoolyard to airplane. Upon touching down in the US, my mother could make a fresh start. Her children, who, like her, were American citizens, could be *her* children again.

Their plan would culminate in an intercontinental flight out of Lagos International Airport, in the west. The typical mode of travel there from the southeast, a short flight, was simply not possible. The closest airport was where the family of her late husband would likely look first.

No, they would need to go by car, and fast, before they were discovered. They would need to hunker down for a while in Lagos, with my Uncle Bertie. Only then could they get on a plane to London, and from there, God willing, to America.

To make all this happen, they needed cars—plural. Remember, this was Nigeria in the early '70s; it couldn't be assumed that if someone had a car, that car worked, or that it could drive miles and miles without stopping. They decided to use four cars and switch them up along the way. This would ensure that each one could go the distance; it would also complicate matters for anyone trying to track them.

They told no one—not even their own parents. The only person in Obosi who knew was Aunty Nkem.

Aunty Azuka sold her Volkswagen to my mother for a dollar: "Just for the bill of sale," she said. That would be the start. They plotted out each meeting place, where, each time, another friend with a better car would be waiting. The last car, belonging to my Aunty Felicia's husband, my Uncle Ben, went the longest distance, all the way to Lagos.

When the time came to leave, Uncle Ben picked up clean clothes for the children: My mother would need to change them out of their school uniforms for the drive ahead.

Then, as usual, my mother drove the Volkswagen to the school.

She saw Onyi first. "For the first time, she didn't cry," my mother told me, "because I told her, 'Today, you can come.'"

When Rich saw my mother and heard her say that it was time to go, he refused to leave the school grounds without proof that Onyi was safe.

There was no time to argue. At any moment, the child keeping watch over my sister would report that she hadn't come back. My mother hustled Rich to the car and rapped on the window. Onyi sat up; only then did he agree to come.

While all this was happening, Aunty Nkem sat by the side of the road, stressed. She had been there all day, worried that the Volkswagen had shown up early, somehow, and she'd missed them. She also felt guilty about the decision to keep their parents in the dark, even if it did offer temporary protection: When the police showed up to ask where the children had gone, my grandmother could—and did—answer truthfully.

"I don't know what you're talking about," she said.

Eventually, the car came into view, and they made the switch. And then again and again. As night fell, and the police began searching at the airport, they were speeding toward Lagos, relieved—and hungry. At one point, Uncle Ben insisted on pulling over to a roadside stand to get some food.

"Let's go!" my mother said to urge him along. By then, she was in no mood to delay. "We can get a plane in the morning!"

My Uncle Bertie was a tough man: "I dare these people to come after us," he said, to reassure her. "We'll rest and then you'll go."

That was what they did. My mother and siblings flew to London, where they stayed for some time, and then, finally, to New York City. With that, they had re-immigrated to the US—a place that they had never intended to leave.

My mother had nowhere to go, but she also didn't want to be a burden to anyone. For a little while, she and my siblings lived in her car. Then Aunty Rachel insisted that they come live with her, her husband, and her four kids in New Jersey. These friends like family did everything they could to help my mother get back on her feet.

With some of the life insurance funds, my mother enrolled in graduate school at Kean College to pursue a master's degree in social work. She found work and moved Rich and Onyi into a place of their own, and then Aunty Azuka joined them to pursue her own undergraduate studies.

When my mother graduated, Aunty Rachel threw her party and invited one of her cousins, my father, a good-looking, single Igbo man who was about my mother's age, with some means and a career ahead of him. Then, at thirty-nine, with two kids and all of that behind her, my mother's next chapter began.

The road was hard, as you can see, but the journey was worth it. When I was born, not long after, my mother called me Uzoamaka. The meaning of the middle name she gave me, Nwanneka, directly translates to "nothing is as important as your siblings." For my mother, the name more directly meant "nothing is as important as your sisters."

By this my mother meant Aunty Azuka, who gave her the car for a dollar. The manager, the woman behind the scenes—the one my mother always called "my FYI." She also meant Aunty Nkem, who finally told my grandparents what had happened, once my mother and siblings had reached safety. The one who forever held my mother's trust—as well as her money, passports, and papers, whenever she returned to Nigeria. She also meant my Aunty Felicia, may she rest, whose husband, Ben, and their car made that fateful drive. Not least did she mean Aunty Rachel, who took the money in my mother's safe and invested it for her, rolling it over and compounding it. And my Aunty Rachel, who brought my father to her, and who had taken us in as her own.

Nigerian children belong not only to parents but to an entire family; most children, including all of my siblings, have blood relations as godparents. (It's also the case that Nigerian parents have so many siblings, there are more than enough godparents to go around!) Still, when I was born, my mother decided to highlight this important story and share that honor with her friends as well as her sisters. Still today, Aunty Rachel and I have this connection.

This is the way of life, for my mother and her sisters, and now for me and mine: Children raise other children, and then they carry one another. For so long, like Onyi and me, my mother and my Aunty Azuka had that bit of space between them, where they were in different worlds and different roles—child and young adult, or child and parent even.

Then there is a window-closing event, after which all the children stand in the adults' places, figuring out how to make something happen.

Chapter 23

B ecause of my mother's condition, there would be no waiting for a wedding—even if we were in the middle of a pandemic. Robert and I picked a date and began to arrange a very small ceremony at Chi-Chi's new home in upstate New York. With speed came simplicity. Details soon fell into place.

I'd long had a real vision for the days—plural—of my wedding: I'd wanted both a trad wedding, with the clothes and the breaking of the kola nut, and another, "white" wedding, officiated by a pastor, where I would wear the dress and the veil and Robert and I would cut the first slice of a many-tiered cake.

It's hard to plan such an elaborate event when you know that the most important person to you, up until that moment, is leaving. Arranging multiple parties over multiple days was out of the question. Our social distancing restrictions were so tight that we needed to keep things as simple and as small as possible. Many of the people dearest to us, including Robert's grandmother, were not able to fly.

While Robert and I wouldn't change a thing, it was quite a complicated way to come together.

Just as Robert had proposed to me in the traditional Igbo way, we planned to incorporate aspects of Igbo culture into our day. This meant the world to me. When our conversations had first turned toward marriage, I had wondered: When I become a part of his house, do I somehow cease being Igbo?

Robert welcomed learning about and embracing my culture so much that he even took Igbo language lessons. He did so not only because he knew it would make me happy but because he valued our history.

Robert's ancestors on his mother's side were enslaved here in the US. Tragically, there is a rupture, an erasure—a limit to what we can know about his own ancestors. He was also raised in Brooklyn in the 1990s, celebrating a shared heritage among Black people, regardless of where you were from.

We chose a wedding date in typically beautiful September, when the leaves in upstate New York are just beginning to turn. When the day arrived, the weather forecast for the East Coast looked grim. Checking off the last few items on our to-do list, fearful of storms, I began to worry that all we had planned would not feel like enough.

I couldn't express any of these concerns to my family; I didn't want to make anyone feel bad. Robert and I had greatly anticipated this day, after all; I just hated that there was a clock ticking in the background.

Time has a sound, and I could hear it.

Love fought through all that doubt, somehow, and the day *did* become my day. The weather—unexpectedly brilliant blue skies— was an outward expression of its perfection. There in this uncertain moment, Robert and I were making our own good news: "A shining spot in a tragedy on top of a tragedy," as he later said.

As skeptical as I'd been about the presence of so many loved ones over a video stream, I really could *feel* everyone surrounding us. After the exchange of vows, rings, and our first kiss, we rushed over to Robert's laptop, where we were greeted by grids and grids of loved ones: some in full tuxedo, others in shirts and ties, T-shirts, even pajamas. All gorgeous. It was the first time in years we'd seen many of them. It wasn't the same, but it *was* enough.

We slipped away once the party was underway, to change into our matching trad. Then we could step out for the first time, officially, as husband and wife. We chose to wear a rich cream color: Robert's outfit had subtle gold touches, in a pocket square and his cap. I wore mine loud, in an intricately embroidered *aso-oke* fabric that would have made my grandmother proud. Plus a fabulous *ichafu* on my head in the most gorgeous coral color. Plus a sequined, golden feathered fan. Plus, plus, plus.

All this coordination was essential, you see: In our Igbo tradition, only a couple can match.

When it came time for Uncle Ifeanyi to break the kola nut, we gathered around the computer once again. We bowed our heads as he did the honors from Cairo, where he and my Aunty Uche had been stranded since the start of the pandemic. My brothers broke our kola nut, passing it to my mother, Robert's father, and his brother.

Every moment and decision leading up to our wedding—the preparations, the logistics, the layers of medical concern—had felt so loud. The inevitable was more than a ticking in the background, if I'm honest; it was a constant, high-pitched scream. September 12, 2020, was the first and possibly only day during that hard season when everything around me dropped into a whispering quiet. I could hear again.

What a gift—one that I know only now how much I needed.

"IF YOU CAN'T COMMUNICATE, then it won't last." That was relationship advice my mother repeated from my living room couch one day, reminding me that she had seen it from many angles as a social worker.

"You and Robert have a lot to talk about as individuals and as married people," she said. She then clarified that she didn't mean I had to share everything. "He may want to know, but if it is something you don't want to tell him or expose, keep it to yourself," my mother said. Autonomy and privacy were important for her, I knew. So was self-reliance.

"That is a most important side," she said. "If you don't want to talk to him, keep moving on. If you're driving in a car, keep moving on."

Motherhood was challenging, she continued, "but not as hard as communication in marriage. It's easier to communicate with your children—especially when they're young. If you don't have any communication with your children by age six, you've lost them."

We had some days like this, stolen days, when the conversation was lively and the hours were ours.

"What do you love about being *my* mother?" I asked later that day, sensing an opening.

"I love you, Uzo, because you are Uzo, and you are mine," my mother said. "No matter what you say, you are mine. People used to say, 'Uzo will kill herself and her brothers' . . . because you did not get ready for school on time. Especially with that big van.

Everybody—Chi-Chi and Junior—would all be ready for school, and you hadn't started."

"I'm still in bed," I said with a laugh, grateful to be there, with her, once again.

MY SIBLINGS AND I began to talk more openly and more often about the realities facing our family. We were honest with our mother and, more and more, she was honest with us.

Still, to me, the words seem disembodied: *As I write this, my mother is dying.*

"Are you afraid of dying?" I asked my mother one day.

"No," my mother said. "I just wish I had a little more time."

The tenor of our conversations was familiar. Faith, work, gratitude. My mother echoed what she'd always said, whenever we'd faced challenges. The year she'd prepared for knee surgery, she had written in my birthday card, "I'm praying to God every day to continue to maintain a positive and upbeat attitude."

Now, as I sat with her, I considered the moments of trial she'd faced and overcome. How could you *not* believe?

I comforted myself with the idea that death meant something different to my mother than it did to me. Then I remembered how she'd always put on a brave face, no matter the circumstance, and I felt fear and worry return. If there was one thing that she was going to hold on to, it was making sure that her kids were protected.

One day my mother told us that her father and her sister and God had all come to her, to tell her about heaven. "God told me I'm going," she said, not for our own comfort but in a way that conveyed true excitement, as if to say, "I'm really glad that I get to go."

I don't know that I've ever felt as much pride as I did seeing the expression on her face. Wow, I thought. You did enough right that you get to go. I don't know how much you need to pour into life's glass to get to go, but you get to go.

"Give us a sign, somehow, when you get there," I told her. "You know—just something to let us know that you've made it."

"I don't know if I can give you a sign," my mother replied. "But if I can, I will."

As the pandemic raged, the premiere and promotion of *Mrs. America* took place entirely online. The only real in-person "appearance" I'd done was a solo mission: On March 18, I donned a mask and rode my bike from Brooklyn into an empty Times Square, so I could see for myself the billboards with our character's likenesses on prominent display. I posted it on social media in a kind of surreal celebration.

The cast was given early access to the show, which I watched with Robert and my mother—or partially watched, in my case. When Shirley's episode came on, I found so many around-the-house chores to do.

They both loved it, lavishing praise; when I learned my work had been nominated for an Emmy Award, we all celebrated together.

The virtual appearances I did to promote the project were challenging, but, given the circumstances, they also provided great relief. Without the responsibility of travel into Manhattan or Los Angeles for a meeting or a photo shoot, I could stay at my mother's and then step away, into a bedroom, when I needed to work.

I prepared for the subdued pomp of the first-ever virtual Emmy

Awards, which were just eight days after our wedding. While it was odd to go forward without a red carpet and exclusive event, I felt so grateful that my mother was able to "join," as she always had in the past, as my date. Her seat might have been on my couch on our lower level, a short flight of stairs below my on-camera perch. Still, in my mind, it counted.

The presenters announced winner after winner; inside their homes, the victors hoisted the coveted statuettes in celebration. As no one had knocked on or lingered outside our door, I assumed that someone else had received the award for which I was nominated. I didn't realize that I won the Emmy until I heard my name announced on the television. I received my award a few months later.

During the commercial break, I bounded down the six stairs to share the news with my mother. She responded with her "well done" and one of her gleeful, awkward, two-handed high-fives—the kind where she held and then wiggled both of our raised, clasped hands in victory. Robert had dressed up for the occasion. I joined him for Italian takeout and the rest of the telecast before jumping into a flood of interviews.

When the commotion died down, I realized how different I felt now than I had when I received previous awards. It was not only the distanced ceremony or even my pride in our truly remarkable, popular, well-received production. From the role to the timing to the recognition, *Mrs. America* held an entirely different value.

A few nights later, I crawled into bed with my mother, as I so often did. I saw, to my surprise, that she was awake. I reminded her of the Emmy win and asked: "Are you proud of me?"

"Very proud of you," my mother said. "I am so proud of you, especially with this last show."

My mother told me that from the moment she first saw Shirley

Chisholm, she knew she loved her very much. "She was so spunky," she said. "Saying, if you don't want to give me this, I have a way of helping myself.

"She took that chair and sat in front," my mother continued. "How many people can do that? Not now, but when America was America. You know what I'm saying?"

It was late, but I had gotten her going, comparing Shirley to the recently departed Supreme Court justice Ruth Bader Ginsburg. "These were people who took the chair and sat in front," my mother repeated. "And she liked to think that she behaved that way too."

We were this way too, I reminded her.

"It's true," my mother agreed. She could forgive many things, she said: People's actions that she despised, for example; there had been moments, when she'd been a student, that people had teased her. Still, however many things—even legitimate things—that she was able to look past, there was one line that could never be crossed.

"You can't step on the toes of my children and get away with it."

MY MOTHER'S DOCTORS DESCRIBED yet another possible treatment option, and they offered another possibility. We could put the hospital behind us and try to be comfortable, they said. We understood that path forward as the only one.

I immediately began making calls—every aunty and uncle, the *adas* and *diokpas* of every line. As hard as we'd tried to live in the moment, we had to share what was ahead.

One day I sat with my mother, helping her pick out the jewelry she wanted to wear for her service. It was unbearable to even consider it; she deputized me anyway. "You're strong like me," she said as a reminder. "You'll be able to get through it."

Soon after, all five of us were together. The conversation drifted back to her service. "What do you want to wear, Mommy?" Onyi asked.

"Not black," my mother said.

"Great, that's what I thought," Onyi said. "I was thinking purple."

"Well, what do you want, Mom?" I asked.

"White," my mother said.

White lace, it turned out. "And very expensive," my mother added. We laughed nervously, fretting over the outfit's specifics for a while, until someone pointed out Junior's silence: "Junior, are you listening?"

Junior looked up with wide eyes. "Very much listening," he said.

We were all quiet after that.

"I want to be buried here in America," my mother said a few minutes later.

We all nodded. This wasn't a surprise; she'd been saying something similar since I was thirteen. I'd always assumed this idea was connected to her long-ago decision to call America rather than Nigeria home. I understood why she would want to rest here, rather than in Achi, my father's place, as tradition would dictate.

"Do you know *where* you want to be?" I can't remember who asked this question. Every word spoken into the quiet room that day had a vivid, almost surreal echo. There we were, after all, talking to a living person about something unbelievable that was most certainly going to happen.

"No, just somewhere close to my children," my mother said. "So that if they have something they want to talk to me about, by the time they get there, they will not have forgotten."

My mother's parents were laid to rest inside the family compound in Obosi, as was customary, close to their home and down a short path to my Uncle Adazie's place. When my mother and I had been in Obosi together, she had spent some time each day standing near their graves. She didn't plan these visits or discuss them; I'd see her out there, standing so quietly, and then watch her walk back to join us inside.

Now, I understood: This decision to rest in America was not about her but about us.

"If you want to sit with me, if you want me to come and bring you comfort," my mother continued, "I want to be somewhere near, so I can do that."

Had she taken so much care in Obosi because she had known it would be her last visit? I would have dismissed this idea then, as I had the reality that my mother might not live to see her own *Ito Ogbo*. She had been seventy-seven years old then, full of life and, as far as we knew it, health.

There were many times when I was a child that I felt helpless when it came to my mother. I could feel all her hopes, and I wanted so badly to realize them. She'd made the choice to live so far from home, to raise us here, knowing that she would miss out on some things. Still, I don't know that a person can fully understand the measure of these losses until they are laid out before them.

"If she gets to March, you guys, we can still do *Ito Ogbo*," I told my siblings, later that night.

Ignoring their sighs and shaking heads, I continued. "Yes. I will get a private plane and fly mom's oncologist, Dr. Spencer. We will touch down in Aba, literally drive to Obosi on the day, and . . . fly back the next day. We can do that." I knew it was that important, not just to her but to me.

"God, I pray she can get there." This is the prayer I prayed every night.

My grandparents' gravestones are two simple, symmetrical slabs of concrete. Each is surrounded by a rim, yet they are still connected. I'd said a prayer there one day, feeling gratitude for my grandparents' lives and their support of my mother. After a few motionless minutes, I'd thought, Well, this is enough.

"OK, I'm good," I'd said.

"OK," my mother had said. Sensing me lingering, she added, "You go. I'm going to stay."

AS THE FRAGILITY of my mother's life became more apparent, vivid memories of my very first visit to Obosi resurfaced. I thought of the brief conversation my grandmother, Chi-Chi, and I had shared, illuminated by our old camcorder's light, which had burned out halfway through our visit.

We still have the tape somewhere; the end is just darkness and audio.

I hadn't known then that my grandmother was dying or how much my Aunty Ifey must have been carrying, as she'd greeted us holding that lantern. Did Onyi's children, my nieces and nephews, now feel the same way I had? This I wondered as I draped my mother's favorite cardigan sweater over her shoulders. Hadn't her own mother worn something similar?

One day, my mother told me where she kept her journals. "Take them to your house and read all of them," she said.

Soon after that, all of a sudden, she started getting stronger. This can be common, they say, but in the moment, it felt like nothing short of a miracle. My brothers and Chudi came down from Boston to visit, and she was up for days, full-on, to the point where I thought maybe we were witnessing a miracle: Cancer, what?

My sisters and I tried to give each visitor as much time and space as possible. In every conversation my mother held her own with energy and fire. I thank God for that time. The Thursday they arrived, she ate a steak.

From then until Monday, when they left, she did not sleep. Not a bit.

She spent all of Tuesday in bed, with her eyes closed. "Just resting," she told Chi-Chi. She was still aware and still nodding in response to what was going on in the room. At one point, Chi-Chi asked what she was thinking.

"I'm thinking about my children and my grandchildren and how much I love them," my mother said.

Later that day, I came in to relieve Chi-Chi. "What are you doing? Are you resting?" I asked my mother, as I put my bag down and pulled over a chair. She nodded. I asked her something else and received no response. "What?" I nudged. "You don't feel like talking?"

My mother raised her eyebrows.

"What? Since when?" I teased. "The only time I've ever seen you speechless is the time we went to the White House." There was her nod, a slight smile. "Silent," I continued. "Like you had no words, and you were all clammed up."

The smile remained, though her head was still.

"Speechless, the only time," I said. "I introduced you. Do you remember?"

Hearing President Barack Obama's voice in my head as I had in 2014, I lowered my own in imitation: "'Mrs. Aduba. Oh, how are you?' And all you could say, Mom, is, 'I'm *fine* . . .'"

Still nodding, my mother fluttered open her eyes. "I really was," she said before closing them again. As I saw her drift back, I closed my own eyes and imagined us there.

A reporter once asked me whether winning my first Emmy Award was the best day of my life, and I had to say no. The best day of my life was actually two weeks before that, when I'd gone to the White House with my mother.

"Get out of here," I'd said, when I'd learned I'd been invited to attend a formal dinner there, to celebrate a week-long US-Africa Leaders Summit. "Can I bring my *mom?*" There was no way that I could go without my mother.

My mother's only response to her invitation was, "Whoa. Whoa." That was how I knew how overwhelmed she was. That's a big Non-yemism, right there.

I would fly straight to Washington, DC, from Los Angeles, and Onyi would give my mother a ride to the train, putting her in the first car. When she stepped off at Union Station, I would be right there on the platform to meet her.

"Please," I texted my publicist from the plane, thankful my hair had been styled for an earlier talk show appearance. "If there is a receiving line, we must, must, must. My mother will lose her mind."

The photo opportunity was confirmed, and I knew there was no way that an action shot, a profile, was going to cut it. "Listen, we're going to turn out," I told my mother, as we were ushered into the event.

"What do you mean?" my mother asked.

"Face out," I said. "They want us to just shake their hands and walk through, but we're going to stop and turn out for the picture. Just follow my lead."

Past the Blue Room, up to the Yellow Oval Room, my mother and I walked past Americana that has been part of my nation's house for generations. Everything there was so top of the line, so beautifully elegant and regal, including my mother—in the traditional *ichafu* my aunty had tied for the occasion—looking like the queen that she was.

For a while we stood in line with all these other somebodies, some of them jumping in front of us, as if we were going to see Santa Claus. My mom fidgeted, straightening up her stuff, asking, "How do I look?" I stared down the line, straining to catch the tops of our hosts' heads or the sides of their faces as we got closer.

"Mom," I whispered to her. "We're at the White House, going to meet the president and the First Lady!"

"I know," said my mother solemnly. "My president."

When we finally reached them, President Obama turned to look at me. I took a breath to introduce myself, and he said, "You were just in our house!"

I felt speechless, but my jaw moved, and I heard, "AH!"

Madame First Lady leaned in, saying, "I've turned him on to it!"

I tried to introduce myself, but the president stopped me. "Uzo, I know," he said. "Good to meet you. Thank you. Who's this?"

God is good, I thought, as I introduced my mother. Never in this woman's life—this woman from Obosi, Anambra State, Nigeria— could she imagine standing at this place. Can you imagine? Standing in the room receiving the president of the United States and the First Lady, hearing from Mr. President, "Thank you for raising such a great daughter."

It wasn't until the First Lady hugged her that my mom found more words: "I love you," my mother said.

To which Mrs. Obama responded, "Let's take a picture!"

"OK!" Oh my God! This was the high. This *is* the high: There we are forever, in the photograph, turned out just as we'd planned.

As we relived this event together in hospice, I, of course, did all the talking. I was so engrossed that I hadn't heard Onyi arrive back at the house. At the sound of my laughter, both of my sisters rushed in.

"That's not the end of it!" I told my mother, as Chi-Chi and Onyi sat down on the edge of the bed. "Don't forget about the dinner." We were now days from the 2020 US presidential election; we couldn't leave out the moment we'd met then Vice President, now Candidate Joe Biden.

"'Oh,'" I said, my voice lowered in my best impression. "'My wife and I love your show.' And then Mom says to him, 'It's not you I want to meet . . .'"

My mother picked her head off the pillow as we both said, at the same time, "It's your wife!"

Of course it had to be Dr. Jill Biden, my sisters and I joked, sharing a silent nod of grateful surprise as our mother's head settled back down on the pillow. Of course Dr. Biden, the woman we now hoped would be our First Lady elect, an educator and a powerhouse in her own right, was the one to impress our mother.

If I am honest, my mother really didn't say much after that. Still, I'll be forever proud that we got in one last joke.

MY SISTERS AND I COULD tell by the hospice nurse's accent that she was Nigerian; when she got up to use the restroom, Chi-Chi and I rushed to scan her name tag and try to place her.

"I think it's an Igbo last name," Chi-Chi said. We weren't sure of the first name, though I was pretty sure it was Frances.

In the end, it was Patricia, and she *was* Igbo—raised just two towns over from where my mother grew up. She had kind eyes atop her face mask and dark, straight hair neatly pulled back.

We told her that our mother was still answering us in ways that she could, mostly by opening her eyes. "Maybe, so as not to scare or worry her, you can speak Igbo to her?" I suggested.

"Nonye?" Patricia Not Frances placed a hand on the blanket just below my mother's knee, using this common pet name in a firm but familiar tone. "Nonyeh . . ."

While my mother had been nearly still, breathing shallowly, her eyes flipped open; her head turned, as if the familiar voice of someone from home had breathed new life into her.

"I'm here to help you," the nurse said. "You're going to be OK. We're just going to take your vitals . . ." As she worked, my mother, who had not spoken, began to respond—just a few sounds and the occasional "Ee," meaning yes, in Igbo.

She was an angel, this woman. Angels are meant to usher people home.

Onyi escorted out the nurse with Chi-Chi following, leaving me alone by the bedside.

"You're doing great," I told my mother for the thousandth time. "I love you."

To my surprise, she responded in a strong whisper, "Iloveyou," as if she were in a rush.

"Oh, I love you too. I love you so much," I said. "I love you with everything. I love you so, so much. You're doing great."

Then she picked herself up a bit, just a touch, though it felt like it took everything to do it.

"Thank you," my mother said.

ABOUT A YEAR before my mother passed, she told me that she had been talking with her father—that she could see him and hear his voice. During my first days of mourning, I pictured the Tower of Babel in the Old Testament: a man trying to build a ladder to the heavens. When God destroyed the ladder, the mother tongue was broken into many languages, as the story goes. The people could no longer understand one another in their communication with God.

The truth is that we don't build ladders to Mars; we build them for things just out of reach. Ladders come in different lengths and heights—the one to get something off the shelf, the one you put up against the side of the house, the one to trim branches or pick cherries. For everything beyond that, we're forced to live with the distance. That was why I cried, mourning the physical as well as the spiritual.

Although: What if my grandfather *had* reached my mother, to tell her? What if heaven really is the best of both worlds, and there is joy, looking to Earth, knowing that the people we love will understand when they come to meet us?

What if, when we die, all this sadness feels laughable? What if the joy to come in heaven was also there somewhere?

Maybe heaven really could just be pizza every day.

In 1980, at the young age of forty-four, my Aunty Ifeoma, my mother's sister and best friend, the one who helped her through polio and so much more, died of cancer. Now I imagined Ify showing my mother around heaven, giving her a tour. *This is where they pound the fufu*, she might say. *You can eat as much as you want, and you won't add weight.*

The look on Mom's face: *You don't add weight?*

That would be heaven for my mom. So would the flowers we put around her bed, after she was gone. For days we kept her room like that, like a shrine to her, vases on the floor three and four deep.

Perfectly straightened. We never slept—or even sat—on her side of the bed.

I did go in there, from time to time, in those liminal days. It was a good place to be, a comforting place. We left her nightstand light on; I turned on her diffuser and her church music, just as I had days earlier, when she had been there.

I was fully aware that my mother was lying in rest at Gleason Funeral Home, but when I was in her room, I felt like she could be in the bathroom or at Onyi's house. I felt like she was still here.

DUE TO THE RESTRICTIONS of the pandemic, many of the people we loved most were not able or allowed to attend my mother's service. With Chudi, there was no discussion: He came down from Boston, just as he had two weeks prior. He was one in a very small circle of people who could show up, in those final days, for my mother and also for us.

We returned from the wake and found the door to my mother's room closed. "Why?" I asked.

"I didn't want the kids to be in there, knocking around the flowers," said my sister's friend Tracy, who'd been watching my brother's two children there.

When we walked in together, we saw the covers pulled back on her side. "Did you sleep in Mom's bed?" I asked Onyi.

"No."

"Chi-Chi." I looked over. "Did you lay in Mom's bed?"

Chi-Chi shook her head. Tracy, with raised eyebrows, shrugged her shoulders. I knew that if the kids had tried to sneak in like that, they would have knocked over at least some of the flowers.

Maybe she made it. That was what I thought, like a child: Maybe she's saying she made it.

The night before, I'd heard my mother's voice in a dream. "Uzo, you are settled," she'd said. I'd heard it—not wind, not air, but a breath. An inhale, full and broad: Uzo. You. Are. Settled.

I don't know what that means, but ever since, it has given me a calm.

Chapter 24

E arlier that summer, a few months before my mother passed, a
new pitch had come in for the lead role in a series called *In
Treatment*—a revival of a television series that had first aired more
than a decade earlier, featuring a psychotherapist treating his patients in intense, closed-door, one-on-one sessions.

I'd been excited by the opportunity to lead, and in a role that
had the strength and power I was looking for. I was also very nervous, for at this point in my career I'd understood, from a distance,
the responsibility of carrying a series—especially one that was crit-
ically acclaimed and recognized for its experimentation.

The best news, to me, was that production was not scheduled to
begin until October, and they didn't need me to decide immediately.
And I wanted to put it out of my head. The summer was drawing to
a close, and my mother's health was clearly deteriorating. "If they
want an answer this week, then my answer is no," I told Kranzler.
My only wish, at that moment, was to be able to continue having the
conversation.

In those days, as I wondered how I could accept an opportunity that would pull me away from my mother, God and I had long conversations, especially when night fell. For months, I'd felt myself being pulled in a direction that I'd understood to be right, but I'd resisted nonetheless. Maybe I didn't want to hear what He said.

Then, one day, a different feeling came over me. I stood up understanding that I wouldn't have to make a decision.

SOMETIMES I THINK that without *In Treatment*, I might have thrown myself into my mother's grave. Instead, I was able to stand at her funeral service knowing that the next day, as my siblings scattered, Robert and I would be on a plane to Los Angeles, for a project I had to study every single day, all hours of the day. That was what I needed at the moment. Thank God.

I dove into the scripts, reviewing them endlessly, doing everything in my power to avoid what still felt like blunt trauma. I justified my round-the-clock work schedule by the fact that the show's pace was like nothing I'd ever experienced. My castmates and I were used to filming an episode over the course of a week or ten days. Now we were to complete each episode in a breathless two days.

My character, Dr. Brooke Taylor, was working through her own grief. While each episode focused on one of her patients, the audience quickly learns that Brooke has just lost her father. Her mother, with whom she was very close, passed many years before.

I am not what is called a method actor, disappearing fully into a role, living as though I were the character. I'd seen others lose their direction, along the way, using a role as rationale for bad behavior. I'd had a filter, in most of my previous roles, whether through a finely drawn character like Suzanne, with whom I shared just a few characteristics, or through careful study of a real person, like Congresswoman Chisholm. I could fill my body and brain with their motivations, understanding that it wasn't my story and that, in the end, I'd feel the separation.

With *In Treatment*, I found myself for the first time dipping into my own well—closing the door of my dressing room for my own virtual therapy sessions and then rushing back to settle into Brooke's chair. I typically needed to stretch to show my feelings, but now I had to work hard to dampen them. As I did, I also had to let others—the camera, the audience, the world—see me and feel what I was going through.

At first, I hated the idea of being this naked all the time. I didn't know what could happen.

"How's it going?" Angela asked me one day.

"I'm scared," I said. "That's how it's going."

When I found myself frustrated by Brooke's behavior, I tried to remember that she was making choices because of past pain.

For close to two years, every part of my life had been tested—my relationships most of all. I lashed out at people at times, even Robert. This difficult season had led me to some destructive and devastating behavior—some of which I also saw in Brooke. Her experience reminded me of a line from the musical *Passing Strange*: Brooke "lost track of her pain."

I could never have imagined I'd have to reach this stage of life in order to play myself. I studied the script every free moment I had, believing that something was meant to come of this process. I sank into the role, delighting in the world the writers, directors, and producers had created, embracing a bold, confident, and sophisticated Black woman with a rich, if complicated, love life. I filmed my first-ever on-screen kiss and my first sex scene.

As the lead, I wanted everyone's experience on set to be joyful—as upbeat and positive as was possible in the middle of a pandemic. The cast didn't know about my mother. No one knew, other than *In Treatment*'s showrunners, producers, and some of the directors. I was adamant about this: I didn't want my castmates to pity or comfort me, or for the focus to be on anything other than what we were supposed to be doing.

Above all, I didn't want to talk about my mother in the past tense.

There was no hiding from my grief on my fortieth birthday. I wasn't expecting to feel so affected; as a grown woman, I'd spent many birthdays without my mom. Still, I awoke that morning at 4:15 a.m., and my eyes landed on her prayer card, which was still on my nightstand. "I wish you were here," I said aloud.

My mother's call had always been the first on my birthday; she woke up early to make sure that would be the case. I dressed for work trying to digest that I would never get a call, or a card, from my mom again.

The day turned out to be lovely, filled with birthday wishes, texts, and calls capping off the birthday celebration Robert and I'd had by ourselves the weekend before. During our lunch break, I snuck back to my trailer to listen to an old voicemail of my mother's—one of a handful of messages I'd thought to save over the course of several years, never imagining that one day they would become some of my most prized possessions. Then I rejoined the cast and crew, who'd gathered everyone together with a cake.

Coming back to the set, I sat down on the couch next to Joel Kinnaman, the actor who played my love interest on the show. One of the male crew members walked by and said, "Happy birthday, Uzo!"

As I thanked him, I could hear Joel's voice over my shoulder, a singsongy "It's Zozo's birthday!"

I turned around. "What did you call me?"

"Zozo," he said, smiling sweetly as if to tease, proud of his new pet name.

"Wow," I said. I was speechless. "My mom calls . . . used to call me that." I hesitated for a minute. "She doesn't call me that now. She once called me that."

"When?" he asked. That was all he said. Something in my face must have told him.

"November 4," I said.

"I'm sorry," he said. "I didn't know—"

"There's nothing to be sorry for," I said. "I just didn't think I was going to hear that name again." My heart felt full, even in its heaviness. She was there; it was clear.

BY SOME MAGIC wonder of God, the last episode of *In Treatment* we filmed was my character giving a therapy session to herself. We illustrated this inner dialogue by filming both sides of the conversation: therapist Brooke, patient Brooke. One completely composed, in fierce work attire, and the other in tears, in pajamas.

In this moment, with the help of her therapist self, Brooke finally addresses some of the trauma she had experienced as a child and its continued impact—the disconnect between her brain and her heart.

I knew it would be a challenge, from an acting perspective. I'd have to remember both sides of the conversation, the words and their order, as well as the reaction that one side would elicit from the other. I had to be precise about how I held my body or moved any props, so that the film could reflect one scene instead of two.

While it was not the last episode of the season, I knew, as I went through the process of filming it, that it was exactly what my last scene needed to be.

There, I understood, was where I was supposed to deposit a lot of pain—some of which I hadn't even realized I was carrying. It was where I needed to tell some of my story, but not only my story. Our society was living through a time of collective grief and isolation; so many had experienced losses of freedom, space, work, and, most significantly, life. I identified with the bulletproof, steel-reinforced concrete walls that Brooke set around herself. She was not the only one to lose track of her pain.

"All I can do is encourage you to sit with your pain," my character told herself. "Have patience with it. Become steadfast in it. Make it mean something."

As I said those words, the camera rolling, I reacted in a way that I didn't even recognize—an emotional response truly beyond my control. The wall didn't come crashing down, for Brooke or for me. Afterward, though, it felt as if a superhero had punched through it, letting in a little light.

It was the catharsis that I did not know *I* needed for my body and life to move on.

Before we began production, Robert and I had taken a road trip to the Grand Canyon. He'd had to pull over a few times on the way because of the force of my sobbing. One of those times was the second we arrived at the Grand Canyon. I didn't think I was going to make it.

I'd tried so hard to hold myself together. I could see and recognize others' grief; still I'd preferred to feel nothing, to distract or numb myself, rather than to learn to accept my own. As I played both sides of Brooke, I held my own life in front of me.

Thank you, I thought, as we wrapped. Message received.

After that, something lifted or left. I knew that I would still be upset at times, and sad most times, but I was no longer afraid. For the first time, I felt that I could find my way back.

"Thank you": When I allowed myself, I could now think back to these, my mother's last words. How fitting they were for a woman so willing to spend her life in a state of constant gratitude. How proud she was to have been blessed with so many children. To have survived polio on two feet. To have arrived in the US, so aware of the opportunities and so determined to make the most of them. To have given each of us the desire to do the same.

Since I was very young, acting has always been where I feel the most free. There are no secrets there; it's life being lived fully, with all the good, bad, and ugly on display. For most of my life, so much of my process, acting and otherwise, was about projecting out—giving something away. On the path I traveled through my own grief, I learned what it means to receive.

FOR A WHILE AFTER my mother's passing, my memories of her final moments and the days following were blurred—almost as if they'd been erased. Then, slowly, they began to return, and I began to get them down in my journal.

I wrote about the moment after her service, when two women I had never seen walked up to my siblings and me. They'd driven in from Maryland, they'd told us. "We just had to pay our respects to our favorite grade school teacher," said one, a doctor. "We loved her so much."

They'd described my mom exactly as I would: smart, passionate, very strict, but also loving. She didn't mince words or play around, her former students and I agreed; still, you understood that she adored you. I was amazed how clearly they'd seen my mother, when I had never even heard their names before.

After *In Treatment* wrapped, Robert and I packed up our Brooklyn apartment for the movers. We loaded up our new car and set off for our new home in Los Angeles, having tucked into the trunk the precious gift of my mother's journals: her story in her own words.

They accompanied us on another long road, with great promise awaiting upon our arrival.

"This is about legacy building," I told Robert, as we finished signing all the papers for our first home. From the tools handed down by our parents, we will forever leave something for our own children.

We settled into our new home and returned to work. I signed a producing deal, naming my studio Meynon Media ("Nonyem" spelled backward), setting an ambitious intention that I know my mother would have embraced: to tell stories that educate and inspire.

I use that word, "ambition," deliberately. The word once made me wince, but now I hear it as unapologetic—not shying away or being falsely humble. Never again will I be small for someone else's comfort or someone else's disguise. I had never wanted to be that way.

Self-deprecation is a habit that has been tough to shake, just like teaching myself to smile after years of trying not to. It helps that I now understand it's neither healthy nor gracious when we diminish ourselves—especially about things we know to be true.

. . .

I LOOKED AT THE STACKS in the cardboard box and on our new carpet, notebooks of all sizes and textures, chronicling countless chapters. Eager to "hear" my mother's voice again, I picked up one journal and put it down, unable to crack it. Then I did the same with another.

Finally, I opened one and read, in an entry dated January 2011, "I am worried, as usual, about the family." This particular passage, I'd see, was about her grandchildren. My mother had been staying with Onyi and looking after her children, decades after she'd last met a school bus, prepared snacks, or corrected homework. In the words I read, I saw her concern, but more than that, her desire to be intentional—and her need for the children to know, truly, how much she loved them.

I finished the passage and then stopped, realizing that if I wasn't careful, I could whip through the journals quickly and get to the end. I continued more slowly, but some of my mother's shorthand sparked questions and painful reminders that she could never again answer.

I put down the books and did my best to rest. I tried not to rush through my pain, as though grief were something from which we move on. I thought: When I am ready, I will open the journals again.

IN ONE EPISODE of *In Treatment*, my character, Brooke, describes herself as "not quite an orphan, and yet there is no one above me." I didn't know the line's prescience at the time, but seven months after we buried my mother, I was myself in this position. I was back in Medfield, helping to lay my father to rest.

I knew that my father had been ill for some time, but his steep decline caught us all by surprise. When the phone rang with the news of his passing, I felt a deep sadness spread throughout my body. Just a few months earlier, I had taken my Aunty Rachel's advice and finally reached out. I'm so glad I did.

My father and I had a challenging relationship; there were long stretches of my adult life when we had not spoken. Much of his life remains a mystery.

He was handsome and gregarious, with one of those laughs that warms a room. He loved to learn and lived to know more; he was always reaching for more—trying to do more, *be* more. He saw in America that there *was* more. Still, sometimes, his efforts fell short. That was my experience, anyway.

My father was not a perfect man. I can only imagine the weight of trying to live up to everything he was positioned to do as an orphan and a *diokpa* by fate, and the first of a family to arrive in America. I cannot imagine the pressure of having so many people relying on you from the time you are a small kid, safeguarding siblings even smaller.

"Your father became the father," my Uncle David told me. "Sadly he became the mother. We stayed together; we took care of each other."

In our brief exchanges before he passed, my father shared the names and histories of his side of the family: father, grandfather, and back even further. I sent him the devotional readings I'd shared with my mother, and together we prayed that we could find our way to salvation.

"Even though you are a daughter, you have always been the man of this house." That was one of the last things my father said to me. Commentary about the patriarchy aside, I understood it as a compliment. For my father's line, after all, I am the *ada*. I knew then that I could truly fulfill my role, when the time came.

My father's funeral service was at the Church of the Advent, where my own faith had taken root. After the service, the eldest son of a dear family friend walked up to us. "I'm getting married next week, but I had to come," he said. "Your parents changed my siblings' and my life.

"Before we met you, all we did was go to school, crack the books," he continued. "And then your parents started hanging out with our parents, taking us to open skates, hockey matches, hockey games, and pizza parties. We'd never have done any of those things otherwise."

My parents were well ahead of their time. Both of them.

If there is one thing that my mother struggled to teach me, it was how to forgive. I've often said that the greatest lessons my father taught me were how to pound fufu, and that there is a difference between being smart and being clever. Above all that, though, my father is the one who taught me the value of forgiveness. I hadn't expected to receive that lesson from him.

During that period of mourning, one of my uncles shared with my brothers the English version of an Igbo proverb: "A boy never becomes fully a man until both his parents are gone."

I think that is true for girls and women as well.

I pray to God that my father is resting. I hope that he's found peace.

IN THE FINAL YEARS of my parents' lives, I'd felt as though I did all the praying—so much praying, as I read the Daily Word for my mother and then my father. During the year to follow, my conversations with God were quite limited.

When I finally unpacked my prayer box in our new home, I felt the magnitude of all that faith. I read through every single prayer card, seeing, sadly, prayers for so many people I loved who are now late: Uncle Bertie, Uncle Uche. I saw prayers of strength for Uncle Uche's widow, my Aunty Oby, and their children.

I hadn't realized how many prayers for my mother I'd put in there during those 495 days. I also hadn't known how many prayers Robert put in there. Time reveals all, as they say.

Now, when I look back at our wedding photos, I can really see the toll of my mother's illness—on all of us.

More importantly, though, I can see my mother looking like herself, which is to say, with a life and a light in her eyes. In one shot, she is sitting next to Onyi, her smiling mouth open wide, while some small child is doing something adorable just off camera. My mom had this big, bright laugh. Until that day, it had been more than a year since I'd seen her laugh like that.

When I rediscovered that photo, it was the Fourth of July, exactly two years after her diagnosis. I'd flipped through my wedding photos countless times; only now, with enough time, could I truly see. Now, as I remember, I can think about the past differently.

I am forever grateful that my mother lived to know Robert and the promise of our future. What a gift, to know that you are reaching the end of something and to see a beginning. I thank God for that.

My entire world has changed. Only now, with time, am I clear enough to say it.

My mother did not live to *Ito Ogbo*, eighty, but for nearly two years, 495 days, she sat on her own throne, in her living room, seeing person after person come through that door. From as far as

Australia to Brussels to everywhere around the world—video calls, endlessly—she did get to see how she would be celebrated. Just how loved she truly was.

The day we wrapped *In Treatment*, a Yolanda Adams song kept coming into my head. A gospel song, called "The Battle Is the Lord's," with a lyric, "God knows what you need before you really need it."

What I wanted was for my mother to live, but what I needed was time to say goodbye. I got that, thank God. I think of that as a miracle now. Imagine turning cancer into a miracle.

Time is a miracle, though, and I got a lot of it.

"YOU'RE STRONG," MY MOTHER often told me. As a child, you hear your parents say things, and you don't realize how deeply they know you. "You're strong like me, and you'll be able to get through it." This was her encouragement during those 495 days and so many others, long before that.

All my life, I had someone pushing me. Now I know that I can push myself.

You'd better believe that this strength will be passed on to my own child. It's the Anyaoku and Aduba way. *This fire is what brought you here*, I will say. *It's also what will bring you forward.*

"You are settled," my mother had said, in my dream. Whatever challenge I am facing, or opportunity or recognition I am chasing, doesn't actually matter. My joy is tied to something else—to my home and my family—and that is what I am now in the business of making more of, spreading, and protecting.

Home, for me, is the space that Robert and I create together, regardless of how far or how often I travel. Still, the older I get, the greater my desire is to live in Nigeria. I have a strong thirst and hunger for my heritage; I want our lives to be steeped in it.

I'm already one removed. I don't want us to be erased.

Let's go back, I tell Robert. Let the code-switch be that way, so the next generation can clearly see from who and what they come. Our children will have Igbo first names, we've agreed, as they will carry his last name.

We can't have our children exist without some of their identity—not in this America. In school, every time they hear their name, and someone asks where those names are from, they will remember.

"I LOVE THIS," I can hear my mother say from the front seat, Simon and Garfunkel's "The Boxer" on the car stereo. "This takes me to Sweden."

Since I was a child in the back seat or at our fabric-strewn dining room table, I have been trying to put together the pieces of my mother's story. I wish so much for even one more day to ask questions. Still, just as I am wincing at death's finality, there inside the journal comes an answer.

One of the notebooks I took out of my mother's stash was from my early New York days. "I worry about Uzo . . . She asked for money, and I know she doesn't ask unless she really needs it."

"I pray this works out," my mother wrote. "I pray to God every night."

Prayer was, for my mother, such a powerful form of care: Even when her children were no longer under her roof, she could always reach us.

With her writing and others' stories, I can close my eyes and reach back. I can see her on that patched-up airstrip at Uli, code-named

Annabelle. She stands there in the dark of night, waiting to meet the planes carrying relief for Biafra, knowing there are just a few precious hours of darkness before the sun rises and the Nigerian bombing campaigns begin anew.

She is there for the aid workers, and for the journalists too—the ones who wanted to write about the war. As she once told me: "They wanted the world to know what was killing everybody."

She is scared, I imagine. She speaks out anyway.

For more than twenty years, I spoke with my mother daily. During the final months of her illness, I grew used to a kind of distance. No longer did we chat on the phone or exchange text messages when we were not together. So much of the time, she was just too tired.

Today, I can hold a journal and hear her voice.

This is my story and my mother's story too. She did what all of us, in this family, come here to do: to see ourselves as connected, strive to reach a place, and then pick up someone else and help them get to their next place.

"I became an optimist instead of an obstacle," my mother wrote in one of her entries. "I didn't think anything could stop me."

It is now, as I close my own book, that I understand: I can still talk with her whenever I want.

Acknowledgments

First and foremost, I want to give thanks and all glory to God for my life, from whom all blessings flow. I wouldn't be anywhere without the work and guidance of The Divine. I pray to continue to be of His service all the days of my life, Amen.

To my husband, Robert, who I couldn't do this life without, thank you for loving me, lifting me, and being the best thing that has ever happened to me through good times, bad times, sick times, and well times.

To my parents, who gave me life and made exceptional sacrifices for my siblings and me, hoping to provide as many opportunities to reach the American dream as possible. May you forever rest.

I'd like extra special thanks to be paid to my mother, from whom I can only say the best of me comes; I am endlessly thankful for her participation and help in sharing for this book and for her bravery in telling her story. Thank you for selflessly sharing countless hours on your great days and not-so-great days.

Thank you to my siblings, Rich, Onyi, Chi-Chi, and Junior, for always being my strongest supporters and champions at every stage of life. I love you guys so much.

To my extended family, who have supported me, to my aunties and uncles—Dr. Buchi and Mrs. Azuka Dike, Mr. David Aduba, Ogbueshi Ationu Mrs. Adora Ekpunobi, Ogbueshi Mr. Ifeanyi, and Mrs. Uche Anyaoku, and to my cousin, Mr. Chudi Ekpunobi, for helping to put this story together.

To my Aunty and godmother, Dr. Mrs. Rachel Iroku, and my cousin, Ms. Obioma Iroku, for giving me a soft place to land when I first moved to New York. Without your early belief and support, I'm not sure where this dream goes.

To my friends, Mr. Mark Crowley, Simi Dube, Angela Wildflower Polk, Lisa Nicole Wilkerson, Dr. Nwamaka Ugokwe, Natasha Lyonne, Idara Victor, Adepero Oduye, and the countless many more who have supported me, cheered me on, carried me and loved me in the hard and happy times. Thank you for always showing up.

To Viking Publishing and Laura Tisdel for encouraging me throughout this experience, and to Sarah J. Robbins for creating a safe space to tell this story. To my team, Albert Lee, Georgia Bodnar, Eric Kranzler, Rachel Karten, James Adam, Scott Winston, and Bria Wade, for their support throughout this journey.

I could not have done this without each of you.